First published in April 2013

Peter Carr has asserted his moral right
to be identified as the author of this work.

A catalogue record for this book is
available from the British Library

ISBN 978 0 85733 231 8

Library of Congress control no. 2012953859

Published by Haynes Publishing,
Sparkford, Yeovil, Somerset BA22 7JJ, UK
Tel: 01963 442030 Fax: 01963 440001
Int. tel: +44 1963 442030 Int. fax: +44 1963 440001
E-mail: sales@haynes.co.uk
Website: www.haynes.co.uk

Haynes North America Inc.
861 Lawrence Drive, Newbury Park,
California 91320, USA

While every effort is taken to ensure the accuracy
of the information given in this book, no liability can
be accepted by the author or publishers for any loss,
damage or injury caused by errors in, or omissions
from the information given.

Printed in the USA by Odcombe Press LP,
1299 Bridgestone Parkway, La Vergne, TN 37086

THE ESSENTIAL GUIDE TO
SURFING IN THE UK AND ABROAD

PETER CARR

HISTORY & CULTURE ■ **BOARD CARE & MAINTENANCE** ■ **FITNESS** ■ **TECHNIQUES** ■ **TRAVEL**

CONTENTS

INTRODUCTION

The "essential guide…."? Purists endlessly rehash the Duke Kahanamoku quote "the best surfer out there is the one having the most fun" and claim that you don't need a book to tell you how to have fun, do you?

It's true that there is no one best board to buy, and no one best way to ride it. But is your wetsuit too thin? Being hypothermic is no fun. Were you sold the wrong board? Not catching waves is no fun. Neither is being stuck in a churning rip current; nor having rocks bounced off your head by irate locals. Missing sessions because of a bad back – that's a downer. Catching your rail every single time you try a forehand cutback can get a little tiresome, too.

It's never too late to get better, and you are never too good to have fun. When you are not enjoying yourself in the waves you know you are not doing something right. That's when it might be worth coming back to the book for a few 'essential' reminders.

As surfer/shaper Bob McTavish said: "Surfing is a lot more fun that it looks. And it looks like a lot of fun."

Pete Carr

Pete Carr
April 2013

'I COULD NOT HELP CONCLUDING THAT THIS MAN
FELT THE MOST SUPREME PLEASURE WHILE HE WAS
DRIVEN ON SO FAST AND SMOOTHLY BY THE SEA.'

James King, lieutenant to Captain James Cook, Tahiti, 1777

CHAPTER 1

SURFING HISTORY

The fact that surfing is essentially a very simple sport makes its roots difficult to trace. Some coastal peoples undoubtedly developed craft that could cope with surf conditions, but only as a necessity for getting safely through the surf line to and from fishing grounds; for most cultures the surf was not an environment in which to mess about.

HE'E NALU: POLYNESIAN WAVE-SLIDING

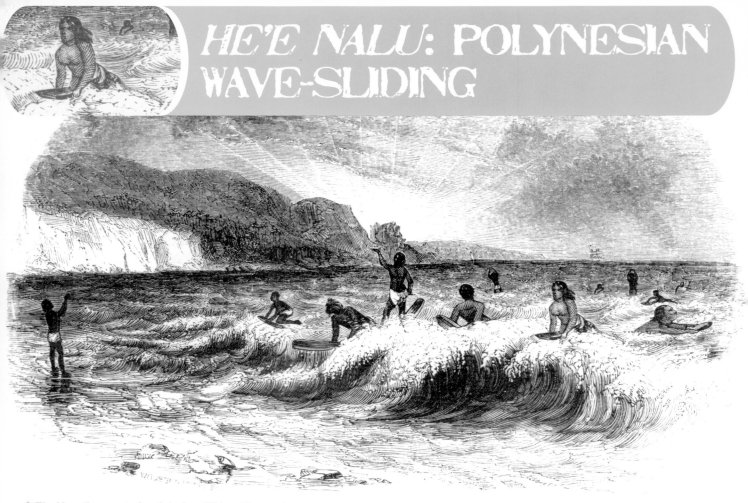

⬆ **The Hawaiian sport of surf playing. (Bishop Museum)**

It's likely that a type of belly-boarding for simple fun was widely practised along the west coast of Africa between what's now Senegal and Nigeria, but it also seems that this pastime remained localised and at a fairly basic level. In Peru, fishermen would sit astride small reed-boats named caballitos and catch waves back to shore – an activity recorded on pre-Columbian pottery.

The Polynesians are the only people for whom surfing assumed real cultural significance. Precisely when they began to surf isn't known, but the great migration of their ancestors from South-East Asia began around 3,000 years ago, and practically everywhere the Polynesians colonised there's evidence of a surfing tradition, from New Guinea to Rapa Nui (Easter Island). European seafarers recorded them enjoying waves throughout the scattered islands of the Pacific Ocean: this wide distribution in itself indicates a long history. However, only among the main islands of Eastern Polynesia (New Zealand, Tahiti, the Marquesas and Hawaii) were the longer boards developed that suggest the sport was more than just a few youngsters frolicking in the waves.

It took the Polynesians some centuries to migrate north-east from the Marquesas to the Hawaiian Islands, arriving between 800–1000 AD. By dating the remains of domesticated animals introduced to the island chain, archaeology reveals that the Polynesians didn't fetch up in Hawaii

> '...ALL THOUGHT OF WORK WAS AT AN END, ONLY THAT OF SPORT WAS LEFT. ALL DAY THERE WAS NOTHING BUT SURFING.'
> Hawaiian scholar **Kepelino Keauokalani** (1830–78)

accidentally, blown off course in their ocean-going canoes. Instead, they were meticulously prepared seafaring colonists who were canny enough to exploit periodic reversals of the normal trade winds and ocean currents that we now refer to as El Niño events.

What they also brought with them was a surfing tradition that discovered a perfect environment to celebrate and develop their favourite sport. In the Hawaiian summer, swells march up from the great Southern Hemisphere storms in the Antarctic Sea; in winter the storm centres in the North Pacific send down swells to the islands' northern shores. All these swells unload on to a series of beaches, points and reefs to provide consistent and varied rideable waves in balmy water.

Surf culture in Hawaii flourished to become as deeply ingrained as it was widespread. Whenever the conditions were right, farming and fishing and daily household tasks were abandoned as entire communities took to the waves. Women not only participated on an equal footing, but frequently carried off the honours in open competition. Always more than just a sport, surfing also had an important social function in courtship ritual: a man and women sharing a wave was considered an invitation to intimacy.

Studies of Hawaiian chants recognise over a hundred named surfing spots dotted around all seven of the Hawaiian Islands; many more probably went unrecorded. Chants were sung at the stone *heiau* – temples that had stone terraces for observing the waves, and stone freshwater pools, evidently for ritual rinsing after a session. A way of celebrating a chief's skill in the waves and a means of summoning waves in flat spells, the use of chants persisted into the 19th century.

BOARD SHAPES

Two distinct types of stand-up board evolved in Hawaii: the *olo* and the *alaia*. Both were lenticular in cross-section (though much more pronounced in the *olo*), and each was designed to enable the rider to trim diagonally across the face of the wave rather than simply heading straight for shore in the white water.

The *alaia* was the shorter of the two, closer to the original belly board, but still long enough – at 6–8ft (1.8–2.4m) – to support a standing rider once he or she was planing across the surface of the wave. *Alaia* were 14–18in (35–46cm) wide and only an inch or so thick, with a rounded nose tapering along the sides to a squared-off tail. A cross-section would show both deck and bottom to be convex, meeting at narrow, even sharp, rails. *Alaia* boards were used in steep fast-breaking shore-break conditions that demanded manoeuvrability. The fact that many examples have survived suggests that most Hawaiian waves ridden at that time were of this type.

Olo boards were longer, 14–18ft (4.3–5.5m) and possibly even more. Lengths of 'four fathoms' were reported – 24ft (7.3m). Cigar-shaped and 18in (46cm) or so at the widest point, an *olo* board was very thick at 8in (15cm) and very heavy indeed at around 160lb (73kg). Their shape is eminently suited to achieving long rides in slack, slow-breaking waves, such as at Waikiki. But it has also been suggested that their extreme length may have been designed to enable riders to catch and ride massive unbroken swells at offshore reefs, kicking out before the wave reached critical steepness.

The distinctions in board shapes reflected Hawaiian social structure. Chiefs (*ali'i*) and commoners (*maka'ainana*) were rigidly divided in Hawaiian society and it may be that *olo* boards were used primarily by the *ali'i*, if not exclusively reserved for them. Commoners seldom shared the surf with chiefs; there is some evidence that chiefs could *tabu* a surfing beach, making it off limits to commoners and so keeping the best waves to themselves.

BOARD MANUFACTURE

Common wood like that of the breadfruit tree was often used to manufacture boards, but the more favoured woods were *koa* and *wiliwili* (the first like mahogany, the second like balsa). *Wiliwili* may have been preferred for its lightness, but examples of boards made of *koa* – being a close-grained and very durable hardwood – are the ones that have survived.

Searching the forest, once the board-maker had found a sound tree he felled it and rough-shaped it on the spot. This 'blank' was hauled to the shore where it was finished under cover. Fine adzes and coral sanding blocks gave the board its final shape, and a smooth finish was achieved with polishing stones. A dark gloss was added by the use of vegetable dyes and *kukui* nut oil. The oiled board was now ready to surf, but had to be dried, re-oiled, wrapped in *tapa* cloth and hung indoors after every session. The care with which this was done reflected the treasured status of their boards amongst Hawaiians.

Hawaiian society was very much a culture of reverence and, within this, surfing had many sacred aspects. Surfing ritual began the moment a tree was selected for making into a surfboard, as a red *kumu* fish was ceremoniously laid at the base of the trunk. After felling the tree, a hole was dug in the roots and the fish placed in it as an offering to the gods. Another ritual was performed once the board had been finished and polished prior to it being taken in the water for the first time.

When the first European explorers arrived in the late 1700s they discovered a people who had placed the supreme skills and long-established rituals of wave-riding at the centre of its culture.

⬆ Engraving depicting domestic life in Hawaii. (Villeroy, Bishop Museum)

HAWAIIAN SURFING TERMS

Ahua – inside the break
'Ale – swell
Alaia – a short thin board
He'e nalu – wave sliding, surfing
He'e umauma – body surfing
Hoe – to paddle
Kakala – a fast curling wave
Kulana nalu – take-off spot
Lala – angling across the wave
Lauloa – a long wave
Muku – the breaking crest of the wave
Nalu – wave
Nalu ha'i lala – a wave that breaks diagonally
Nalunalu – big waves
Olo – a long narrow board
Papa he'e nalu – surfboard

⬇ **Hawaiian man with surfboard at Waikiki Beach; Honolulu, Oahu, Hawaii. (Bishop Museum)**

'TO HAVE A NEAT FLOATBOARD, WELL-KEPT, AND DRIED, IS TO A SANDWICH ISLANDER WHAT A TILBURY OR A CABRIOLET OR WHATEVER LIGHT CARRIAGE MAY BE IN FASHION IS TO A YOUNG ENGLISH MAN.'
Lord Byron (cousin to the poet), commander of HMS *Blonde* in the early 1820s

DISCOVERY

↑ **A view of Karakakooa, in Hawaii.**
(Engraving by W. Byrne, Bishop Museum)

Captain James Cook had already remarked on the water skills of the Polynesians after watching a lone wave-rider in an outrigger canoe in Tahiti in late 1777. But by the time Cook arrived in the Hawaiian Islands in 1778, the islanders there were angling across waves riding all types of boards, prone, kneeling and standing up.

Although it's probable that European explorers had visited Hawaii prior to the 17th century, Cook's visit was especially significant in that he brought eminent scientists whose sole purpose in the expedition was to minutely record whatever fascinated and surprised them. So it is Cook's lieutenant James King who in 1778 provides the first published account of Hawaiian surfing:

'The boldness and address with which I saw them perform these difficult and dangerous manoeuvres was altogether astonishing and is scarcely to be believed… Whenever, from stormy weather or any extraordinary swell at sea the impetuosity of the surf is increased to its utmost heights, they choose that time for their amusement, which is performed in the following manner: Twenty or thirty of the natives, taking each a long narrow board, rounded at the ends, set out together from the shore. The first wave they meet they plunge under, suffering it to roll over them, rise again beyond it, and make the best of their way, by swimming out in to the sea. The second wave is encountered in the same manner as the first… as soon as they have gained by these repeated efforts, the smooth water beyond the surf, they lay themselves at length on their board, and prepare for their return.'

For Western sailors the sea inspired not fun, but fatalism.

Traditionally they refused even to learn to swim: if you were lost overboard, why prolong the agony of inevitable drowning? So not only were the skills that the Polynesians had developed profoundly impressive; but the very idea that the sea could be enjoyed for its own sake seemed almost unimaginably exotic and difficult to comprehend. That's why so many early records, like King's, have such a detailed technical flavour: the explorers were, in effect, writing the first surf manuals, trying to explain to themselves precisely how it could be done.

Although the arrival of the Europeans was, mostly inadvertently, to bring Hawaiian surf culture to its knees in the following century, in King's description we can also see what was to save it – the fascination and seduction of surfing.

↑ **Polynesian men and women equally enjoyed the thrill of wave-sliding.**

DECLINE

The long-isolated Hawaiians had virtually no natural immunity to epidemic diseases carried by the Europeans. Within a century from Cook's visit in 1778 the native population had dropped from an estimated 300,000 to less than 40,000 – a figure which by then included part-blood as well as pure-blood Hawaiians. This period of population decline was also a time of great social, economic and political upheaval in the islands.

Using European arms and advisers, a single kingdom was imposed upon the various tribes by the warrior chief Kamehameha, but it failed to bring stability and cultural coherence. Instead, in 1819, under the impact of the new socio-political realities, Kamehameha's heir declared an end to the ancient *tabu* system so important to regulating Hawaiian social and religious life. Surfing – an integral part of this system of social and cultural cohesion – was about to go into steep decline.

Adding to the cultural melange of the established whalers, sandalwood traders, settlers, sugarcane growers and Asian labourers, American missionaries descended on Hawaii in 1820. Stepping into a spiritual vacuum, they quickly set about making Christians of the pagan Hawaiians.

It isn't difficult to see why the strict Calvinist missionaries should have disapproved of Hawaiian surfing: it appeared to celebrate false gods, gambling, wanton intermingling of the sexes and neglect of domestic duties. Opposing all pagan rituals, the missionaries also inevitably opposed surfing. If they didn't ban the sport outright, the missionaries strongly discouraged any participation in it.

Quick to see the benefits of reading and writing in this new era, the Hawaiians weren't entirely passive victims of all these momentous changes. Instead, they were largely happy to adapt by attending schools. But nothing so poignantly illustrates the changing of their ways as a report that recorded Hawaiians chopping up their once-revered surfboards to make seats and desks to be installed in the new missionary school on Kauai.

By the middle of the 19th century surfing was coming to be a rare sight around the islands, and by 1890 the ancient culture of the Hawaiians was hopelessly fragmented. Their population decimated, much of their land owned by foreigners, the Hawaiians' final indignity was having the entire kingdom annexed by the United States.

Surfing's last bastion was Waikiki beach. Waikiki was then on the outskirts of Honolulu, the capital of the new United States Territory of Hawaii, and its major port. This is what saved it from going the way of many other extinct Hawaiian sports: by 1900 Honolulu was where a quarter of the surviving Hawaiians lived, and where shiploads of tourists descended, looking to sample authentic Hawaiian culture – including, naturally, surfboard riding.

So surfing survived – an orphan sport rescued from oblivion by the very forces that had nearly extinguished it. The old boards, like the old board shapers, were largely gone. *Olo* boards weren't being made at all. The new boards were poor imitations of the old *alaia*, crudely shaped from imported woods. They had ugly, boxy rails that wouldn't angle across the wave, but would only allow the rider to, as Charmian London put it in 1907, 'make straight to the beach'. Surfing had regressed, but it had survived.

'THE SPORT OF SURF-RIDING POSSESSED A GRAND FASCINATION AND FOR A TIME SEEMED AS IF IT HAD A VITALITY OF ITS OWN AS A NATIONAL PASTIME. THERE ARE THOSE LIVING... WHO REMEMBER THE TIME WHEN ALMOST THE ENTIRE POPULATION OF A VILLAGE WOULD AT CERTAIN HOURS RESORT TO THE SEASIDE TO INDULGE IN, OR TO WITNESS, THIS MAGNIFICENT ACCOMPLISHMENT. WE CANNOT BUT MOURN ITS DECLINE. BUT THIS TOO HAS FELT THE TOUCH OF CIVILISATION, AND TODAY IT IS HARD TO FIND A SURFBOARD OUTSIDE OF OUR MUSEUMS AND PRIVATE COLLECTIONS.'
Nathaniel Emerson, 1892

← **With the arrival in Hawaii of the Calvinist missionaries, surfing was banished to the margins.**

RESURGENCE

The belief among the *haoles* (whites) up to this point had been that surfing was a sort of 'voodoo sport'. Risky and mysterious, it was fun to flirt with, but whites could never truly master surfing even if they were inclined to try. There was a kind of cultural defeatism propagated by Mark Twain in the 1860s in his widely read *Letters From Hawaii*. 'I tried surf-bathing once, subsequently, but made a failure of it,' he wrote in 1866. 'I had the board placed right, and at the right moment, too; but missed the connection myself. The board struck the shore in three-quarters of a second, without any cargo, and I struck the bottom about the same time, with a couple of barrels of water in me.'

Twain's comically pitiful efforts are contrasted with the ease with which 'the heathen' (as Twain calls the Hawaiian surfer) 'comes whizzing by like a bombshell'. 'None but the natives ever master the art of surf-bathing thoroughly,' he pronounced, and for much of the 19th century surfing continued to be presented as exotic but dangerously alien.

As Hawaiian population decline was gradually halted, the islands' close social and political links with the USA following annexation brought a fresh influx of settlers towards the end of the 19th century. These *haoles* were more sensitive to surfing culture than had been the early wave of missionaries, plantation owners and speculators. The Waikiki 'beach boy' lifestyle became massively in vogue. But where boards had once been innocently stashed in the bushes of an empty beach, developers now tried to restrict access to the beachfront acres that were fast becoming desirable real estate. The booming popularity of Honolulu threatened to close down the resurgence in surfing just as it had got under way. It took a group of enlightened settlers to realise that surfing was a valuable resource that must be preserved if it was to be successfully exploited, both as a healthy pastime and a tourist attraction.

Led by Alexander Hume Ford, the group campaigned to keep open access to the beach in order to boost the sport. A club was formed – the Hawaiian Outrigger Canoe Club – with the express intention of 'preserving surfing on boards and in Hawaiian outrigger canoes'. Lessons were provided; youngsters were encouraged. A beachfront lot was leased to provide changing and storage facilities. Surfing had a new home, both literally and figuratively: part cultural artefact, part mainstream tourist attraction.

The mainstream appeal of surfing was exploited by Jack London, then America's foremost cultural celebrity. In 1907 he wrote an article – 'Riding the South Seas Surf' – for the widely read journal *A Woman's Home Companion*. Surfing had become thoroughly democratised: now the masses had their own royal pastime in exotic tropical islands that were actually a part of the USA.

But the revived sport was still in its infancy. The boards were short and barely floated the rider. Only the expert few even scrambled to their knees, and all, it seems, rode straight to shore, not angling across the waves as they'd been doing for centuries when Cook and King arrived.

Interest in the sport blossomed. Surfing contests and exhibitions were held at Waikiki that gained national publicity in the United States, and surfing became a top tourist attraction in Hawaii. Hundreds would be in the water at Waikiki at the weekend. Jack London returned to the Islands in 1915 to find that the Outrigger club boasted 1,200 members and that the mostly *haole* institution had established a friendly rivalry with the native *Hui Nalu* ('Wave Club'). Board design and surf skills were regaining the lost arts and then some: as Charmian London wrote of that trip, 'The newest brood of surf-boarders had learned and put into practice angles never dreamed of a decade earlier.'

'WHEN YOU SEE IT COMING, STAND READY TO LAUNCH THE BOARD ON THE GATHERING SLOPE, SPRING UPON IT, AND – KEEP GOING IF YOU CAN. LIE FLAT ON YOUR CHEST, HANDS GRASPING THE SIDES OF THE LARGE END OF THE HEAVY TIMBER, AND STEER WITH YOUR FEET. THE EXPERT, HAVING GAUGED THE RIGHT SPEED, RISES CAUTIOUSLY TO HIS KNEES, TO FULL STATURE, AND THEN, ERECT WITH FEET IN THE CHURNING FOAM, HE MAKES STRAIGHT FOR THE BEACH.'

Charmian London, *Jack London and Hawaii*, 1918

← Jack and Charmion London at the Outrigger Canoe Club on Waikiki Beach with Apuakehau Stream and the Moana Hotel in the background; Honolulu, Hawaii.
(Photo by Ray Jerome Baker, Bishop Museum)

↑ Surfboards and canoes at the Outrigger Canoe Club, next to Apuakehau Stream; Waikiki, Honolulu, Hawaii.
(Photo by Ray Jerome Baker, Bishop Museum)

That decade of rapid evolution marked the birth of modern surf culture; the sport had been more than just saved, it was now ready for export. But how would the hedonistic pastime of the South Seas translate to places like California and Australia? These were civic societies then largely in the grip of frowning moralists, where bare-chested male swimmers still faced the possibility of prosecution.

CALIFORNIA

The first surfers in California were three Hawaiian princes, Jonah Kuhio Kalaniana'ole Piikoi and his brothers David and Edward. Whilst attending military school in San Mateo in 1885, the brothers shaped boards from milled redwood logs and astonished a crowd at the mouth of the San Lorenzo River. In the cold Californian waters they made plenty of headlines but no converts. It was to take the promotional savvy of a major corporation to establish surfing on the mainland.

As part of a sophisticated marketing strategy, in 1907 the Pacific Electric Railroad Company paid for an Irish-Hawaiian surfer called George Freeth, the champion of Waikiki, to come to California. His demonstrations of the new sport were designed to lure rail customers to new resorts such as Redondo Beach, the aim being to promote the new beach lifestyle and sell a good few plots of land into the bargain. Surf lessons were part of the package.

Freeth was to remain in California for the next 12 years, spreading

KAHANAMOKU 52

the word. This blend of corporate boosterism and laid-back beach lifestyle was something distinctly Californian, and became the blueprint for the dynamic of surfing's development into the coming century.

Five years after Freeth had arrived in California, another Hawaiian water sports ambassador appeared on the mainland scene. Keen surfer Duke Paoa Kahini Mokoe Hulikahola Kahanamoku was only 21 when he visited Southern California for the 1912 Olympic swimming trials. He breezed through them, went to the Stockholm Olympics and, in his first heat, sliced three seconds off the world record for the 100m freestyle. His subsequent gold medal made him famous, but it was his skill at the exotic sport of surfing that made him fascinating.

Off he went on a series of swimming exhibitions around the US, and when conditions were right he was more than happy to demonstrate the newest skills in surfing. In 1912 Duke surfed waves in Florida, New Jersey and California. Measurably the world's best swimmer, by demonstrating and spreading his enthusiasm for the missionaries' 'devil's pastime' Duke pulled off a difficult feat: his status as a disciplined and accomplished Olympian helped legitimise surfing as a worthy sport, whilst his exoticism as a regal brown Hawaiian 'beachboy' lent surfing ever more romantic appeal.

In 1920 Duke Kahanamoku was touring the mainland US on the back of another Olympic gold medal won at Antwerp when he met a competitive swimmer called Tom Blake. Kahanamoku advised him to take up surfing, and Blake soon moved to Oahu, bringing a fresh perspective to the stalled evolution of board design there. That the old Hawaiian boards were so heavy was related to prestige in Hawaiian eyes – weight reflected the wealth and power of the owner. But Blake soon made himself a hollow board with which he won numerous paddle races. The board being hollow was not in itself a startling advance – even Blake's new boards still weighed 100lb (45kg), a mass that restricted surfing's popularity – the significance was more that mainland surfers adopted a mindset of innovation and were beginning to challenge old assumptions.

After the First World War the centre of innovation in surfing development began to shift wholesale to California.

In the early 1930s Bob Simmons (an engineer by trade) was recovering in a Californian hospital from a road accident that had badly mangled his arm. He was told that if he didn't exercise it constantly it would require amputation. He heard about surfing from a fellow patient, determined to try the new sport, and was soon hooked. By 1934 he was something of a surf vagabond, roaming the coast of California absorbing the culture and trying to find a way to get rid of the 100lb redwood boards that he found impossible to manage with his withered arm.

Experiments had been ongoing with balsa wood shipped in from South America, but the quality of shipments was unreliable and even the best wood, whilst being light, was soft: movement allowed the coating of varnish to crack and let in water. Simmons tried to get around this limitation by taking Blake's hollow board principle but sandwiching

← **Duke Kahanamoku: first ambassador of surfing.**

'IT WOULD TAKE ME FORTY-FIVE MINUTES JUST TO GET THE BOARD IN THE WATER. IT WAS MADE OF SOLID REDWOOD AND WEIGHED ABOUT A HUNDRED AND TEN POUNDS – TWENTY POUNDS MORE THAN I DID! I NAILED SOME ROLLER-SKATE WHEELS ON TO A WOOD PLANK AND USED THAT TO PUSH THE BOARD DOWN TO THE BEACH. MY MOM WOULD HELP ME PUSH IT TO THE STEPS AT THE PIER. THEN I'D GIVE THE BOARD A SHOVE AND WATCH IT BOUNCE DOWN THE STEPS. THE FIN WOULD COME OFF EVERY TIME, SO I LEFT A COUPLE OF SIXPENNY NAILS AT THE BASE OF THE STAIRS NEAR A ROCK THAT I'D USE TO POUND THE FIN BACK ON. THEN I'D DRAG THE BOARD TO THE WATER AND TRY TO SURF IT.'

Greg Noll, *Da Bull: Life Over the Edge,* 1989

polystyrene foam between the wood veneers. He subsequently sealed his boards with the new fibreglass cloth and resin then being used in the marine industry. The plywood layers were necessary still to protect the polystyrene foam from being dissolved by the polyester resin.

One great benefit of fibreglass was that, finally, fins could be attached rigidly to the bottom of boards – previous fixing methods had been unable to withstand for long even the torque generated in the water, never mind the impact of frequent collisions. But Simmons' experiments with fibreglass and resin were to revolutionise board design in just a few short years after the end of the Second World War.

During that conflict much essential war industry had relocated to the safe blue skies of California. One result of this move was a disparate coastal community of iconoclastic draft-dodgers, enthusiastic students, boffins, engineers and disillusioned veterans. All were keen to experiment with a different lifestyle; those drawn to surfing could now get their hands on newly developed wartime materials such as polyurethane foam and plastics to apply to the board-making process. They also had 840 miles (1,350km) of surf coast on which to try out the results, most especially at the long perfect point break at Malibu. Here designs were tested and refined to such a degree that a local shaping community put down roots and the new super-manoeuvrable craft became known simply as 'Malibu boards'.

By the time of Simmons' premature death in 1954 boards were down to 25lb (11.4kg) – lighter yet with more buoyancy than the old logs. The increase in buoyancy allowed for a shorter board and this in turn enabled greater manoeuvrability.

The plastics revolution was the real boom – polyurethane foam (first used in the board industry in 1955) could be moulded, and its density controlled by tweaking the chemical formula. Whatever can be moulded can be mass-produced, so plywood veneer and even hand-shaped balsa were effectively gone within a few years as surfing plunged into the mass-market mainstream.

By the mid-1950s there were dozens of surf clubs in California, most of them tapping into an image of the laid-back lifestyle of the Hawaiian beachboys. Pioneering surfers were by now having to scour the coast to discover new, less crowded breaks in 'surfaris' that equally contributed to the zeitgeist of post-war liberalisation, escapism and freewheeling idealism.

AUSTRALIA

When Duke Kahanamoku took surfing to the Antipodes late in 1914, Australia was certainly ready for it. This was a continent-sized country that had 12,000 miles (19,300km) of coast – most of it beaches with breaking surf. Bodysurfing had been successfully introduced by a Tahitian lad known as 'Tommy Tanna' in the 1880s, but the birth of surfing on boards was less straightforward.

Early tales of Hawaiian surfing crossed the Pacific and led some of the bodysurfers to experiment with what they imagined these surfboards to look like. Liners bound for Australia stopped at Hawaii; passengers would spend an enchanted few days at Waikiki beach, perhaps buying a board there to bring home. So up and down the Australian coast in the early years of the 20th century learner surfers were not an unfamiliar sight. But most gave up the difficult struggle to control the logs in the testing conditions of East Coast beach breaks. These waves were much less forgiving than the gentle rollers of Waikiki. Imported Hawaiian surf craft had a tendency to end their useful lives as shelving or ironing boards.

In the Christmas holiday season of 1914–15 Duke Kahanamoku was invited to Australia as an Olympic gold medallist, to race against Australian swimming champions in pool meets. As usual, the added

BOARD EVOLUTION IN THE 1930S

Tom Blake's improvements led to longer boards being made, allowing surfers to ride new spots around the coast of the Islands. However, these boards still tended to slip out and tail-slide in steep sections, severely limiting their functionality. How could this be remedied? The details are contested, but some time during the 1930s the answer gradually emerged.

The V-tail cross-section was designed by Honolulu surfer John Kelly in 1937. This was a long V-section extending along the tail that gave the board directional stability. Add too much 'V', however, and it was impossible to turn at all. This innovation was superseded by Blake who – inspired by boat keels – may well have been the first to stick a fin on the bottom of a board, enabling much greater control. Blake's experiments with fins had been ongoing since the mid-1930s.

'NOBODY PAID ANY ATTENTION TO IT, AND IT TOOK TEN YEARS BEFORE THAT THING REALLY CAUGHT ON.'
Tom Blake

attraction was the extensively promoted surfing demonstrations. When Kahanamoku arrived he found that Sydneysiders had surfboards but, as he said, 'no one had the knack'. Hobbled by inappropriate equipment and lacking instruction, Australian surfers were getting nowhere fast.

Having been forewarned that surf riding was prohibited, Kahanamoku had left his board at home. Some seaside councils had indeed imposed local bans: they had justifiable safety concerns following numerous injuries inflicted by out-of-control 150lb (68kg) tankers crashing through the bathers in the shore break. But seeing the quality of the surf, Duke knocked up a board out of a length of sugar pine, took it to Freshwater Beach and showed off to the crowd on 23 December 1914. The holiday event garnered massive news coverage. Kahanamoku extended his tour to New Zealand, with similar demonstrations to similar effect on both North and South Islands in February and March 1915. When he finally left Australia his board stayed there and a nation was hooked.

The established traditions of the surf lifesaving clubs in Australia took board design towards the rescue and racing scene. The resulting boards were big, long and buoyant and weren't particularly suited to manoeuvring. Not that the Australians were bothered: although the design revolution of the fin had arrived in Australia it wasn't used to manoeuvre on to the shoulder but just to hold the board in track as it sped straight to the beach.

After the Melbourne Olympics in late 1956, however, a group of dedicated American surfers arrived as part of a sporting goodwill tour. Although sponsored by the US government to take part in lifesaving carnivals and paddleboard races, they also brought with them a quiver of the new 'Malibu' boards. Exhibitions were given to stunned crowds at surf carnivals around the coast, and the Americans surfed in the Australian national championships at Bells Beach, Victoria. The effect was dramatic. Demand for the new boards was enormous but

KAHANAMOKU'S FRESHWATER BOARD

The 8ft 8in (2.6m) sugar pine board that Duke made and rode at Freshwater now resides behind glass, on show at the Freshwater Surf Lifesaving Club. It was actually in regular use up until 1976, when the Club decided it was perhaps better off being retired. It is now insured for around $1 million.

there was no balsa in Australia, so plywood copies were quickly slung together. Meanwhile, urgent enquiries were made to Californian board suppliers, and Australian manufacturers tooled up in anticipation of a whole new local industry. In 1959 board-makers in Australia knocked out 1,500 foam and fibreglass boards; by just 1962 that figure was up to 7,500. Modern surfing had well and truly arrived Down Under.

'TRADITIONS DEMANDED THAT SURFERS RIDE THEIR BOARDS STRAIGHT TOWARDS THE BEACH THROUGH THE CHURNING WHITE WATER. CUTTING TOWARDS THE GREEN SLOPING SHOULDER OF A WAVE RAISED QUESTIONS ABOUT ONE'S MANHOOD. THE RELATIVE SAFETY OF THE SHOULDER OF THE WAVE WAS OUT OF BOUNDS AND WAS ONLY USED BY SCOUNDRELS AND COWARDS.'

Murray Walding, Australian surfing journalist

EUROPE

Somewhat surprisingly, the birthplace of surfing in the UK may not have been the rugged Atlantic coast of Cornwall, but the genteel North Yorkshire resort of Bridlington. Letters discovered in the extensive files of the Bishop Museum in Hawaii show that two of the same Hawaiian princes (Jonah Kuhio Kalanianaelo Piikoi and his brother David Kahalopouli Piikoi) who took surfing to the US in 1885 also took to the water in Bridlington in 1890 whilst being educated in England.

A letter dated September 1890 describes how they 'enjoy surf riding very much and surprise the people to see us riding the surf.' It isn't known exactly what type of board they rode, but it's certain they would have been cold.

The Jack London article that kicked off US interest in the Polynesian Sport of Kings was also published in Britain in 1908 in the society magazine *Pall Mall*. There, however, it didn't have quite the same effect. The media were certainly curious, but who would surf in the British climate? It's hardly surprising that the first British surf club was established as far south as geographically possible, in Jersey in 1923.

But most of the early experiments with surfing took place in the Cornish resort of Newquay. In 1929 Londoner Lewis Rosenberg saw newsreel footage of Australian surfers at Bondi Beach and had a go at fashioning his own balsa board. Cine footage exists of him trying it out in the summer waves of 1930 around Newquay, although he lacked wax and a fin. A genuine Tom Blake 14-footer was imported from Hawaii in 1938 by Jimmy Dix, who used it for years with modest success on his summer trips to the Cornish coast. It was in 1938 that Newquay local Pip Staffieri saw the Blake board and built his own hollow version of it, but had the idea of adding a keel fin to enable him to trim across the waves.

At the end of the Second World War servicemen from the Royal Australian Air Force stationed near Newquay staged a celebratory surf carnival that attracted 5,000 spectators. Alongside the exhibitions of lifesaving and sea swimming were demonstrations of surfboard riding.

Some servicemen had by that time fabricated boards locally; others had already brought over their own boards from home.

Although a few visiting surfers showed up here and there over the years, the UK for long lacked a local knowledge base. Surfing only became firmly established in Britain with the import of Australian lifeguards and their boards into Cornwall in the early 1960s. In

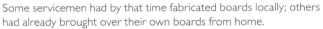

🏄 **Two Surfing Hawaiian princes in Bridlington 1890!**

⬆ **Charlie Force rides one of the first British surf craft in Newquay'. (Charlie Force)**

⬇ **Bells Beach, Australia.**

THE FIRST SURFING LESSON

Peter Viertel recalls what was, in effect, the first surf lesson in Europe:

'How does it work?' they would ask. 'You lie on the board and the boat pulls you?'

'There is no boat.'

'But what makes the board move?'

'The waves.'

'The waves? I don't understand.'

'You paddle with your arms and once you have enough speed, the waves take over, and you get up and ride the board, steering it with your feet.'

'Aha, I see. *C'est comme le ski nautious.*'

'Not at all.'

Peter Dixon's *Men Who Ride Mountains*, 1969

1962 four Aussies came down from London, caught sight of the Cornish surf and immediately arranged to get themselves hired on the privately owned local beaches to stave off the recent spate of summer drownings. Where the early Cornish pioneers were struggling with their wooden logs, the Australians had their own foam and fibreglass boards and were good surfers even by Australian standards of the time.

The sight of surfing lifeguards regularly enjoying the waves created a demand for boards that could only be met by a local industry. A few individuals had a go at fashioning boards for the local market, but it wasn't until one of the original four Australian guards – Bob Head – teamed up with local man Bill Bailey that the industry really blossomed, with Bilbo Surfboards leading the way.

The sport then spread up the English and Welsh coasts, and across the Irish Sea. Three clubs were established in Ireland by 1964, although the first Irish surfer was probably a 14-year-old lad called Joe Roddy, who in 1949 saw a pattern of a surfboard in his father's woodworking magazine and set about making his own model out of old floorboards and tea chests.

Surfers in France experimented with their own boards after having seen movies and heard stories of Hawaiian and Australian surfing. Again it was the travelling Australians who consolidated surfing in Continental Europe (amongst them the lifeguards from Cornwall, who headed down to Biarritz at the end of the summer in 1962), but it was moviemakers who brought the first boards.

Californian screenwriter Peter Viertel claims to have introduced the Malibu board to France in 1954. Visiting Biarritz for locations for a Hollywood film, Viertel – a beginner surfer at Malibu – was amazed to find that both the climate and the waves in south-west France were a match for those in Southern California. He immediately requested that two boards be airfreighted to France.

Surfing in France was quickly chic, but slow to spread far beyond the popular resort of Biarritz. Travelling professionals kept its profile relatively high in the world of surf movies, but all this did was encourage yet more temporary blow-ins. For the French it remained

really a marginal sport until the Lacanau Pro contest opened in 1979, whereupon it expanded rapidly.

The surf industry established a European headquarters in the Basque region in the 1980s, encouraging more contests and more crowds. The region was to become *en vogue* with disillusioned and burnt-out American and Australian professionals in the 1990s, which ensured that surfing standards were always high enough to intrigue the media and keep a spotlight on the area's formidable waves. By the 2000s France had a batch of home-grown professionals on the World Tour.

The spread of surfing into Spain has been traced to the day a French board (with the logos removed to pretend it was Australian) was brought to Santander and ridden at Sardinero Playa in May 1962. From Cantabria, surfing spread along the northern coast and eventually to the rest of the wave-rich Spanish coastline. It was the discovery of the world-class river-mouth break at Mundaka and the consistent waves of Spain's own version of Hawaii – the Canary Islands – that consolidated the reputation of and participation in Iberian surfing.

Portugal's history is less clear-cut, but by the 1970s it had received widespread mainstream attention for the power and consistency of the waves on its Atlantic coast. A premium destination for travelling surfers in its own right, Portugal is a hotbed of surfing talent whose major contribution to global surf culture is perhaps the introduction of surfing to its former colony – and future surfing powerhouse – Brazil.

Today there's barely a European country that doesn't have its own surfing community. The Mediterranean, the Baltic and the North Sea all get waves that are eminently rideable and the coastal nations all have locals ready to ride them. The relative affluence of the European nations means that wherever you travel in the world you'll bump into German, Dutch, Scandinavian and Swiss surfers all on the hunt for quality waves.

LATIN AMERICA

Although the *Caballiteros* of Peru were amongst the first recorded surfers, modern wave-riding in South America again owes its birth to Duke Kahanamoku. In 1930s Waikiki he first inspired, then taught, the son of a wealthy magnate from Peru, who returned home and near Lima promptly formed the rather exclusive Club Waikiki. The first national championships were held in 1950 and Peru's position was consolidated when selected to host the first World Championship under the auspices of the newly formed International Surfing Federation. It was won by local boy Felipe Pomar.

Surfing then stalled slightly in Peru; it was maintained as the preserve of the wealthy who, taking the Sport of Kings at face value, had little interest in spreading it to the masses. Not until surfing moved into the newly opened beach resorts of the 1970s and '80s did it spread more widely. The 1990s saw the creation of the Latin American Surfing Association (ALAS), and by 2004 Latin America had its first world champion in Peru's Sofia Mulanovich.

The sleeping giant of Brazil probably witnessed its first surfing before the Second World War, at Santos. Here, the first to turn on to wave riding were not lifeguards, as elsewhere, but a community of scuba divers. In the 1960s and 1970s the scene moved to the Rio beaches of Arpoador and Ipanema Pier, where it became trendy amongst the hanging musicians and intellectuals. In the 1972 *Verão da contracultura* Brazil held its first surf championship at the Pier and never looked back. In 1976 the newly formed Professional World Tour chose Brazil to host one of its stops – the Waimea 5000 (named, rather confusingly, after the local sponsoring surf shop, which was named after the Hawaiian surf break) – duly won by a local. The very next year both contestants in the final were Brazilian. Ever since then Brazilians have been a permanent fixture in the top 30 world-ranked professionals.

AFRICA

Body surfing and belly-boarding had been reported by seafarers along the African West Coast in the 1830s, but this was probably little more than the spontaneous fun of local kids. Political unrest, poverty and disease are the everyday realities for many Africans, and this has always kept the leisure pursuit of surfing at a very low priority. Consequently, surfing began – and has tended to remain – confined to the tips of the continent: European travelling surfers migrating south took surfing into Morocco, and travelling Australians explored the relative affluence of Apartheid-era South Africa in the early 1960s.

The earliest documented example of surfing in South Africa occurred in 1919. Two US Marines on a naval vessel heading home at the end of the First World War had with them wooden boards and surfed the break at Muizenberg.

This seems to have been a rather isolated incident that had little cultural knock-on effect. But by the 1920s boards were being made that were crude copies of Hawaiian craft seen in pictures. They were again ridden at Muizenberg, tested, and rapidly improved; but, as in Australia, the establishment of surf lifesaving initially directed most design trends towards better rescue boards. Not until the 1938 Empire Games revealed the advances that Australians had made in stand-up surfing did South Africans sit up and take notice.

Exoticism is what led most travelling surfers to South Africa once Bruce Brown's seminal movie *Endless Summer* was released. The established urban spots around Cape Town and Durban were the bases from which surfers fanned out on to the coast to colonise famed breaks such as Cape St Francis and Jeffrey's Bay. Certainly, in 1963 Brown was able to sell the idea of the African coast as a vast unexplored wilderness, and for many surfers that's how much of it remains.

↑ *Caballitos de totora* – **Peruvian reed watercraft.**

ASIA

After building a hotel in Bali and paddling out to ride Kuta Beach in late 1936, transplanted Californian Robert Koke may have been the first surfer in the whole of the immense Indonesian archipelago. Cultural attitudes meant that surfing didn't catch on: the ocean was a place in which spirits resided, some of them threatening and evil. Indonesia remained a surfing backwater until Australians and a few hardy Americans started to arrive in the late 1960s. Through the 1970s oil industry workers in Indonesia, Sumatra and Kalimantan regularly visited Bali to surf. The first locals borrowed boards to try in 1971 and by 1973 a local club had formed to promote Balinese participation in the sport. The first contest was held in 1976.

It wasn't until the professional era had ushered big money into the surf industry that surfing was widely promoted in Asia in an effort to exploit a potentially enormous new market. The first Indonesian Championship was held only as late as 2004, but now Asia has its own Tour – in 2011 the first professional Asian Surfing Championship was held, comprising nine events in four countries (Indonesia, Malaysia, Taiwan and Thailand).

← **Cape St Francis in South Africa.**

THE MODERN ERA

During the growth years of the late 1950s and the 1960s the surfer was largely considered a low-class bum. To the media, surfers were vagabonds exploiting relative post-war affluence and freedom by just wandering around looking for nothing other than kicks and waves. The surfing self-image, however, was that of a unique tribe of confrontational non-conformists escaping the increasing regimentation and stale contentment of society.

Inflated images aside, there remained the uncomfortable reality of out-of-control boards becoming a genuine hazard in the crowded surf of many popular beaches. Some US beach authorities and local councils responded by legislating to separate the surfers from the bathers – surfers were banished to the margins. Segregation quickly became alienation. So surfers sought recognition in other ways: hip language, outrageous clothing, hooliganism and vandalism. Surfing movies were banned in many cities in the US after a destructive series of near-riots and general mayhem. Some beaches were then entirely closed to board-riding.

The bans led to the formation of the US Surfing Association to try to resolve the growing problem of the poor image of surfing. The Association managed to save many further beaches from closure to board-riders. Using the Association as a model, other clubs reformed

and began a slow journey towards respectability. It was becoming hard to surf without it.

It was even harder in Australia, where there was the added schism between the community values of the well-established surf-lifesaving clubs set against the scornfully individualistic Australian surfer. The low esteem of the surfer changed to reluctant respect only once Bernard 'Midget' Farrelly won the unofficial world title at the Makaha, Hawaii, International Surfing Championships. His victory made the front page of every major Australian newspaper.

Just as surfing was struggling to define itself and gain respectability, mass acceptance was thrust upon it when Hollywood awoke to the fascinating sub-culture existing right under its nose. Never mind respectability, what about the marketability? When in 1959 the teen surf-movie *Gigdet* became a smash hit, the full force of mainstream exploitation was focused on the hip subculture of surfing.

First came the sequels and spin-offs, then came the music. With the establishment of surf fashion as the height of cool, the clothing industry also took off. Surfing accessorised itself. To some sceptics, surfing had lost its innocence and become just another product in the youth marketplace.

Surfing split into the cynical purists and the new go-getters. But

⬇ **The 'Look' in the 60s – when checking each other was more important than checking the waves.**

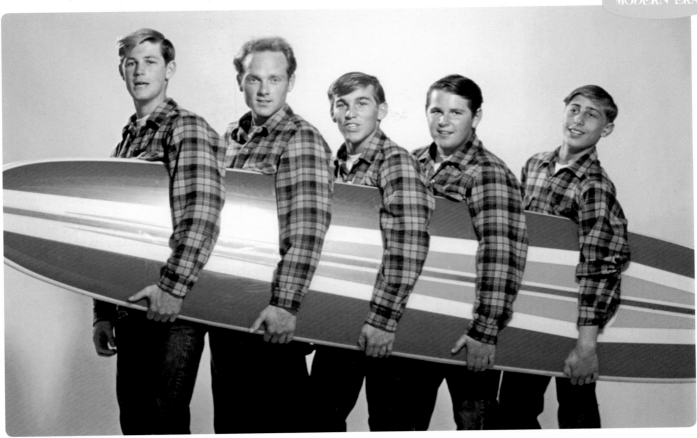

even the splits within the surfing community helped fuel its popularity: whether it was Miki Dora set against Phil Edwards in California, or Midget Farrelly at loggerheads with Nat Young in Australia, the various personalities and concocted rivalries served only to make surfing ever more fascinating to the public. Like it or not, by the late 1950s surfing was firmly in the mainstream.

THE TRANSITIONAL ERA

Style-wise, where the cool pose of nose-riding remained sacrosanct in California, it was quickly superseded in Australia once the surfing population expanded beyond the enclaves of Noosa, Byron and Crescent Head. Most Australian waves beyond these early surf centres were less suited to nose-riding, being shifting peaky beach breaks or heavy sucking slabs.

California remained nose-riding heaven until the 1966 world championships in San Diego, where Australian Nat Young demonstrated a range of power-surfing manoeuvres that humbled the complacent Californian favourites.

The Young result drove surfing into more radical experimentation in equipment, led by shapers Bob McTavish and George Greenough. Californian Greenough had come to Queensland with an overcoat stuffed with camera equipment and a head stuffed full of ideas. The Aussies quickly got over their preconceptions about Greenough – notably, he didn't stand up to surf – when they saw how innovative he was. McTavish would watch Greenough's radical approach on his kneeboards and inflatable mats, and try to translate that into surfboard design. They rapidly set about hacking feet of redundant foam off the old logs. Such was the frenzy of innovation that McTavish now claims that 'three-quarters of the development of the shortboard' took place in that single year of 1967.

⬆ **The Beach Boys only needed one surfboard because only one of them could actually surf.**

⬇ **John Kelly was a persistent innovator: this is his radical hydro-hull.**

SURFING HISTORY 23

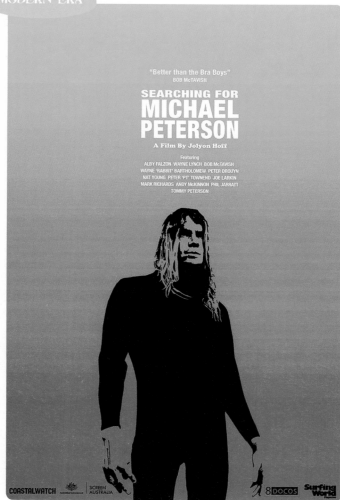

"Better than the Bra Boys"
BOB McTAVISH

SEARCHING FOR
MICHAEL PETERSON

A Film By Jolyon Hoff

Featuring
ALBY FALZON · WAYNE LYNCH · BOB McTAVISH
WAYNE 'RABBIT' BARTHOLOMEW · PETER DROUYN
NAT YOUNG · PETER 'PT' TOWNEND · JOE LARKIN
MARK RICHARDS · ANDY McKINNON · PHIL JARRATT
TOMMY PETERSON

COASTALWATCH   SCREEN AUSTRALIA   8 DOCOS   Surfing World

← **Michael Peterson in the mid-1970s might have looked like our modern conception of a soul-surfer but was a ruthlessly fierce professional competitor.**

This period of accelerated experimentation and innovation – begun in 1966 and lasting until around 1972 – has come to be known as the 'transitional' era. Australian surfing writer Tim Baker has described it as 'a confused time in surfing's history. Some still see it as a golden era of design innovation, alternative lifestyles and counter-culture consciousness. Others see it as a dark, shameful era of drug-induced design lunacy and a period in which surfing fell from grace.'

By 1970 Australians had lost the world titles by competing on untested designs as short as 5ft 6in (1.68m).

1970s SOUL

Through the 1970s the line-up remained fairly stable, if somewhat split into factions. The traditionalists favoured single-fin shapes in subtle variations of the rounded pintail; more experimental-minded surfers used the wider swallow-tailed twin fins.

As a hangover from the countercultural late-1960s, however, a schism appeared in the whole philosophy of surfing. On the one hand, professionalism beckoned, backed by an industry in full corporate swing and focused on contests with thousands of dollars in prize money; on the other hand self-styled 'soul surfers' rejected what they saw as the prostitution of the professionals and sought to preserve surfing as an art-form rather than a sporting circus. Many rejected materialism, consumption and competition in favour of free-form creativity and self-expression.

In the confusion, some top surfers – World Champions like Farrelly and 1970's Rolf Arness – gave up the sport because they could see no career path, no money, no clear future. If there was something of an apocalyptic feel during this time, it wasn't entirely nihilistic, but at its most optimistic called for the fraternal individualism of surfing to provide an alternative possible utopia. Critics, however, argued that 'soul-surfers' were little more than undisciplined, self-indulgent druggies and that surfing would always be held back until it truly professionalised itself.

Despite the naivety of some of the pronouncements of the time, the 'soul era' was an important period of introspection for surfing. Ever since this time, the ethos of the 'soul-surfer' has lent a counterweight to the rampant corporatisation of surfing: its potency revealed in the way that since the 1990s the major corporations have sought to appropriate its imagery and mores into their own marketing strategies.

THE PROFESSIONAL ERA

Making a determined bid for legitimacy and public acceptance, the first Professional World Championship was a global tour of competitions undertaken during 1976. Australian Peter Townsend was proclaimed the winner. Despite the emergence of some colourful competitors and consummate athletes – most of them (with a few noble exceptions) articulate, photogenic and fairly well-groomed – the professional game failed to ignite the passions of the public. The stagnation ended when Peter Drouyn introduced man-on-man surfing with no-rules heats in the Stubbies Classic at Burleigh Heads, Queensland, in March 1977. It was a format that was simpler

So, rather than being constrained by the Californian fads of the time, Australian board designs grew from scaled-up versions of Greenough's kneeboards, well adapted to fit the short, steep Aussie waves. The collaborative efforts of Greenough and McTavish illustrate the global fusion that was bubbling along in the surf world underneath various crude national and personal rivalries promoted by the media.

By 1967 in Australia, big nose-riding boards were old hat; the new extreme V-bottom boards, such as McTavish's Fantastic Plastic Machines, had become all the rage. This style of board was down to 8ft (2.4m) long and 20in (0.5m) wide with a flexing fin. Very manoeuvrable in beach breaks, they were nevertheless tricky to control and had yet to prove themselves in really big waves.

Late in 1967 top Aussies Young, McTavish and Ted Spencer, with George Greenough, travelled to Hawaii, taking along their V-bottomed plastic machines. But the boards failed dramatically to cope with the power of the North Shore; the young Hawaiians had boards that were longer, racier, thinner, narrower and sleeker. It did turn out, however, that the plastic machines were fairly well suited to the reeling breaks of Maui. Eventually both sides were impressed. This meeting of the minds, in what's now known as the Honolua Sessions, became a design watershed: the deep V-bottomed plastic machines were instantly obsolete, and plan shapes were pulled in the tail. The deep V was replaced by more subtle curves, and rails were down-turned for more bite.

WORLD TITLES

The first international surfing championships were held at Makaha in 1953, organised by the Waikiki Surf Club. Judging criteria included sportsmanship, grace and deportment, and the event was as much a fraternal social gathering as a rigorous competition.

Although not convened under the auspices of an international governing body, the first so-called 'World Championship' competition was held at Manly, Australia, in 1964. Entrants came from Hawaii, California and Australia. Corporate sponsorship was provided by Ampol, and a crowd estimated at 65,000 saw local surfer 'Midget' Farrelly take the title.

Shortly after, the International Surfing Federation was formed, so the first fully sanctioned World Championships were those held in Peru in 1965, again won by a local favourite, this time Peruvian Felipe Pomar. The 1966 title contests held in San Diego, California, provided the first real upset when Nat Young's radical carving style was scored higher than the contrasting nose-riding of Californian David Nuuhiwa.

The first Professional World Championship Tour was held during 1976 – won by Australian Peter Townsend.

to score, simpler to follow, and simpler to dramatise. As the season's first event, the success of the Stubbies was crucial: as it happened, the waves turned on, the event was a massive hit and the man-on-man format was introduced with no further ado to three-quarters of the world tour venues that year.

Pro surfing marched towards the neon 1980s on the back of supremely marketable world champs such as Shaun Tompson and Wayne Bartholomew. 'Bugs' Bartholomew's portrayal of himself as a bona fide rock star was just the spur that sponsors Quiksilver and Rip Curl needed to break out of the local Victoria scene and become huge corporate players on the global stage.

Professional surfing itself became a global brand and was taking competitors not necessarily always to the best surf, but to the biggest potential markets: in 1979 four of the thirteen tour events were held in Japan.

Everything to do with surfing was getting bigger, bolder and brasher – contests, sponsorship, budgets, colours. By the end of the 1970s, whether you were a travelling feral soul surfer or a fully-sponsored professional you had some status, some self-belief, comfortable in the validity of your sport.

THE 1980S

In 1981 Simon Anderson evolved an experimental three-fin design into what he called the iconic 'Thruster'. Proven and dominant in competition, it's still the default design decades later. Equally significant was the development of America's National Scholastic Surfing

↑ **Barton Lynch and Tom Curren share the honours in France in 1988.**

Association. Posited as a kind of academy towards progress to the IPS, competitive surfing in the US was now underpinned by a rigorous coaching structure led by two Australians, Ian Cairns and Peter Townsend.

Cairns was to take the reform of professional surfing even further when he replaced the old Hawaiian-based IPS with a new governing body, the Association of Surfing Professionals. Significantly, the ASP found a new home in the heart of big money and surf media – Orange County, California.

A new international sporting rivalry of Californian Tom Curren and Australian Mark Occhilupo further boosted the profile of professional surfing, and resulted in unprecedented levels of performance in the many man-on-man heats they fought. But it also led to a riot at Huntington Beach in 1986; now surfing was international news once again for all the wrong reasons. The media enjoyed rehashing the old question of whether surfers were dedicated athletes or just a bunch of antisocial hooligans.

NOW

Since that last stutter at the gates of mainstream acceptance, surfing has gone on to become an almost inescapable element of Western culture, particularly in the spheres of imagery, music and clothing. The unprecedented sporting achievements of multiple world champion Kelly Slater have certainly helped, as has his high celebrity profile.

Heading into the new century the acceptability of surfing has never been higher. The prevalence of manuals, surf schools and surf camps continues to increase the number of people actually getting in the water; the prevalence of surfing imagery in the mainstream media exponentially raises the number who'd love the chance to try. Live Internet streaming of professional contests frees the organisers of the ASP and WQS to take their surfers to the best waves – not necessarily to the most physically accessible venues – knowing that huge audiences are happily following the spectacle online.

Increasingly, surfers don't even need to visit the ocean. The jury is still out on whether the boom in indoor arenas siphons off the crowds of would-be surfers or creates yet more people heading for the beach looking for the thrill of the real thing. In the 21st century surfing is available to all and acceptable to all. It is no longer an escape from real life, it *is* real life.

When Captain James Cook arrived in Hawaii in 1778 after crossing thousands of miles of empty ocean from the Society Islands

Kelly Slater collected his 44th elite tour victory in the men's Rip Curl Pro, Portugal, 2010.

Pro surfer Kelly Slater in action.

he was astounded to find the natives paddling surfboards out to meet him and conversing in a language he had heard spoken all across the Pacific. 'How shall we account for this Nation spreading itself so far over this Vast ocean?' he marvelled. Well, by now the surfing tribe is 23 million strong and is still spreading across the oceans of the world. This is your chance to join it.

'IT IS POSSIBLE THAT NO SPORT PRACTISED BY FEWER PEOPLE HAS EVER HAD THE INFLUENCE OF SURFING ON AMERICAN STYLE.'
Guy Trebay, *New York Times, 2006*

'EVERY WAVE IS A PERFECT EXPRESSION OF THE PRESENT TENSE: IT CAN'T BE GRASPED OR PROLONGED, ONLY RIDDEN.'

Fiona Capp from *That Oceanic Feeling: a surfing odyssey*, 2003

CHAPTER 2

THE ELEMENTS

Nowadays you can pay good money to ride artificial waves indoors, but to most surfers the raw and elemental nature of surfing is still much of the sport's appeal. Great satisfaction can be had working out how all the elements conspire just to produce a clean wave that reels off at your local break. For free!

Not every surf spot is covered by surf-spy cameras and helpful mates with mobile phones, so if you want to be in the right place at the right time (not just at the same place at the same time as everybody else), get yourself a thorough understanding of weather systems and wave patterns.

WINDS

Surfing great waves on a day that's overcast without a breath of breeze, you have the Sun and the wind to thank for the swell. How does that work?

Simply put, if air temperature was constant across the entire planet we'd never have any wind and therefore no swell. Thankfully, striking the Earth's poles obliquely and the equator square on, the Sun cannot heat the atmosphere of our spherical planet with uniform intensity.

The Equator is closer to the sun so it receives more heat than the Poles. The heat that does arrive at the Poles is distributed over a wider surface area.

More heat energy will always be received at the tropics than at the poles. Air isn't warmed directly by the Sun's rays, however, but by heat radiating from the Earth's surface; therefore rates of warming vary, also depending upon the type and aspect of the surface.

Due to ever-present temperature differentials, our atmosphere is volatile. Heated air will rise; rising air has reduced pressure, thus allowing cooler air to rush in beneath it. Cooled air sinks, its increasing pressure displacing warmer air. Wind is simply currents of air moving along pressure gradients as the atmosphere seeks equilibrium. These

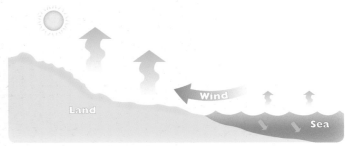

winds might be steady and predictable throughout the year (as in the Trade Wind belts) or ferociously seasonal (the word 'monsoon' is derived from an Arabic term signifying 'season').

Amongst the strongest winds are those associated with frontal disturbance. Depending upon their origin and the surface they

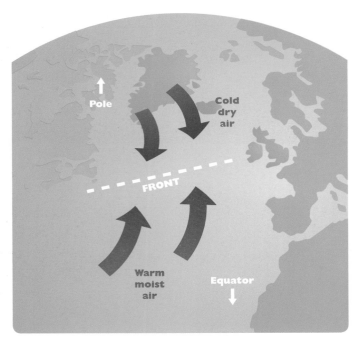

travel across, air masses can differ starkly in terms of temperature, pressure and humidity; these masses of air tend not to mix readily when they meet.

One example of frontal disturbance of particular interest to surfers is that of a mass of warm, moist, tropical air advancing to meet an area of cold, dry, dense, polar air. Generally the warm air is forced gently upwards, but should there be a spot of particularly marked pressure differential along the front (perhaps due to some external factor, such as surface temperature) winds will increase and the front will develop a distinct kink in it. In any weather system air always moves down the pressure gradient from high pressure to lower pressure; the sharper the gradient, the stronger the resulting wind. But it cannot rush in directly: as the wind is deflected and sent spinning by the rotation of

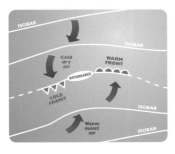

↑ The beginnings of a frontal depression. The front kinks at an area of particular differential in the two air masses.

↑ A fully-developed low pressure system. Winds follow the isobars. In the warm sector winds blow in a steady direction giving the best conditions to bear a swell.

PREDICTING THE WIND

Winds may be mercurial but they're not entirely unpredictable. There are principles and patterns that you can interpret to predict wind shifts and so anticipate good surfing conditions.

Coastal winds experienced in a stable atmospheric system (as in a blocking anticyclone) are a result of fairly simple temperature differentials between the land and the sea. During the daytime, the land heats up more than the reflecting sea (water has a higher specific heat capacity), so air will move from the sea to replace the warmer air expanding and rising over the land – an onshore breeze. The sea retains what heat it has stored

from the Sun into the night-time, whereas the land rapidly cools; so eventually during the night the cold land air rushes down to displace the warmer air rising over the sea – an offshore breeze. The offshore wind will persist into the late morning, giving ideal surf conditions until the Sun gets hot and the air above the heating land begins to rise again.

If the weather system is actively travelling over your position – as with a frontal depression – the winds are still predictable to a large degree. The length of time the wind blows from a certain direction depends upon the speed and proximity of the system, but the way the winds shift around the points of the compass follows a set pattern. In the northern hemisphere the approach of a low-pressure system is signalled by a wind slowly backing to the south or south-east due to the impending warm front. As the warm front passes, winds will be steady from the south-west with dull conditions in the warm sector. When the following cold front comes through, the skies will clear and the wind will veer sharply to the west and then north-west or even north. There may well be a few hours of relatively light winds before the north-westerly really starts to blow. The cold front is unstable, so clouds will be vertically extended and winds will initially be very gusty. Applying this kind of knowledge to your own stretch of coast can give you just enough of a weather window to get in a good session at a sheltered spot.

↑ Early morning offshore breeze.

An unstable cold front means looking for a sheltered cove.

WEATHER MAP

A weather map – either online or in newsprint – displays all the information a surfer needs, if you learn how to interpret it. The lines on the weather map are isobars joining areas of equal barometric pressure: the closer the lines, the steeper the gradient and so the stronger the winds. Weather fronts are shown by red lines with red semi-circles (warm front), and blue lines with blue triangles (cold front). Weather systems are clearly marked 'L' (low) for a depression and 'H' (high) for an anticyclone. Arrows indicate a system's direction of travel. A glance at a single weather map will give you some indication of how severe a disturbance is over the ocean, its extent, and its direction of travel: with just this information you could make a reasonable stab at guessing the arrival of any swell.

A more assured guess can be made by looking at three-day weather charts online. Now you know how rapidly the storm is moving your way. If you take a guide of swell travelling approximately 600 miles (960km) in 24 hours, you can work out whether the clean swell is likely to reach you much before the mother system arrives and trashes it.

Maps known as WAM (wave model) charts are also available online, and feature in many surf prediction websites. They graphically display swell direction and mean wave height/significant wave height, and, most importantly, the period of a swell. The higher the number for the period, the better quality the swell.

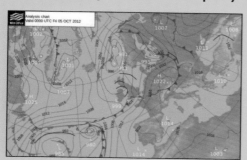

← Weather map showing isobars, weather systems and fronts.

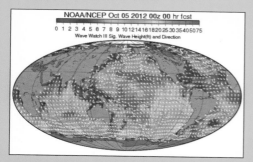

← Wave model chart showing wave height and direction.

the Earth (a phenomenon known as the Coriolis effect), the kink in the front becomes more and more pronounced until it's the shape of a wave. We now have a classic mid-latitude depression swerving across the ocean with the winds churning away inside it, the whole system a spinning vortex of energy.

The swirling winds at the centre of a storm produce chaotic conditions, but a depression will advance by means of the cold front chasing a warm front ahead of it. In this sector the isobars are relatively straight, so here winds will blow strongly in one direction for a sustained period of time, giving the best conditions to bear a swell.

So a deep depression over the ocean is the midwife of swell, but how does that wind energy transfer itself to water?

When air starts to move over water some interesting things happen. Cooling your cup of tea by blowing across it provides a simple demonstration of the ability of wind to make waves, but the actual process is so complex that it's still imperfectly understood.

Water is heavier and more viscous than air and is bound by the powerful inertia of its own surface tension; so why doesn't the air just slide smoothly across the flat surface of the water, leaving it undisturbed? In fact, water barely registers air *beginning* to move, but

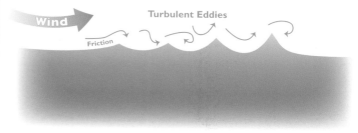

⬆ The effect of air moving across the surface of water.

the smallest amount of friction acting on the lowest layer of moving air slows it down slightly; enough for the layer just above to 'trip' over it, creating eddies that press down on the surface of the water.

The surface level of any liquid is in equilibrium between gravity acting downwards and buoyancy pushing upwards. When a force presses down on the surface of the water, creating a dip, then a counterforce – buoyancy – forces the water to spring back up. This trips up more air, establishing a positive feedback loop: the wind is disturbed by the very waves it has created, so creating higher waves which will trip up more wind, and so on.

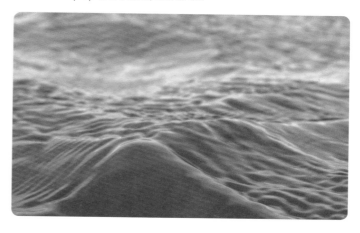

⬆ Wind on water.

SWELL

These wavelets might increase to eventually display whitecaps (a whitecap will form when the angle of the wave crest steepens to less than 120°), but you cannot surf them. How do whitecaps grow to be surfable waves?

Whitecaps close to the source of their generation seem chaotic and directionless and have various wavelengths – their random frequency and direction merely correspond closely to individual strong gusts of wind. Sailors – closer to this kind of energy – would call this a 'sea' or a 'wind-sea'. A 'sea' is described as being 'fully developed' when the amount of force input by the wind is cancelled out by the energy lost by the waves breaking – instead of growing higher, they'll just keep breaking and spilling their energy as foam. But these conditions are unsurfable – so much so that surfers barely have terms to describe them: perhaps 'chop' or 'junk'. We can barely interpret this sea, let alone ride it.

Thankfully, nature has a way of ordering this wind-sea into regular swell for surfers to use. Steeper wavelets of shorter wavelength will always break first, and this transfers part of their energy to the larger, faster wavelets that overtake them. Smaller waves thus inexorably disappear by becoming part of longer, higher ones that store more and

↑ A 'sea' only becomes 'swell' once it propagates away from the storm that generated it.

← Waves organise themselves over time.

more energy. Therefore, as long as the wind blows, energy is always being marshalled into longer waves with lower frequency.

The total amount of energy input depends upon three factors: the speed of the wind, the duration of the blow, and the distance over which the wind blows (fetch). A force eight gale (winds of 20m per second, or 68kph) blowing unobstructed over the open ocean would eventually develop a sea with a significant wave height of 9m and a peak period of 15 seconds. That would create quite a swell.

In order to spawn good, rideable waves a low-pressure system in the Atlantic needs to be deep enough to generate winds of over 32kph for a couple of days, and far enough away to allow radial dispersion to clean up the swell. Applying these criteria to, for example, a surface pressure chart of the North Atlantic, a low pressure of 996mb established for at least 48 hours 800km west of Ireland would make a lot of Western European surfers very happy indeed.

When the waves simply cannot grow any higher but the wind keeps blowing, that extra energy has to go somewhere. It's then that surplus energy is dissipated by the waves beginning to travel out into the surrounding ocean, a process known as propagation.

Waves propagating away from the storm that generates them become 'swell'. Whatever may happen to the storm it's escaped from, the swell will continue to disperse in two ways: circumferentially and radially. Think of a pebble dropped in the centre of a pond: the ripples spread out around the pond and across it.

Circumferential dispersion describes how large the circles have to be in order to fill the pond – the swell moves from its point of origin in a spreading circle getting larger with distance, trying to 'fill' the ocean.

The further it travels, the more it spreads out. But as a swell disperses circumferentially it will lose power – assuming the storm centre to be a single point, the height of a swell is reduced by roughly a third for every doubling of the propagation distance. Of course, a storm centre is rarely a single point; usually it's spread over many miles and often follows the swell it's generating – in this case, the energy in swell is much extended, the loss being in the order of only 15% for every doubling of the propagation distance.

Radial dispersion describes *crossing* the pond rather than *filling* it; that is, how far across the pond the circles have to travel in order to get to a point on the other side. It's during radial dispersion that the swell cleans up and organises itself, a phenomenon crucial to surfers. In practical terms, this means that for a good solid groundswell we need the generating storm system to be far enough away for radial propagation to clean up the swell, but not so far that circumferential propagation will significantly decay it.

One law of dispersion of surface waves on a liquid dictates that different wavelengths travel with different velocities. Shorter waves

⬇ Each parcel of energy has to expand radially and circumferentially as it moves to fill the pond.

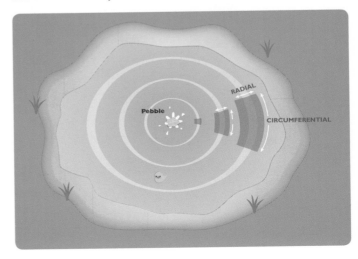

CALCULATING
SWELL SPEED

If you know the period of a swell you can work out roughly the speed at which it's travelling, and when it's likely to reach your surf spot. Simply multiply the period (in seconds) by a factor of three to give you a figure in knots. Knowing the wavelength (expressed in feet) will also enable you to calculate the speed: in knots it's 1.34 times the square root of the wavelength.

A few examples:
Period (T) of 8 seconds = wavelength (λ) of 328ft = speed (c) of 24kt.
T of 12 seconds = λ 737ft = c of 36kt.
T of 16 seconds = λ of 1,310ft = c of 48kt.

A swell usually has a period of between 7 and 12 seconds. The longest period ever timed was 22.5 seconds. That swell would have been travelling at a speed of 67.5kt with a wavelength of 2,500ft, or roughly half a nautical mile. Good luck paddling into that one!

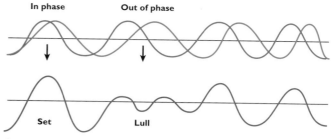

In phase   Out of phase

Set   Lull

⬆ **When two swells of differing wavelengths combine their energies, the result can produce distinct sets and lulls at the shore.**

insignificant waves – between them. Understanding sets is crucial to your whole surfing experience: not so much how they come about, perhaps, but how to cater for them. Sets are slightly mysterious but are most likely the result of two or more apparent swells (or wave trains) being superimposed upon each other in their propagation journey. These swells may well be from the same storm as it intensifies, abates, then re-intensifies in various locations. Where the peaks of the differing wavelengths closely coincide, a set will be formed; where the wavelengths are out of phase, they'll nearly cancel each other out, resulting in a slump of energy – a 'lull'. The greater the propagation distance, the more 'setty' the swell will be. A lull might last for ten or twenty minutes – take the time to scramble back out after a long ride. A set might be ten waves deep, so don't paddle lamely and miss the first one or you'll get nine on your head.

A wave's speed depends on two factors: its own wavelength, and the depth of the ocean across which it travels. In deep water the swell expends only a tiny fraction of its energy in 'lifting' the surface of the water as it passes beneath. Once water depth is less than half the wavelength, however, the wave begins to 'feel the bottom': its energy can no longer pass unobstructed.

Friction against the seabed causes several things to happen. Most notably, the wave as a whole slows down; this results in the wavelength shortening so that a swell concertinas against a shore as the waves in front have the brakes applied. But also the wave becomes asymmetrical as the front slope slows and is pushed upwards by the slightly quicker back of the wave. So a long period swell not only moves faster than a short swell but will also feel the bottom earlier. Forced to rear up sooner, it therefore creates higher waves at the shore.

Speed increases with wavelength (or with the period, as $T = \lambda/c$), but is independent of a wave's height. A long swell might not have great amplitude out at sea, but as it'll feel the bottom earlier it'll jack up higher into a bigger wave.

travel more slowly and lose their energy – 'die' – more quickly than longer waves. So, in effect, the waves are 'filtered' over time and distance. The further from the storm that generated them, the more regular the swell will seem with regard to height and wavelength.

Because longer wavelength swells travel faster, they'll arrive at a distant shore sooner than those of a short wavelength. This often makes it seem as though a swell has come from nowhere – there's no gradual build-up. The better the swell, the more bang with which it arrives; so get to the beach early when the swell first arrives in order to get the most power out of it.

One thing that surfers pick up on as soon as they're ready to leave the shallows and head out the back, is that waves come in groups, or 'sets'. This phenomenon is another result of wave propagation: waves organise themselves into groups of anything between three and a dozen powerful waves, with nothing – or a series of very

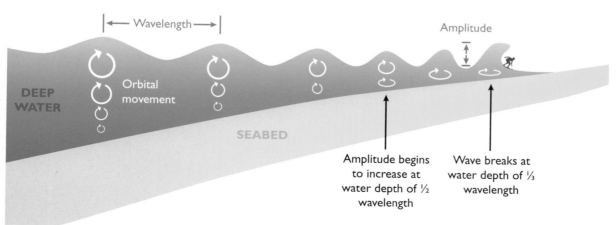

|← Wavelength →|

Amplitude

DEEP
WATER

Orbital
movement

SEABED

⬅ **Amplitude increases whereas wavelength decreases as the swell feels the influence of the bottom.**

Amplitude begins to increase at water depth of ½ wavelength

Wave breaks at water depth of ⅓ wavelength

On its journey across the ocean a swell may encounter a following wind that increases the amplitude of the swell (but it won't increase its wavelength). An adverse wind may diminish it. Swell will gradually lose energy over time (amplitude diminishes in inverse proportion to the square root of its distance from its origin), but in general the most likely thing to stop a swell in its tracks is land. And this is where surfers come in.

When the depth of the water falls to less than half of the wavelength, the wave's mode of travel is modified. As swell approaches the coast, friction on the bottom causes it to slow down, but until the wave breaks at the crest it can only lose a small part of its energy through friction. Therefore, as it slows, it grows higher and amplitude is increased.

Amplitude increases in proportion to how steeply the seabed rises from the bottom – that is, how quickly the brakes are being applied to the lower part of the swell. Friction will affect the swell earlier at the trough than at the crest, so the crest advances relative to the base of the wave: it begins to 'pitch'.

A wave will actually break when the water depth is about 1.3 times the height of the wave. It has now changed from being a wave of oscillation to a wave of translation – one that surfers can actually ride.

TSUNAMI

The destructive force of a tsunami is due to its incredible wavelength – usually over 60 miles (95km). In the ocean, this means it'll be travelling at around 400kt, roughly the speed of a jet airliner. All that that enormous force will do to a boat at sea, however, is swiftly but gently raise it about a metre or so and keep it up there on a long flat crest that may extend for many miles. The amplitude of a tsunami is only magnified once it feels the bottom as it approaches the coast. There it may reach 30m (100ft) high and do incalculable damage.

⬇ **Very little can survive the destructive force of a tsunami once it reaches the coast.**

Although, strictly speaking, speed is independent of wave height, a wave just 1m high will travel at roughly 7kt. No one can paddle that fast for long, if at all, so how then do surfers paddle into waves? Obviously we need some kind of assistance, since we cannot 'match' the speed of the wave by paddling alone. That assistance comes from gravity.

In an unbroken wave the water itself does not travel. Imagine sweeping a broom handle along beneath a rug – you create a wave moving through the rug, but the rug itself is going nowhere. Sitting out back on your board, when a swell passes underneath you you're lifted up and around in an orbital motion to end up exactly where you started. The only way you could travel forwards would be if you were to actually tumble down the face of the wave: this will only happen if the wave is critically steep, because friction is sticking you to the wave surface.

You'll see surfers catch waves barely paddling at all, maybe just one or two strokes, sometimes just using the buoyancy of the board to pop themselves on to the face. They time it so the wave's steep enough for gravity to do all the work for them. They're certainly not paddling at 7kt. All they need to do is 'unstick' themselves.

You don't paddle to match the speed of the wave. You paddle for two reasons: firstly to get in the right position so that gravity can do most of the work; secondly to break the surface tension on the board, to get it to plane so that frictional drag is reduced to the point where gravity can take over. The rest of the ride involves manipulating the board so that the forces of gravity (falling) match the force of friction (sticking) and you stay in the pocket. Paddling force is added at the start only in order to get you out of the sucky, sticky water.

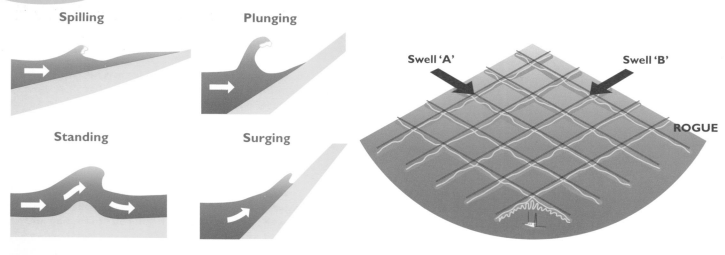

Spilling   Plunging

Standing   Surging

Swell 'A'   Swell 'B'

ROGUE

WAVE TYPES

Waves are classified into five types of which three are surfable, two commonly so:

Spilling – If the slope of the bottom is gentle, the swell is slowed gradually and the resulting wave will merely spill over. This type of wave is common on shallow coasts with a large tidal range, and is the most forgiving wave on which to learn to surf.

Plunging – If the slope is steeper, then the crest will suddenly apparently accelerate, so 'plunging' over into the trough. This type of wave demands more skill to pop up to your feet and negotiate the steep face. The consequences of a wipeout are also potentially more serious.

Standing – When moving water is forced over an obstacle, a 'bump' in the surface of the wave will form which can be steep enough to surf. The water is moving but the wave is fixed; you can surf, but you won't be going anywhere (until you fall off – then you're faced with a long trip downstream). Many indoor artificial surf arenas are based on the principles of standing waves.

Surging – If the coast is 'steep-to' then the swell won't break at all, but will merely surge unbroken up the shore and retreat. It cannot be surfed and it presents a danger to the unwary on the shore.

Rogue – So-called 'rogue' waves have a mythic air about them, but they do exist. They aren't something that need concern the average surfer, however, as they're found far out to sea, where two or more swells from differing directions meet and magnify each other's energy. By the time interfering swells have made it to shore, the effects have invariably been much moderated.

SUPERPOSITION

Handily for surfers, dispersion organises swell into nice, cleanly distinguished lines. But a perfectly even wave is just a close-out. We need something to pull swell into a focal point where the energy is concentrated, where we can catch the wave and ride along it to the channel. A reef or a sandbank usually does this job.

A phenomenon known as linear superposition can also create a focal point. Here, two crests meet each other and produce a spike of energy that combines their heights. But how can this happen? For surfers, it's rare that you get a meeting of two distinct originating swells; sailors might be familiar with its disturbing effects (rogue waves), but by the time the swells reach shore their energies have fused or even cancelled each other out. What's more likely to be of interest to surfers is when a single swell is disrupted by a coastal feature in such a way that the resultant effects – two different *apparent*

swells – re-combine shortly afterwards, often to spectacular effect. This is called lateral superposition.

Lateral superposition could be the result of a small island diffracting swell around, only for it to recombine on the other side. What will also do it is reflection off a cliff or a wall, so long as the wall's set at a fortuitously oblique angle to the incoming swell. Then the wave will hit it, bounce back into the path of either itself or one of the subsequent waves of the swell, and jack up in a startling, but nevertheless fairly predictable, manner. The shape and height of the resulting 'wedge' will be affected by swell angle, wavelength and any sandbank or reef that might have formed near the obstacle.

In small swell conditions, thanks to the doubling effect of lateral superposition, a wedge might be the only place to offer a rideable wave. But bear in mind that with all that focused energy, take-offs will be twice as testing, with a peak that's lurching and difficult to read.

Amplitude is increased when the wave meets the coast, but equally the swell may change its orientation to the shore by means of refraction. Due to friction on the bottom, swell lines always bend to accommodate, or 'echo', the contours of the coast. Refraction describes the way a wave bends when it meets an obstacle, such as a headland or a reef.

Picture a swell advancing in a straight line towards a shallow reef fringed by deep water: that part of the swell striking the reef will be forced to slow down; the rest will advance at the original speed past the reef in deeper water. The result is a pronounced bend in the swell – it 'wraps' around the reef. This concave refraction has the effect of

MAN-MADE

So many board-riders have seen favourite waves compromised or destroyed by ill-advised coastal engineering projects that surfers traditionally have a suspicious attitude to meddling with nature. But it's also true that some breaks have been inadvertently improved by man-made structures or interventions.

Today there are extra pressing needs to understand and apply the mechanics of wave action. The increase in storm action and the rise in sea temperatures attributable to global climate change demand more effective barriers to coastal erosion. Handily, an explosion in the surf population has created not only the desire for more surf breaks but also the money to construct them.

Once policy-makers realise it makes sound economic sense to combine the two needs, surfing could enter an era of radical change, with sea defences designed to take energy out of storm waves by turning them into rideable surf breaks.

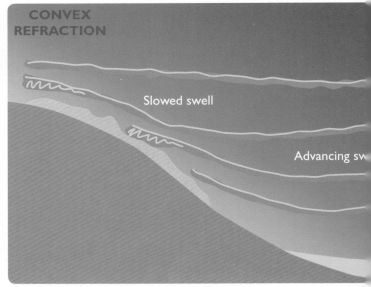

focusing the energy and producing a wave of concentrated power.

When the swell is slowed by a headland or promontory and curves into a deep bay (convex refraction), the energy is more dissipated. Here the amplitude and power of the waves won't be maximally focused as on a reef, but the waves may be more lined-up, enabling longer rides.

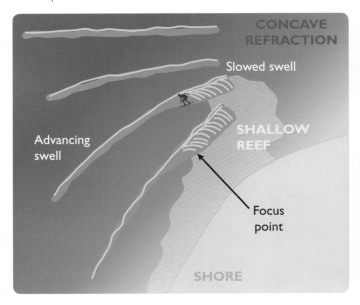

CONCAVE REFRACTION

Slowed swell

SHALLOW REEF

Advancing swell

Focus point

SHORE

CONVEX REFRACTION

Slowed swell

Advancing sw

GEOLOGY

A rock such as the granite of West Cornwall tends not to lie in horizontal beds, and its vertical jointing precludes long surfable reefs. But once broken down by the battering of the ocean, the quartz and feldspar that partly compose the rock produce coarse grains of sand: good for creating very surfable shifting sandbanks. So, visiting West Cornwall, where granite monoliths and large tides dominate the coastal landscape, you could reasonably expect to find beaches with promising sandbanks, but you wouldn't invest too much time searching for reef breaks. In England's North-East the opposite is the case – fingers of flat slate beds have created excellent reef breaks and long point breaks, but the water is murkier and beaches browner, with fewer sandbanks because of the finer sediment.

BEDROCK

Bedrock comprises sedimentary, metamorphic and igneous rocks:

Sedimentary rocks are those unchanged in composition (uniform lithology) since being formed by deposition in horizontal or shallow-angled strata or beds. Potentially they offer the optimum profile for nice even waves and easy landings if you fall off, but they can be *too* even, leading to miles of reef where waves close out or back off. Also, since being laid down flat, sedimentary strata may have been subject to deformation or folding; depending on the various rates of erosion within the differing strata, this could result in jagged rows of rocks at forbidding angles waiting to snag you and your board.

Metamorphic rocks are the widest range of rocks covering the majority of the Earth's surface. They're the result of pre-existing rock (the protolith) being subjected either to heat or pressure so intense that the mineral composition is transformed. Metamorphic rocks offer a wide spectrum of reefs, but irregularities are the rule, more so than with sedimentary rocks: be on the lookout for unpleasant surprises in the shape of the occasional 'board-stop rock'.

Igneous rocks are produced in the crucible of volcanic activity. Volcanic reefs are most often found in oceanic archipelagos and are most renowned where they've been formed by a tongue of lava that's flowed into the sea, cooled, and set into a shape perfect for A-frame peaks. When lava cools and sets it forms a basalt rock that's very hard and rough, and although generally fairly even it can be riddled with potholes and caves to trap the unwary.

A bedrock reef offers waves that are, to a large degree, predictable. The only time the bottom would be subject to change is when a swell may deposit sand over the reef.

Despite the inherent stability of rocky breaks, variables such as wind, tide and swell direction can alter the nature of the break quite significantly: don't expect it necessarily to be the same from one swell to the next.

An adjacent deeper channel means you can often paddle out without getting your hair wet. But beware: without the built-in filter of the white water to contend with you may be tempted to paddle out in conditions more testing than your modest abilities would normally allow. So the advantages for surfing – predictability, less susceptibility to local wind effects – are mitigated, from a learner's point of view, by the qualities of extra power and, of course, the unyielding nature of the bottom.

Predictability also means that the take-off area becomes a single take-off spot, and is therefore crowded, with competition more intense.

BOULDERS

A boulder bed can offer excellent surfing. Boulders are where they are due to gravity, and therefore lie as flat as their complex interlocking shapes will allow. The waves they create are often regular, but before you can ride them you tend to find that the greatest obstacle is in getting into the water in the first place. Boulders can be smooth and slippery and have a nasty habit of leaving foot-sized gaps between them, making snagged leashes and twisted ankles a real possibility. Great care is essential on entry and exit – you cannot rush into the water no matter how good the waves are looking.

On the Atlantic island of Madeira, *fajas* are massive boulder slides that have tumbled down the precipitous cliffs, fanning out into the sea in a neat semicircle. These offer a perfect point set-up upon which the Atlantic swells wrap and unload.

⬇ **Sedimentary rocks subjected to folding can create a very nasty uneven reef.**

⬇ **Usually smooth due to wave erosion, boulders look less threatening but are often very slippery to walk across.**

→ **Sandbanks can emerge or disappear over the course of a single tide.**

SAND

Sand is the end product of erosion and presents fewer obvious dangers to the surfer. It's a relief to be able to walk casually out to a beach break after days of dealing with rocky entries. It won't cut your feet to ribbons, but the danger of sand lies in its shifting, unpredictable nature. Sand cannot be trusted: a bank can alter in shape and profile so radically from one swell to the next that the inattentive surfer can be badly caught out. Expecting yesterday's mellow crumbling waves, you could casually be paddling out to confront today's super shallow death-pits.

Sand is soft when it's aerated. Underwater, this usually won't be the case; once the water has expelled the air and allowed the grains to settle, it can be more like concrete. More surfer neck injuries occur in beach breaks than on rock – a phenomenon that can be partly explained by participation figures perhaps, but is also partly due to complacency.

CORAL

Surfers tend not to be complacent when it comes to coral, as its reputation precedes it. Extremely rare outside the tropics, it's nevertheless everywhere in the surf media. Covering only 0.1% of the earth's surface, surfers are exposed to coral disproportionately because, for a couple of reasons, it creates excellent waves in conditions that are extremely photogenic.

Firstly, the water is crystal clear, because coral struggles to survive if salinity and sunlight fall below certain levels. So there'll be no coral near the sediment and run-off associated with freshwater estuaries, and little of it in consistently sunless regions. Secondly, the waves are super predictable, not just because of the shape of the coral reefs, but because in the tropics the reefs are distant from the main storm tracks' mid-latitude depressions. Arriving swell tends to be cleaned up by having undergone a lengthy journey.

Coral reefs have all the advantages and disadvantages of rock reef but with one extra hazard – a coral reef is alive. Although they look like plants, corals are simple animals that can act as predators capturing prey, but have also developed the plant-like ability to photosynthesise to cope with the barren clear waters of the tropics – which is why they like the Sun. The animal symbiotically lives with a single-celled algal plant lodged in its tissues that provides it with oxygen and glucose. The reef is its outgrown calcified skeleton. The reef cuts you, the organism infests you, and the tropical heat and humidity fester the whole thing.

THE BASQUE WAVE

The famous Basque wave at Mundaka was trashed in the winter of 2004/5 when the bank at the river mouth disappeared entirely. The cause remained mysterious. Whether it was due to heavy dredging some miles upriver or was part of some natural cycle no one was entirely sure. Certainly there had been a marked lack of swell that winter. The phenomenon showed how sensitive sand and silt deposits are to a complex array of factors. The loss of the bank also demonstrated the fragility of surf tourism: 10,000 annual visitors to Europe's most famous left-hander suddenly weren't visiting any more.

MUD

River mouths will often produce excellent banks because the silt carried in suspension is dropped just where the speed of the river current is baulked by the tide. This finer sediment allows little aeration, so river-mouth banks have inherent stability. This is great if the shape of the bank happens to be a good one, not so good if the bank is laid down too uniformly and produces nothing more than a close-out. If it's closing out today, then it'll probably be closing out tomorrow, maybe even this time next year.

Once you get to the coast, whatever its composition or configuration, you won't be able to surf if there's no water on the reef; nor, for that matter, if there's too much. Tides make a huge difference to the waves – more so in some regions than others.

Tides may be predictable, but regional discrepancies seem very puzzling. Britain's Severn estuary and the Bay of Fundy in Canada receive very large tides on opposite sides of the Atlantic (over 10m/32ft in range), but the tide in the middle of the Atlantic rises and falls only about a metre. Then again, the entire Mediterranean Sea experiences average tides of just 20cm (8in).

The answer to this puzzle has to do with natural periods and resonance. If you take a bowl of water and give it one quick shove, the water surges to one side then back again, oscillating like that until it slowly settles. Visualised in cross-section, the movement is like a see-saw: the water is displaced vertically far less at the centre of the system than it will be at the edges. The time it takes the surge to travel from one side to the other is called the period. The larger the bowl, the longer the period.

If you echo that natural period by continuing to shake the bowl rhythmically in time with the surging water, you create resonance and will get wet feet. Whenever the force used to excite the water (the shove, or the Moon) has the same period as the system being excited (the water in the bowl, or the ocean), the amplitude is magnified to its greatest extent and the water sloshes out of the bowl (or surges up the coast).

It just so happens that the natural period of the Atlantic basin is

↑ A tide dropping back six or seven metres, as it regularly does in Cornwall, would have most Pacific Islanders convinced there was an approaching Tsunami.

about 12 hours, which is close to the period of excitation due to the Moon's pull (12 hours 25 minutes). This correspondence exaggerates the amplitude of the tides at the edge of the bowl that is the Atlantic Ocean. If you then add in local features such as the funnel-shape of the Bay of Fundy or the Severn estuary, then that resonance is further amplified.

The opposite is the case in the Mediterranean. Here, the Strait of Gibraltar is so narrow that the tides of the Atlantic barely penetrate. The Mediterranean is therefore isolated from the bowl of the Atlantic, although it's still a significant body of water subject to the influences of the Moon and Sun. But the Mediterranean is effectively two small basins separated by the shallow Strait of Sicily, and each basin has a natural period of only two to three hours. This period is much shorter than the forces of excitation of the Moon (12 hours) or the Sun (24 hours), so there's no resulting resonance. Instead of any amplification, the two forces actually damp each other out. A similar damping effect produces the small tides experienced in the Gulf of Mexico and the Baltic Sea.

Where there are large tides, water level not only has practical implications (a swell will only steepen when water depth is half of the wavelength), but safety concerns also. A reef that was easily makeable at high tide will become steadily more critical as the tide ebbs, leaving less and less margin for error until it starts to suck on to dry rock. A fast-moving tide can also create strong currents that might drag the unwary surfer away from the break and toward a hazard.

Thankfully, apart from occasional adjustments due to local weather conditions (lower or higher atmospheric pressure, strong onshore or offshore winds) tidal levels are entirely predictable, so a local tide table is a prerequisite. Look in shops for the common booklet form, look in local newspapers, search the Internet or watch TV bulletins.

Where printed tidal information isn't available, you can learn to *read* the coast. Study the tide line – is the tide advancing over a dry bottom, or does it seem to be receding, leaving a wet shoreline behind it? Where the growth of barnacles or seaweed ends will mark high water, so where is the tide right now?

Try to predict hazards or difficulties that might present themselves to you when you exit the water after a two-hour surf. During this time the tide may race 200m (220yd) across a flat beach or climb 2m (6.5ft) up a steep cliff. Will those steps be underwater, will that beach have entirely disappeared, or will that dry gulley in the sand have been replaced by a raging rip current? These scenarios could have implications far more serious than just your unattended clothes being washed away.

WHAT CAUSES THE TIDES?

Most surfers intuit that the Moon has something fundamental to do with our tides, but why should there be two tides a day? If it's the Moon that's attracting the seas due its gravitational effect, then why should there be another high tide in the 12 hours when the Moon's on the opposite side of the Earth? Or – another way of putting it – how can there be simultaneously a high tide on opposite sides of the globe?

Countering the inwards force of Earth's gravity, there are two main forces acting on the waters of the Earth. The centrifugal force of our orbital movement around the Sun *throws* water out from the planet, whilst the gravitational attraction of the orbiting Moon *pulls* water away from it.

On the side of the Earth nearest the Moon the oceans will be more affected by lunar gravity, so water here will bulge outwards towards the Moon. On the opposite side, lunar gravity is weak but centrifugal force dominates, throwing water outwards away from the Moon. Each bulge produces a high tide on opposite sides of the Earth.

Another way of conceptualising it is that, in effect, our would-be spherical sea level is stretched into a permanent ellipsoid along the Earth–Moon axis. The tides then *seem* to flood and ebb, but it's the Earth that rotates into, then out of, the bulges, giving us two tides per day.

THE SUN

The Sun has enormous mass, but it is also enormously distant. The tide caused by the Sun is consequently about half that due to the Moon. Overall, then, two-thirds of the tide is due to the Moon and one-third to the Sun, but there are places on the globe where the positions of land masses modify the general rule. The Moon dominates entirely the tides of Western Europe, and dominates mostly the coasts of much of the world. But the lunar influence is overwhelmed by the effects of the Sun in the Gulf of Mexico and Western Australia: here they experience diurnal tides – just one tide per day.

The presence of the continents complicates the model of a tidal bulge moving simply around the Earth; in effect the bulge is contained within oceanic basins. The spinning of the Earth imparts a rotation to the bulge within the basins, so the total effect is not unlike getting a bowl of water and tipping it around in a circular motion: a small crest of water will surge around the rim of the bowl but the water at the centre will actually remain at a fairly constant level. This is called an amphidromic point. Tides here are barely perceptible; surfers in Tahiti will be familiar with this phenomenon. The further your location is from an amphidrome (and there are a dozen scattered around the oceans), the larger your tides will tend to be.

Moon's gravitational force

Sun's gravitational force

Centrifugal force

RIP CURRENTS

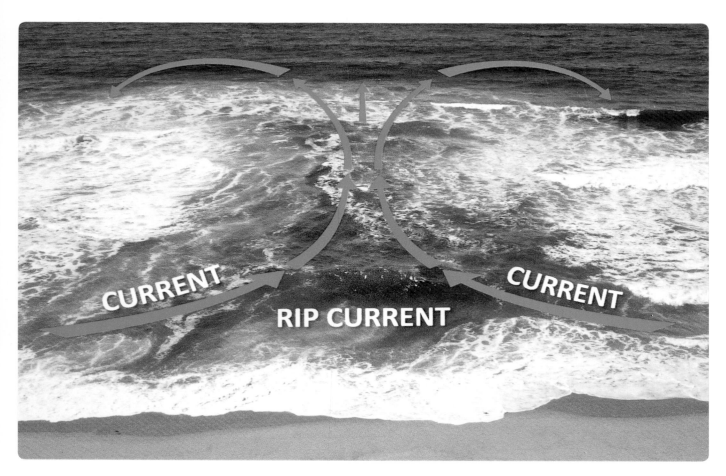

CURRENT

RIP CURRENT

CURRENT

A rip current is a body of water running parallel to the shore or washing out perpendicularly from the shore to the sea. Depending on where you're headed, rips can be your best friend or your worst enemy. They can offer a free ride out the back or send you flailing a mile down the coast; they can churn a good peak to pieces in a few seconds, but also dump enough sand to later create an even better peak. Come to terms with rips by learning firstly how to recognise them, then how to exploit them.

Although they all look pretty much the same to the casual observer, rips can be categorised:

Permanent – A permanent rip is one caused by an obstacle or natural feature that's immobile – examples could be a jetty, a channel in a rock bed, or a headland. The presence of any wave energy will always activate a permanent rip. Its predictability makes it relatively simple for surfers to utilise or avoid, but set waves will produce corresponding surges in rip strength that can be difficult to counter.

Fixed – A fixed rip is likely to exist in a break with a sand or mud bottom; it can persist for days, weeks or months. In sand, rips tend to be self-perpetuating because the action of the water moving steadily seawards scours a yet deeper channel into the sea bottom. Only when the sandbanks are shifted wholesale – by heavy storm action, perhaps – will the fixed rip disappear.

Travelling – Travelling rips are some of the most relentless because their energy is often drawn from local winds in tandem with the angle of swell. Waves striking the shore obliquely due to refraction or swell

HOW TO SPOT A RIP

Rip currents are identified by the following:

- ☐ **Discoloured brown water caused by sand stirred up from the ocean.**
- ☐ **Foam on the surface extending beyond the break.**
- ☐ **A rippled appearance, with waves breaking on both sides of the rip, but not inside the rip.**
- ☐ **Items on the water's surface, floating seaward on the surface of the rip.**

⬇ **A permanent rip formed by a man-made feature.**

COLD WATER

Cold winter swells undoubtedly feel heavier than summer waves even if they have the same amplitude and period. Is this perception accurate? Extra density (more tightly packed molecules) does mean more mass. Kinetic energy is proportional to mass times the square of the velocity, so a wave in winter travelling at the same speed as a summer one of the same size will have more energy.

A colder wave *will* hit you harder, but only slightly: it's been calculated that the increase in kinetic energy would be in the order of only 0.2%, or an extra 4kg in a lip weighing a couple of tons. Of course, the water that you're landing on is also denser, but even so, any perceived effect is more likely due to the way our bodies react to cold water – we're stiffer, slower, and tend to be more apprehensive.

direction will push water along the coast in a steady stream, taking the unsuspecting surfer along for the ride. It is often referred to as 'longshore drift', which describes the action very well.

Flash – Flash rips are the result of water pile-up after a particularly heavy set of waves. Depending upon where a set of waves has focused its energy – next to a jetty, or over a sandbank – there will be a high spot of water that'll suddenly surge back to sea like someone tipping over a giant water tank. Although likely to be short-lived, a flash rip is unpredictable and dangerous due to the amount of energy focused in a small area.

HOW ARE RIP CURRENTS FORMED?

We know that in the ocean, deep water is just the medium through which the wave energy travels – the water itself isn't transported anywhere. Once the swell meets the shore, however, that 'wave of oscillation' becomes a 'wave of translation': white water spills down the wave and its momentum is towards the shore. As a sequence or 'set' of waves casts its load of water at the coast we get a condition called 'wave set-up' – water gets piled up at the shoreline significantly higher than the sea level behind it. That water cannot stay there; gravity dictates that it will always need to find an escape route back to

an area of lower set-up. The route it takes becomes the rip current.

Sensible surfers understand that rip currents aren't something you can afford to spend too much time fighting. At a point break with a strong travelling rip you get out of the water after a long ride and save energy by walking back to the point. At a headland or jetty you often paddle out right next to the rocks to take advantage of the permanent rip offering you a free ride to the peak. At a beach break you scan the area for the fixed rips to take you out the back, or even wait for a big set to sweep through and then position yourself to jump in, hoping to ride the flash rip out to the break. Easy.

So when you realise the many ways in which nature has made surf rideable for us, it's almost impolite not to grab a board and learn how to use it.

'I PUT RESIN ON IT. I PUT ACETONE ON IT. I GLASSED IT...AND THAT NIGHT I TOOK THAT LITTLE BLOCK TO A PARTY, PULLED IT OUT OF MY POCKET AND SAID, "THIS IS IT, BOYS – THE FUTURE OF SURFBOARDS IS RIGHT HERE."'

Surf manufacturer **Hobie Alter** remembers getting his hands on polyurethane foam in 1954.

CHAPTER 3

EQUIPMENT

Getting kitted up is something of a minefield. How do you know if that shiny thruster you liked in the shop will be any better for you than that cheap old pop-out you saw at the car boot sale? How will you avoid the humiliation of striding down the beach with your new wetsuit on back-to-front? Keep your wallet in your pocket until you have a basic grasp of the huge range of surf equipment available.

THE BOARD

'I DESERTED THE COOL SHADE, PUT ON
A SWIMMING SUIT, AND GOT HOLD OF A
SURFBOARD. IT WAS TOO SMALL A BOARD. BUT I
DIDN'T KNOW, AND NOBODY TOLD ME... I TRIED
FOR AN HOUR, AND NOT ONE WAVE COULD I
PERSUADE TO BOOST ME SHOREWARD.'
Jack London, *Riding the South Seas Surf,* 1907

The ideal board for you is simply the one that gets you in the water and riding waves. Not any old thing will do, however. If you get the opportunity, your first contact with the surf should be on a soft foam board, often known as a 'foamie' or 'Swellie' (after manufacturer Swell Surf Products). Designed for safety, stability and durability, soft boards ease the absolute beginner into the business of catching waves. The Swellie features a soft and forgiving EVA skin wrapped around a foam core: you can't damage it, and it can't damage you.

Very wide and very buoyant, the limitations inherent in the construction and design mean that the Swellie is perfect only for your first few sessions. As soon as you start to think about performance, pass the Swellie on to someone else.

Performance boards come in a whole spectrum of shapes and sizes, but can be broadly categorised into four main classes:

Shortboards – Under 7ft (2.1m) in length, low volume, refined, sensitive to weight shifts, requiring constant rider input: for performance in the pocket.

Longboards – Above 9ft (2.7m) in length, high volume, stable width, longer parallel rails: for cruising or hot-dogging.

Hybrids – 6–8ft (1.8–2.4m) in length, fuller in the nose with a forwards wide point, integrating borrowed attributes of the other classes: for fun in compromised conditions.

Guns – 7ft and over in length, narrow nose, forwards wide-point and volume, parallel rails into a drawn-out tail: for getting in and out of big waves.

Each distinct shape is designed either to function maximally on a certain type of wave or to facilitate a certain style of riding. The most

DESIGN BASICS

■ **Width provides stability.**

■ **Length provides speed.**

■ **Curves provide manoeuvrability.**

■ **Thickness provides buoyancy.**

■ **Fins provide projection.**

advanced manoeuvres are done on a shortboard: that type of radical surfing may or may not be what you aspire to, but the best guideline is to try everything and go with the style that makes you happiest.

DESIGN PRINCIPLES

Compared to the frantic innovation of the late 1960s, the design fundamentals of the modern high-performance surfboard have changed relatively little in the past 25 years. Partly this is due to hydrodynamic principles, partly to the macro-economic demands of an industry now leaning heavily towards mass production in the Far East. But even though the principles of board design change little, there might still seem to be a bewildering variety of boards available to you.

Understanding the principle of board design – how a board works – will provide some insight into what will work for you.

All of the above qualities are desirable – so why not have the widest, thickest, longest, curviest board with as many fins as you can fit on it? Because with each element there's a trade-off: gains in one area will compromise another. The art of surfboard design lies in blending the qualities to match board, waves and rider.

Width

Stability is usually considered the single most important factor when you're learning: a wide board provides a steady platform on which to struggle to your feet. You have a bigger margin for error – if your feet aren't quite planted in the right spot, then you have a nice platform to shuffle them around without tipping the board over.

So, what is wide? For an adult, 20–23in (51–58cm) at the widest point would be considered wide and stable. The dimensions of the board should be written on it somewhere, probably on the bottom

SHORTBOARD

LONGBOARD

HYBRID

GUN

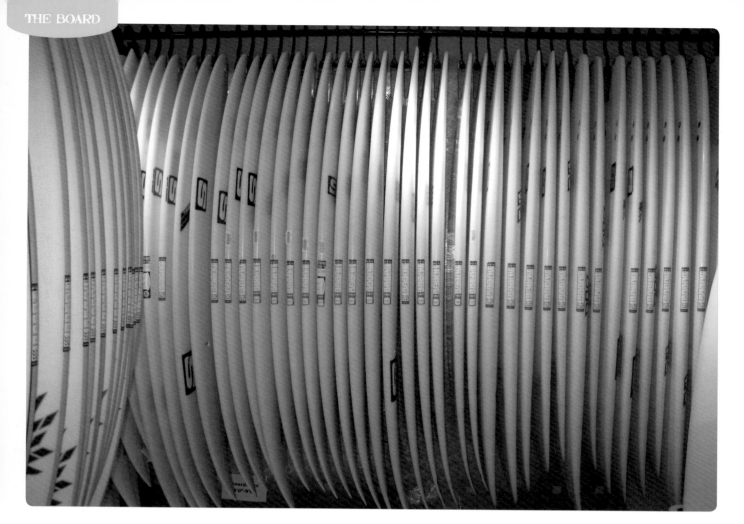

along the stringer. If not, then do the underarm test – pick the board up and hold it under one arm as you would to carry it down the beach. Can't reach? Then the board's probably a little too wide for you.

And what is narrow? Almost any shortboard will tend to feel tippy at first, but you can quickly come down in width if you're looking for more response in your board. Being able to get the board on its rail easier means quicker turns, and also means the board will feel grippier in sucky waves. In reasonable waves, good surfers will be riding shortboards of around 18.5in (47cm) width; for an adult learner that would be too narrow. A board narrower than that would be used by experienced surfers only in critical waves.

Thickness/volume

The more waves you catch the faster you learn; and the better your board floats then the more waves you'll catch. Foam is your friend: but only up to a point. Once you're bored of catching white water and want to paddle out the back, then all that foam can be a hindrance. All that the white water wants to do is push you back to the beach, and the more buoyancy you have the harder it is to stop that from happening. What's the point in having a board that could potentially catch 50 clean waves in a session if that very board is preventing you from getting past waist-deep water?

The heavier you are then the more buoyancy you need, but anything thicker than 3in (7.6cm) will perform like a barge. At the other end of the scale, anyone bar the lightest grommet would swamp a board less than 2in (5cm) thick. Look around you in the line-up: if you're sat way

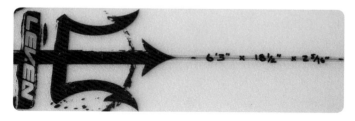

⬇⬆ **Manufacturers have universally adopted imperial measurements for board dimensions.**

higher than everyone else and your shorts are dry, then your board is too thick; if you're up to your armpits in the water, then your board is too thin.

Remember that volume isn't the same as buoyancy. A cannonball may have the same volume as a beachball but only one will float.

As soon as polyurethane foam was developed, chemists began formulating different densities. With the myriad new materials now being used in surfboard production it's particularly important to consider buoyancy. There's been talk in the industry of a standard test to provide a buoyancy value to go alongside other fundamental board measurements such as width and length. The difficulty of applying such a test universally means that it's unlikely to be imposed, so as a general guide remember that EPS foam is more buoyant than polyurethane foam – so an epoxy board will float higher and give a significantly different feel to a poly board having the same dimensions.

You can carry a lot of foam so long as it's distributed nicely through the board. A good chunk of volume should be under your chest in order to give lift to the centre of effort when paddling. But feel the rails – too much thickness carried into the rails will make the board 'catch' when turning. The body of the board can be thick but a good shaper will 'pinch' the rails to prevent them from being too boxy. Some of the thicker short hybrid boards now in favour are being shaped with concaves in the deck, bringing the rider's feet closer to the water, so helping eliminate that 'gondolier' sensation of being perched too high up.

Check the thickness that's carried into the tail; thickness here is often justified on the grounds that it will help the wave lift you on to it as it passes underneath you, and it's true that a board with a thick chunky tail will feel flatteringly stable and fast in junky waves. But it will quickly become a liability when the waves get steeper – a steep wave wants to spit the board from its face. If you have too much thickness in the tail, when you try to turn the tail will just slide out; you have no 'bite'.

Thickness and width in the nose of the board is again a trade-off – a thick rounded nose will provide buoyancy and stability but also provides resistance: to air in a stiff offshore wind, to white water when paddling out, and to chop when surfing in less than clean conditions. The general principle to apply is that thickness is welcome only so long as it's *refined* thickness.

Length

Hydrodynamics dictate that hull length is directly proportional to speed, so a longer board will paddle faster and allow you to catch waves earlier. A longer board also allows you to have width without your board looking, and performing, like a Frisbee. Width of 23in (58cm) is perfectly feasible on a 9ft (2.7m) longboard but would look and feel faintly bizarre on something under 6ft (1.8m).

A common mistake is to go too short too soon: this will only set you back in the long run. Try this as a guide: start surfing with a board that, with an outstretched arm, you can reach up and cup the nose of. As you progress, aim to *gradually* work down to something that's the same height as you, or perhaps a tad more. Stop wherever you feel most comfortable, and the board most manageable.

⬆ **A little bit of extra width carried from the nose right through to the tail makes this shortboard fun in gutless conditions.**

If you never go shorter, but instead feel as though you want to go *longer*, then that's fine – you're a natural longboarder! Shorter boards are necessary for tighter-radius manoeuvres, but longer boards are great for developing correct technique in turns. There are no shortcuts with longer boards.

Curves

The curves of a board's shape are found not only in its outline as seen from above but also in the 'rocker' – the amount of bow it has as seen from the side. Generally, curves help break the board from its track and enable it to change direction. But a board that wants to change direction all the time will have to lose speed to do it. Generally speaking, straighter and flatter is faster.

'Rocker' can be explained in this way: imagine a flexible board 9ft (1.7m) long. When that board is flat all 9ft of its hull length is in the water, enabling you to go faster but offering maximum resistance to changes in direction. If you could bend that board into a U-shape then the board would be able to pivot on its belly more readily to change direction, but you'd have reduced its effective hull length in order to achieve this manoeuvrability, compromising your speed. The same principle can be applied to the rails in plan shape: rails parallel to each other indicate a fast section on a plan shape, whereas sweeping curves foster turns at the expense of pure speed.

⬆ **Try not to learn on anything shorter than your outstretched arm.**

⬆ **After a year aim to be riding something as tall as you.**

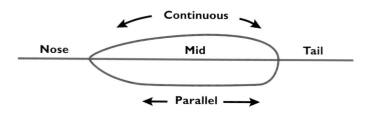

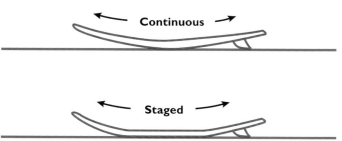

ADVANCED BOARD DESIGN

Outline (plan, template)

Plan shape is the way the board curves from the nose, through the midpoint to the tail. A board will have either a full nose, square nose, needle nose or no nose. The midpoint can be narrow, wide, forwards or rearwards. Tails can vary from round to pin, squash, swallow or square. The curve linking the nose, midpoint and tail (the rail line) is either parallel or continuous. Parallel rails extend the width forwards or rearwards from the midpoint to draw out turns and provide down-the-line speed. Continuous curve on the rails tends towards the elliptical, and facilitates a tighter turning radius. Matched with rocker, the various outlines dictate ease of turn, radius of turn, speed and projection.

Bottom rocker

Bottom rocker (the bow of the board from nose to tail) is fundamental to performance. Rocker can be continuous (a steady smooth curve) or staged (inserting a relatively flat spot somewhere in the curve). Continuous rocker facilitates turning; the flatter section of a staged rocker generates speed and projection.

Rails

The rail is the board's true interface with the water; rail profiles are subsequently complex and refined, because they have to support, penetrate, grip and release. Shapers have almost endless permutations of profiles to play with up and down the rail, but a few generalisations can be made. Thin rails allow more penetration and will be found nearer the nose; tucked-under rails permit bite with an edge for a little release; 50/50 rails allow the water to wrap around them for greater grip in the face; and hard rails are found on the tail of the board rearward from the back fins, to generate release and speed.

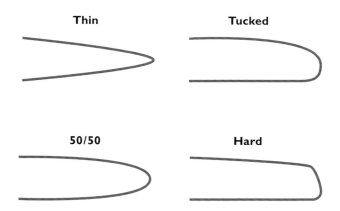

Flat   Convex   Tri-plane   Concave

Bottom contours

Gauged across the board from rail to rail, these can be flat, convex or concave. Performance-wise, a flat bottom is considered neutral, and is ideal for solid, conservative surfing. A slight modification to the flat bottom is the tri-plane hull: faster than a flat bottom because of the reduced wetted surface area, it can help initiate turns by getting on to the rail more easily. A convex bottom (where the lowest point extends *below* the level of the rail) is basically a displacement hull, so is good for stability, control and smooth rail-to-rail transitions. Concaves ascend into the board *above* the rail line and are designed to create a laminar flow, feeding, compressing and directing water in tandem with other features such as fins, rocker, rails and template. Concaves are the fastest but least stable of the bottom contours.

Again, bottom contours are nuanced by the shaper from front to back so the boards offer more of either speed or stability with subtle shifts of the rider's body weight. Single into double concave is common, as is single concave into flat into vee.

Tail

The tail reconciles the rail line, and dictates how much surface area you have under your back foot, the power foot. More surface area equals more release, more lift, easier speed; less surface area equals greater penetration and control. Basically, tails belong to one of two families – round or square. The round family comprises the round tail, the rounded pin and the pintail. In the square family are found the squash tail, the chisel and the swallowtail.

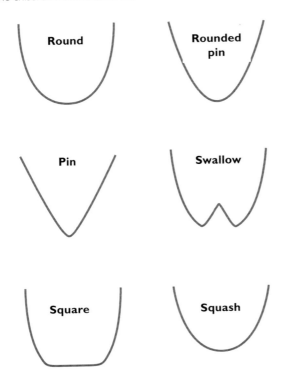

Round   Rounded pin   Pin   Swallow   Square   Squash

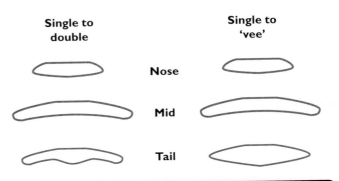

Single to double   Single to 'vee'   Nose   Mid   Tail

MACHINE SHAPING

Board-shaping machines have been around since the 1980s. Known then as pre-shaping machines or profilers, they could mechanically rough-shape a blank template to take out much of the unwanted volume. This was a time-saver, allowing the skilled shaper to focus on hand-finishing more pre-shaped blanks.

The technology was first developed for the much larger blanks of the windsurfing industry. By the early 1990s the early pioneers had machines that could carve out 10,000 boards per year, and the technology had cross-pollinated to the surfboard industry. By 2001 the first three-dimensional shaping programs were available. A couple of years later the software had developed to the degree where a shaper could design a board on screen, tweak it to his satisfaction, position the screen design on the blank, press a button and watch it go. The fully hand-shaped surfboard is now pretty much a bespoke relic of a bygone era.

EGG

TRADITIONAL FISH

BONZER

SINGLE-FIN

PERFORMANCE FISH

UNCONVENTIONAL SHAPES

Traditional fish – Defined by its wide swallowtail, keel fins and short hull. 'Trad fish' are best in point breaks on your forehand, on long walls with juicy sections where their natural speed can be exploited. Noted for quick acceleration, they can feel a little stiff, with a distinct way of turning that often feels awkward on your backhand. For that reason, and because of their reduced rocker, they're perhaps not ideal for beginners.

Performance fish – Its shortness, width and flatness are borrowed from the trad fish, but usually there are three fins and a less radical swallow – although the performance fish can have a number of variants of fins and tail. Faster than a conventional shortboard on flatter sections, they're a little less positive in manoeuvres. Flatter rocker means that all fish are best surfed in clean, less-than-critical waves less than head-high.

Egg – Unlike the fish designed from a shortboard up, egg-type boards are designed from a longboard down – very flat rocker, full nose, parallel rails and wide round or squash tail. They generally sport a central single fin in a box for drive, with two side trailing fins for bite when up on a rail. The extra volume means that they're hard to handle in critical waves.

Single-fin – The main characteristic is sheer drive, so long as they're nursed through the turns, which have to be long and drawn-out. They simply won't let you go vertical and will spin out if you try. Reassuringly positive or frustratingly conservative depending on your perspective, the single-fin is great for nailing the fundamentals of solid turns.

Bonzer – A three- or five-fin configuration based on a single box fin with steeply canted side fins and deep concaves. This distinct combination provides unmatched drive and hold which will get you anywhere fast on the wave. Once in the critical spot, however, the Bonzer doesn't quite have the radical edge of the modern performance thruster.

More and more models with appealing funky names regularly appear on the market: the slipper, biscuit, fishcuit, potato/sweet potato, gravy, neckbeard etc, etc. When faced with a bewildering variety of hybrid boards, start by trying to work out whether the shaper has taken shortboard principles and added bits, or started with a longboard and taken bits away. That will give you some idea of where the strengths and limitations of each particular hybrid will lie.

FINS

A board with no fins has the directional stability of a turntable. In the absence of fins, the only foiled edge to provide something against which to pivot is the rail, and rails alone simply cannot grab enough water to do the job. Configurations of deep concaves and a sharp 'V' have been tried in a bid to develop a new generation of finless boards but these features severely compromise other aspects of the board's performance. Fins are the best means of offering lateral resistance.

When you're learning, fine-tuning your fin system isn't a major issue; just make sure you have *something*. But, depending on how big you are, and what type of turns you want to execute in which types of wave, there's a set of fins designed just for the job. So how do you choose which fin set-up to adopt?

The two fundamentals in fin design are template (outline) and cross-section (foil).

TEMPLATE

The outline of the fin, when viewed from the side, dictates how much surface area is presented to the water in the turn. The greater the surface area, the more force can be applied to the turn and the more drive will result. More drive is ideal for:

- Larger, more powerful surfers, to avoid overpowering the board in the turn.
- Surfers wanting to draw out the lines of their turns.
- Holding in on large, sucky waves.

Reduced template surface area should be considered by:
- Smaller, lighter surfers who have less power to apply in the turn.
- Surfers wanting to slide and waft the tail in turns.
- Small days when more release from the face is desired.

Just *how* the area is distributed is important. A wide base provides the most drive, whereas a narrower base will free up your turns. The width of the tip fine-tunes the principle of area distribution: a fuller tip, fuller turns; smaller tip, slidey turns.

⬆ **Base profile.**

⬆ **Tip profile.**

The next consideration in template is the *attitude* of the fin, usually referred to as 'rake'. Rake describes how swept back the fin is. More swept back fins provide resistance or traction for extra drive by translating effort into forward momentum in the direction of the turn; a more vertical aspect means greater release, allowing more pivotal turns but less effort transmitted into forward drive.

⬅ **Rake profile.**

Other considerations include:
- **Cluster** – Fins set closer together allow sharper turns; a wider cluster means more stability.
- **Toe** (angled in towards nose) – Less toe is good for setting a firm line (tracking). Too much toe results in instability.
- **Cant** (splay) – Fins canted outwards will tend to stay in the water when banking on a turn, but too much cant reduces down-the-line drive.
- **Stiffness** – Rigid fins provide more speed in powerful waves; more pliability is good for surfer-created speed.

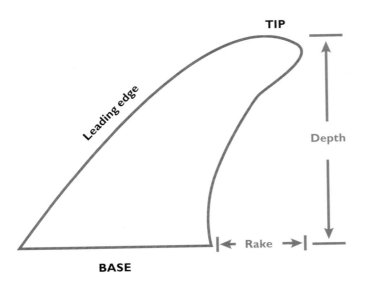

CROSS-SECTION

Much recent fin research focuses on 'foil', the cross-section of the fin from front to back (or the distribution of thickness). As with a sail or an aeroplane wing, foil provides lift. But this only works so long as the water is in contact with the fin surface, so designers work on how to keep the water in contact to maximise lift; when contact is lost the fin stalls and cannot do its work of driving the board. So actually the aim is not to reduce drag around the fin (as shapers used to do with fine edges and flat-sided foils), but to permit optimum drag for the fins to be fully functional at all angles of attack. Flat-sided foils persisted partly because they were easy to lay-up by hand; modern manufacturing techniques have changed that prejudice. Complex asymmetric double-sided foils are now in mode, with various concave and convex features.

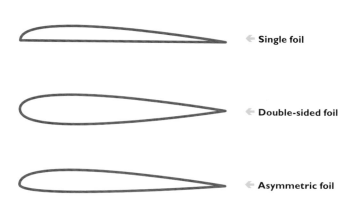

← Single foil

← Double-sided foil

← Asymmetric foil

BUYING

Fins are usually rated by the manufacturer with regard to three properties: hold, pivot and drive. If you tend to be heavy on your back foot, like to feel a rock-solid tail underneath you, and surf fast waves in a down-the-line style, then a fin set with high scores in the hold and drive departments will suit you. This requires a larger overall area, a good proportion of it in the base of the fin, and the fins swept well back from the base.

↓ **A set of wide-base fixed fins, with high vertical aspect – designed for hold in the pocket of very sucky waves.**

← Foil.

COMPOSITION

From solid redwood to bamboo ply, from plastics to carbon fibre, a variety of materials have been used in fin construction. Moulded polycarbonates now offer a cost-efficient way of achieving a lightweight fin that's reasonably stiff yet simple to adapt to the recent trend for complex double-sided foils. Composite materials such as carbon fibre glassed in layers over a foam core are the lightest way of achieving maximum stiffness in a removable fin, particularly significant when the latest five-fin systems have to be rigid without adding too much weight to the tail.

↖ **Since Tom Blake fixed a metal boat keel to the bottom on his board in 1935, fins have been fashioned out of anything that comes to hand**

→ **When shopping, offer up a variety of fins to compare profiles**

FIN EVOLUTION

A more skatey style of tail slides and floaters on weaker waves will require fins with a vertical aspect and less overall area, enabling them to break from the water – scoring high on pivot, low on hold.

Pulling into deep barrels on sucky waves that don't demand much in the way of drawn-out turns requires fins with a lot of hold, deep and vertical.

Fin systems aside, glassed-in fins are undoubtedly strongest. They have more inherent stiffness and transfer energy directly to the tip. For this reason you'll notice that many professionals, whilst endorsing removable fin designs, often use boards with fixed fins. But that's because they can afford to have a quiver of boards from which to select, and have the experience to know exactly what type of fins they like. You don't have that luxury. Experiment where you can – the differences can be subtle, so try fins that lie towards the ends of the design spectrum, then work back to a set of fins that really works for you.

Removable fins offer you several advantages: you can swap fins with friends to work out how designs differ in performance; you can keep favourite fins from a board when you sell it on; you can store your board flat; and you can travel more easily with it.

Fins can transform performance, but try to see them as complementing an already well-chosen board. They can never completely override very bold design features in the board itself.

INSTALLATION

Removable fin systems usually rely on one or two grub screws tightened up against a tab on the bottom of each fin. The tabs locate into a glassed-in fin plug. There are a few weaknesses in the system: the grub screws can round fairly easily, making extraction difficult; over-zealous tightening on the screw can lead to fracturing of the tab, particularly on carbon-fibre fins; and a knock to the fin can break the fins off at the tab, or crush the fin plug through the glass and into the foam – even a small crack here will lead to significant water ingress and subsequent weakness.

Many of the quantum leaps in the history of surfboard design are a result of reconceptualising the fin:

- **Tom Blake added a keel in the 1930s to enable lateral trimming on steep waves.**
- **In the 1950s glass fibre permitted fins to be refined in shape and size and fixed more securely, ushering in the hotdog era.**
- **George Greenough's innovations with foil and flex were the vanguard of the experimental late 1960s and 1970s.**
- **The early professional era was dominated by Mark Richards' radical reinvention of the performance twin-fin.**
- **The competitive edge of the 'twinnie' was bettered only when Simon Anderson came up with the three-fin thruster in the mid-1980s, still the default design an entire generation later.**
- **Reliable removable fin systems have made plan shapes almost secondary in importance to multi-fin configurations in the 21st-century board market.**

THE RIDER

Like boards and waves, people come in all shapes and sizes. A board that's an ideal learning platform for your six-year-old son might feel like a toothpick to you. If a board is going to have to do double or treble duty in your family, then think very carefully about all the compromises that will have to be made – you're looking for a Swiss-army-knife of a board, one that fulfils many roles tolerably well, rather than being a specialist tool.

But even if shopping just for yourself, consider a few things before you settle for one board, because although the board can't change, you might. Are you likely to lose or gain much weight in the near future? Try to be honest with yourself before you assume that the pounds are going to fall off as you get into the sport and spend hours in the water. How much is your paddling ability going to improve in a few weeks? Again it's a compromise, this time between the absolute beginner that you are and the surfer you expect to become. Best err on the side of caution: a good learner board can easily be sold on, but the second-hand racks are full of shortboards that were bought then rapidly discarded by over-ambitious novices.

And where are you going to be using this new board of yours? Will you be riding predominantly at a single break? If so, what type of wave is usually encountered there? Slack, mushy waves require extra volume and length to get you moving and across the weak sections – here extra width is a good idea. Punchier waves work the other way; more power in the wave means you need to provide less power yourself. Here you can get away with less volume, so you can go a little narrower and shorter.

Are the take-offs steep? A little more nose rocker might be a good idea. Do you have to travel to get to your break? Detachable fins take up a lot less space. Are there regular crowds? A bit more length will help you catch more waves.

If you surf a rock entry and exit then perhaps consider an epoxy board for its extra resilience, or a cheap throwaway polyurethane one which it won't break your heart to ding. If you're likely to use your board up and down the coast at differing breaks then consider a good all-rounder: a board with a fin system that can be easily changed with a contrasting set of fins is a wise investment.

But why have only one board? In real terms used boards are cheap, they don't rust or seize up over time, and they're certainly nice to own and to look at. So if you have room, why not keep a quiver of boards to suit your mood or the mood of the ocean? In small gutless waves you need to avoid the style crime of flapping the nose of a too-small board in a desperate effort to generate some speed. On days like this you need more buoyancy and glide – whether you find that in a fish, egg, longboard or old gunny single-fin doesn't really matter as long as you're not fighting but gliding. You can still manoeuvre, and it'll engender good habits: making solid turns using the proper distribution of body weight over the rail instead of jerking the board around a reduced pivot point. Surfers who persistently ride boards too small for them tend to have style similarities – pivoting in scratchy direction changes rather than arcing in power turns. Sudden random arm flapping and head twitches might look impressive caught in a single-frame shot, but interrupting flow means sacrificing speed. Picture yourself surfing in a movie, not a set of stills.

MATERIALS

Double world champ
Mick Fanning once revealed
that he could get through
100 boards a year.

Materials are the current focus of major developments in the board-manufacturing industry. Performance shapes have received little more than the occasional tweak for years now, although the vogue for retro boards has seen a few newer ideas and concepts applied to older designs. It's materials research that has revolutionised the industry, and will likely play a big part in your choice of equipment.

As a learner, your first board might be the 'foamie' or 'Swellie', made from a foam core usually with a wooden stringer for strength and a thick EVA (vinyl) skin wrapped around and bonded on the rails. If it looks a lot like a giant bodyboard that's because the early versions had exactly the same polyethylene construction. Today, many 'soft' manufacturers use an EPS core topped with a quarter-inch (6mm) soft foam skin and a harder plastic base.

You might equally pick up an old-style 'pop-out' where two moulded fibreglass halves are bonded at the rail before liquid polyurethane foam is injected into the hull. The result is a tough but relatively heavy board.

The manufacturing processes of these beginner boards limit much refinement of the shape, particularly on the all-important rails. Each has a place in the learning curve, but these boards aren't designed for performance.

There are two major types of performance surfboard mass-manufactured in the industry: polyurethane/PU boards (otherwise known simply as 'conventional' surfboards), and epoxy/EPS boards.

Polyurethane has been the primary material used for boards since the 1960s. The usual manufacturing process involves a polyurethane foam blank being shaped by hand (or, more recently, CNC machined); the result is then laid up with fibreglass cloth, soaked in polyester resin, allowed to cure, then hand-sanded and polished. The process is fully customisable; shapes are infinitely variable, flex and strength are built-in by the wooden stringer and layers of glass. The foam is closed cell, compression-resistant, and fine-grained enough to be shaped easily to very high tolerances, then airbrushed for an appealing cosmetic finish.

← **A beginner board has to be tough.**

↑ **Don't begrudge paying good money for boards – shaping and glassing them is a dirty, dusty, messy business.**

Epoxy/EPS boards use either expanded polystyrene or extruded polystyrene. Expanded polystyrene is the rather coarse-beaded foam (known initially by its early brand name of Styrofoam) that you might find insulating a beer cooler. It's inexpensive (so will be found in the cheaper range of epoxy boards), but shapers don't favour it, as its relatively large individual spheres aren't easy to draw a shaping plane across smoothly. Its structure is based on open cells, so although it's extremely lightweight (just one to two pounds per cubic foot) water will wick through it, and it breaks readily. Consequently boards with a solid glass job are fine, but more fibreglass is required to provide the required strength. Any fractures in the glass have to be repaired immediately, otherwise the foam core sucks up water like a sponge.

Extruded polystyrene (EXPS or XPS) is more expensive, so will be found in the top end of the epoxy board range. It has a finer closed-cell construction that makes it easier to shape, provides better resistance to impact and compression, and doesn't allow water absorption. The newest versions could, in theory, be taken into the water and surfed without even being glassed. Extruded foam cores have been found to provide excellent response to flex patterns, unlike the expanded foam that was so stiff that to many surfers it felt rather dead.

There are two ways of shaping epoxy boards – hand-shaping and moulding (or 'pop-out'). Hand shaping is pretty much the same, fully customisable process as with conventional PU boards, the only differences being those inherent in the materials themselves. The process is well understood and problems have been few.

Pop-out boards involve a mould being created from a plug of a hand-shaped original. EPS foam is injected, then layered up with cloth and resin and sandwiched with a high-density foam layer (or with a layer of PVC). This is either pressed or vacuumed to suck out excess resin; extra heat applied during this process will add strength. A stringer can be added to supply extra resilience. The result is spray-painted as you would a car, then more resin, lacquer and polish are applied. This is a mass-produced item, with limited scope for options. Being labour intensive, most production is currently in the Far East. The major teething problem has been delamination in high temperatures – this is being overcome by the use of venting systems. The lack of flex and the cosmetic issues have also been challenging, but new foams are now being developed possessing better flex patterns, and fine enough to be airbrushed.

FINISHING

With early foam and fibreglass boards, pigment was added to the laminating resin to create a 'solid' panel (whether to the whole board or just a stripe). This would have been applied purely to cover up imperfections or defects in the foam. Only a relatively small percentage of the shaped blanks would be candidates for 'clear' treatment – glassed to look as though the resin and glass simply weren't there. In that case all that the customer would see was the foam, with the mahogany, balsa or redwood stringers either glued through the blank or multiple stringers routed into the foam. With the wooden tail blocks and nose blocks and a wooden fin, these were the most cosmetically desirable early boards.

Paint was seen as an admission of imperfection – pure white foam and solid wood was where it was at. The lack of UV stabiliser in early resins and foam blanks, however, meant that prolonged exposure to sunlight would leave them looking unhealthily brown and prematurely aged. By the time foam formulas were tweaked to reduce this problem, the freaky custom-car culture of the California

MATERIALS DEVELOPMENT

Recent trends in materials and construction include:
- **EPS and EXPS foam.**
- **Epoxy resins.**
- **Parabolic stringers.**
- **Dialled-in flex.**
- **Exact, precise replication.**
- **Ecological and environmental concerns (fewer VOCs – volatile organic compounds).**

PU resin cannot be used with EPS foam – the foam will melt. Epoxy materials are less polluting, having fewer VOCs (volatile organic compounds).

highways had migrated to the beach and brought with it a riot of colour work.

But unlike metal car bodies, the foam of the surfboard blanks was an extremely unstable medium upon which to apply colour – there were early concerns about delamination, collapsing foam due to incompatible chemicals, and shortened lifespan of resins. Experiments led to paint being applied either straight on to the foam or on to the sanded board prior to the gloss coat. Initially restricted to sober pin lines, with the advent of the spray gun and aerosol can anything became possible, and the late-'60s era of radical customisation got under way.

Since the advent of machine-shaping and mass production, surfers have responded to the standardisation of factory surfboards by individual customisation. Eye-catching results can be achieved with stickers, laminated images, chinagraph pencils, posca pens or spray cans, graffiti-style; mostly they're impermanent too, so the next owner can easily erase or change the decoration to suit his or her own style.

DURABILITY

For all but the professionals, durability is a crucial performance criterion. A fully sponsored surfer can accept breaking six boards on a trip to Indonesia, because he can afford to take eight. Demanding a board exactly the same as the professionals ride will get you one that breaks easily, it's as simple as that.

Developments in the industry as a whole have given rise to concerns about the durability of boards designed even for the general surfer. Some board glassers have turned to using all UV-cured resin, which allows for a rapid glass job but is 30% weaker than catalyst-cured resin. Resin manufacturers have been forced by environmental legislation to use less and less styrene in their resin, which again weakens it. Try to ensure the materials used in the manufacture of your board are of the best quality.

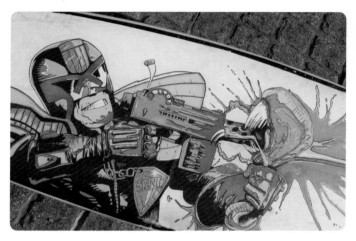

⬆ **What can be done with a flat spell, some Posca pens, and a lot of talent.**

⬇ **A board with a pro-weight glass job can't be expected to last forever.**

SHOPPING

Poldhu Cafe Surf Hire

	1 hour	3 hours	5 hours
WETSUIT	5.00	8.00	12.00
BODYBOARD	5.00	8.00	12.00
SURFBOARD	7.00	10.00	15.00
BOARD & SUIT	10.00	16.00	22.00

All Hire Equipment Is Taken At ... OWN Risk ... Deposit Of

WHEN BUYING...

DON'T
- [ ] **Be dishonest with yourself about your ability.**
- [ ] **Be dishonest with your retailer or shaper about your ability.**
- [ ] **Underestimate your weight.**
- [ ] **Overestimate your fitness.**
- [ ] **Copy the pros too slavishly.**

DO
- [ ] **Listen to advice.**
- [ ] **Borrow and try as many boards as you can.**
- [ ] **Read up on board design.**
- [ ] **Buy what you like.**

You now have a good idea of what board is best for you, but how do you get hold of it?

Borrowing a board sounds like a no-lose situation. Trying as many boards as you can is undoubtedly the best way to discover what works for you in different conditions. Until the distant day when you're a fully sponsored professional, borrowing boards from friends is the only realistic way to do this.

Study closely the shapes and the contours of the boards you borrow and try to figure out how the various design features contribute to the performance properties that you can feel beneath your feet.

The only drawback with borrowing is the ever-present prospect of damage. Even if a ding of yours has been well repaired at your expense and in no way affects the performance of the board, dings are unsightly, and the resale value of any board depends largely on cosmetics. A small hole in a board can put a big hole in a friendship, so make sure you have an understanding before you borrow.

Renting a board is a sensible option if trips to the beach are likely to be infrequent. You know what you need, so don't grab something unsuitable from the first rental outfit you come across. Many surf

outlets will be geared up to cater for the learner surfer, and it's in their interests to supply a rental board good enough to get you hooked: the idea being that you'll then come back ready to spend some serious money in their shop.

Buying a board reveals just what an optimistic bunch surfers are. There aren't many transactions in which you'd happily spend a couple of weeks' wages on an untested item. A lot of faith and an experienced eye is what's required here. By definition, as a learner you don't *have* an experienced eye, so you need to rely on someone else. If you don't have absolute trust in the vendor, then take along an experienced friend.

The resale value of a new board plummets as soon as some wax is rubbed on the deck, so the best way to get a bargain is to buy a used board. But do your homework. Is the board a reputable make, or has it been knocked up in a garage somewhere? A 'garage' board can be perfect for you, but remember to think about resale value, as this is a board you're aiming to rapidly progress beyond.

Where was the board made? Some countries have a reputation for weaker finishing/glassing standards than others. Ask the usual questions of the vendor – how much use has it had, why are they selling it, do any dings need to be fixed?

As with everything else, the best bargains are to be found on Internet auction sites. But unless you're in the vendor's neighbourhood you're relying on a couple of photos and a few lines of description, and then a courier for delivery of a fragile item at the end of the deal. It can be worth the risk if you're careful. But if you do your shopping online, remember that you're not in a good position to complain when surf shops on your local high street go bust.

In a surfing town you'll have options: adverts placed in the local press, posted in shop windows, and of course second-hand boards in the racks of specialist surf shops. Shops will have a rack of used boards that they're either selling on commission or have taken in part-exchange for a new board and are hoping to chop out for a modest return. Ask the salesperson direct, 'Is this a good board for a learner?'

Check for hidden dings. There might be nothing sinister about a strangely placed sticker or an unusual sudden splodge of paint, but it's up to you to discover whether or not they're there to hide an ugly repair job. And what if you *are* looking at a board that's cheap

↑ **Spoilt for choice.**

because of an ugly repair job? Has it been fixed with care, or is it a bodge? Is it something you can easily improve the look of?

Even a board that's been broken in two and then fixed isn't necessarily a write-off – if it's been fixed well, with the proper attention paid to correct alignment, then it could give many more years' service. It may seem counterintuitive, but the best place for a board to break is right in the middle – the added weight of a strong repair isn't a major problem in itself so long as it doesn't unbalance the board.

BUYING FOR A GROM

'Soft-top' boards are good for the younger surfer (or 'grommet') and start at sizes under 6ft (1.8m). Safety being paramount, these foam boards come with rubber fins, soft foam deck and rubber 'bumper' rails. After safety, buoyancy and stability are the key qualities; so something small but wide is desirable.

Buy the grom something too small, however, and he or she won't catch enough waves to be encouraged, and will develop a jerky and twitchy style. Once they're genuinely ready for something a little more performance-oriented, the extra durability of an epoxy shortboard is something parents could consider.

↖ **At ten quid for a morning's hire, there is no sense buying your own board until you are sure you want to take your surfing further.**

→ **An ugly but surprisingly sound repair might make this learner board a bargain.**

BUYING OFF THE RACK

Because of the perilous depreciation of new boards, there's no chance of trying before buying. But some of the larger surf shops may have a demonstration board of a model you're considering: if so, take the opportunity.

Don't be dazzled: buy what you know you need, not what you think you fancy. The surf industry is big business, and a few shop owners are sophisticated salesmen first and nice guys later. Reputation and experience are your only guides, so take along someone knowledgeable if you can, and don't be impulsive. Shop around; there will always be more boards and more waves.

← **Have you got one like that but in pink?**

BUYING CUSTOM-MADE

The pros all have their boards custom-made for them, but wouldn't that be rather presumptuous for you? Well actually, no. A custom-made board will seldom cost more than off the rack, so if you're going to buy new, then why not?

You need to be close enough to a reputable shaper to establish at least a dialogue with him, but his experience will be invaluable – so long as you're honest about your abilities and expectations. Don't bluff, pretending you know more than you do. Ask; don't be afraid of revealing the limits of your surf knowledge – a good shaper is a guide, not a judge. And know your weight; this is key to getting the buoyancy right. Take along your current board and describe its limitations and how you'd like to see yourself progressing.

The only downside is the wait – and the better the shaper, then the longer that wait is likely to be. But it'll be worth it. If you build a relationship with him, over time your boards will be fine-tuned to you, and you'll be the one getting preferential treatment; the rest can wait.

⬆ **Take an old favourite board to the shaper...**

⬆ **...and discuss what it is you like about it.**

⬆ **In the shaping bay...**

⬆ **...he can measure it up...**

⬆ **...and go about shaping up a new version.**

⬆ **Many hours and a lot of dust later, the shaped blank will be ready to glass.**

CARE AND REPAIR

Despite the best efforts of the surf industry, boards are still fragile items designed for use in a tough environment. Just getting the board out of the garage, off the car and across the car park is fraught with danger, never mind surfing the thing.

Dings have got to be fixed early before much water gets into the foam. A proper repair demands fibreglass cloth and resin, but a desperate stopgap measure can be attempted by stuffing a plug of wax scraped from the deck into the hole. Tape or even stickers can also be used. These types of 'repair' tend to have a horrible inertia, however, and tape can stay on for years; years in which water will inexorably be seeping into the board and turning the foam to a brown mush. Retire the board for a while, get it well and truly dry and do the job properly. Your local surf shop will have the name of a ding fixer, but why not do it yourself? The materials are cheap, and it's fun and rewarding to develop a useful skill.

FIXING A DING

- ▣ Dry thoroughly (for days, not just hours).
- ▣ Dig out rotten foam.
- ▣ Cut and fit replacement chunk of foam if necessary.
- ▣ Sand the area to provide a key.
- ▣ Mask off the area.
- ▣ Prepare resin: UV-activated resin is easier, though slightly weaker; resin with catalyst provides more control over the process. Holes can be filled with resin mixed with lightweight Q-cell powder or micro-balloons.
- ▣ Prepare fibreglass cloth – cut to fit.
- ▣ Apply resin, forcing out any air bubbles.
- ▣ Apply two layers of cloth; soak in resin.
- ▣ Allow to cure.
- ▣ Remove masking tape, and sand back.
- ▣ Apply gloss coat; polish to fine finish.

↑ **Sand the damaged areas to remove delaminated glass and to get a key.**

↑ **Dig out rotten foam.**

↑ **Mask up the area to retain the liquid resin that needs building up.**

↑ **UV-cured resin can be applied directly to the ding...**

↑ **...then masked over to retain the shape.**

↑ **Then a layer of figreglass cloth is applied...**

↑ **Soak in a little more resin before adding a second layer of cloth.**

↑ **It doesn't have to be too neat – it will all come out in the sanding.**

↑ **If you are using catalyst-cured resin, you can add colour.**

↑ **Add q-cell powder as a lightweight filler...**

⬆ ...before adding the correct volume of catalyst.

⬆ Mix it up thoroughly.

⬆ Now the resin will begin to set, so don't hang about.

⬆ Rough sand the hardened resin into shape...

⬆ ...then add two layers of cloth soaked in more resin.

⬆ Once all the repairs have set, it is time to rough sand again.

⬆ Take care not to sand right through the new layers of glass, otherwise you will have to start all over again. Use a finer sander for finishing work.

⬆ Using fine-grade paper, gradually get back to the original lines of the board.

⬆ A final check of the lines of the repair...

⬆ ...and you can finish off with a light coat of clear lacquer.

⬆ Wash off the dust and the board is ready to go back in the water.

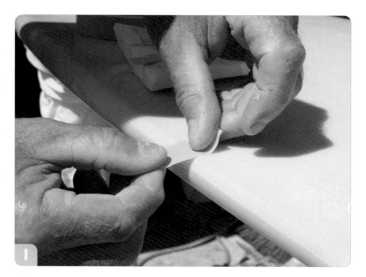

⬆ The principles (and cloth) are exactly the same for an epoxy board...

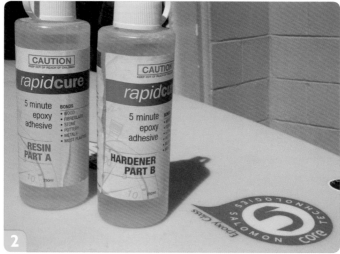

⬆ ...but make sure you use epoxy resin!

WETSUITS

↖ **Suited up and ready for winter.**

↑ **A local wetsuit factory will be able to offer you custom suits, after-sales service and speedy repairs.**

Y ou have to be extremely hardy to remain un-insulated for long in water much below 20°C. Add to that the wind-chill factor acting on a wet surfer perched on their board, and it's a miracle that surfing ever escaped the tropics.

In temperate countries the development of the wetsuit has been the biggest single factor in the explosion of the surfing demographic. You simply don't need to be cold any more. Being warm makes you feel good, but warmth isn't all that a wetsuit provides – you have far more buoyancy in a wetsuit, so will have greater confidence in the water. You're also protected from scrapes and grazes.

Feeling warm and safe is fundamental to learning, so get a good suit. As the different brands compete for ever-larger market shares, wetsuits are becoming more and more technical and prices have been forced down in real terms. So with careful selection and advice you can get a fantastic deal.

FIT

Wetsuits were originally designed to allow for a very thin layer of water to be trapped and then warmed by your body. This was partly by default, as limitations in materials and design meant they couldn't be made to fit any better. Modern wetsuits are now so well sealed that practically no water gets in – you're virtually encased in a single neoprene cell. Removing a well-fitted wetsuit after a hectic couple of hours in the water, you should find large areas of the interior still completely dry.

With regard to fitting, assistants at reputable surf shops are your best bet. It becomes hot and sweaty work, but try on as many suits as you can bear, and shop around – you need to able to make comparisons:

■ A suit that's too loose will allow too much water in. You'll use too much body heat to warm the water up, and lose warmed water too easily out of the suit.

■ A suit that's too tight will rub you raw. Make sure it fits snugly, but try a full range of movements to ensure that it's not too restrictive.

■ If nothing fits you perfectly, it's better to have something that's a snug fit in the body and around vital organs but an inch too short in the leg, than compromise the warmth of your torso by getting a baggy larger size just to cover that last inch of skin at your ankles.

■ There should be no slack neoprene in the small of the back, under the arms, behind the knees or around the neck.

Off-the-peg wetsuits now come in a wide range of sizes – you can get a 'large-medium-tall' if you want – but if you're an unusual body shape then you might want to consider getting a suit custom-made. The vast majority of wetsuits now get made in the Far East, but some surf towns have local wetsuit manufacturers. Do your research, look online, ask around and talk to the company – the warmest suit is always one that fits the best, and getting one custom-made should ensure that.

DESIGN

Neoprene is remarkably well insulating, but individually shaped panels have to be joined together. The ultimate suit would be one with no seams: minimal leakage, optimal stretch. The seamless suit isn't quite with us yet, but seams have been minimised and ways of joining them have been improved. Stitching is strong but destructive; gluing is non-destructive but inherently weaker.

Suits designed for warmer conditions can get away with flatlock stitching – the stitches go all the way through the neoprene but the seams will rarely come apart: a strong method, but not the warmest. Where warmth is at a premium, the stitching should be blind (ie the stitching goes halfway through the neoprene then returns); the rest of the join is glued. Taping the glued side of the join provides extra strengthening and some further waterproofing. All-glued no-stitch seams are the warmest, but probably the least durable at the moment, although technology here is advancing rapidly.

↑ **Blind stitched seams.**

↑ **Liquid taped seams.**

↑ **Taped seams on the inside.**

SEAM TIPS

Seams should run away from muscle zones so that there's no restriction on flex.

BACK CLOSURE – There are lots of systems to combat back drip, but whichever you choose make sure you can secure it on your own.

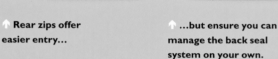

⬆ **Rear zips offer easier entry...**

⬆ **...but ensure you can manage the back seal system on your own.**

ANKLE CLOSURE SYSTEMS – The raw seal is best for ease of entry but needs good-quality fabric as it has least longevity; the rolled-over finish is the most durable but makes a slightly less snug-fitting seal; half-and-half is the best compromise, but should always be complemented by a well-contoured ankle panel.

⬆ **A raw ankle seal with a well-contoured panel.**

More air in modern neoprene equals more flexibility and warmth, but as it stretches further it becomes thinner and therefore colder; remember that when trying on a suit in the warmth of a shop.

➡ **A back zip is easiest to get into but slightly less flexible than a front zip.**

GETTING IN AND OUT

A suit with a vertical back zip has the advantage of being easy to slip on and off, but you may feel that the zip creates some restriction in your back and shoulders. Also, because the zip bisects the neck seal you're subject to the dreaded flush every now and then and the possibility of bad rub if the closure system isn't flawlessly designed.

Zipperless suits were in vogue for a few years because of their comfort and flexibility, but the neoprene around the closure systems suffered from memory loss, leading to unacceptably saggy neck areas. A mini front zip on the chest panel (a short transverse zip across the top of the chest) allows you to seal a one-piece neck, so eliminating flush and the cold spot of the back zip. But these suits can be tricky to get in and out of: exit involves much contortion, and this subjects the neoprene around the narrow neck opening to some stress which will tend to reduce its life a little. There will be greater comfort and flexibility with a front-zip wetsuit, but durability may suffer.

Take care when getting in and out of the suit. A suit has to be a snug fit to work, but try to ease into it. Try to keep zips clear of sand. Pull the zip only in the direction it's designed to travel, and never yank on the zip to try to force it. Don't pull on the centre of the neoprene panels, pull steadily on the seams – these are the strongest part. Roll the cuffs off your wrists and ankles; don't yank them.

⬆➡ **A mini front zip means no restriction on the back of the suit.**

Getting out of a mini-zip wetsuit can be something of a struggle, so to minimise wear and tear don't yank on the neoprene.

If you're finding it difficult to climb into your suit, then there are tricks to help your feet slide in nicely. You could try rubbing a little baby oil on your feet, but oil inevitably finds its way to the wax, so making your board incredibly slippery. The best method is to wrap your foot into a supermarket checkout plastic bag, slide it through your suit, then whip the bag off.

MATERIALS

Neoprene can be lined or 'smoothskin'. The lining is bonded on to the neoprene to add durability and colour, but it also retains moisture, so is more subject to wind chill. A smoothskin suit sheds water instantly, but will be much more susceptible to rips and tears, wear from chafing and ultraviolet damage. Warmer but less durable, smoothskin panels are often used in areas of the suit that are exposed to wind-chill but not subject to much wear – the chest and the back, for example.

Whatever the method used in the joins on the suit you're looking at, bear in mind that the seam can never be as flexible as the neoprene itself – so the design of the suit should take into account that panels need to be joined at areas of least movement. A suit may feature all sorts of funky technical panels, but a seam located right in your armpit is likely to rub horribly after 20 minutes of paddling.

⬆➡ Smoothskin panels should be clear of areas of chafe.

CARE & REPAIR

Suits don't last forever, but the usable life of a wetsuit will be extended by taking good care of it. Care instructions are usually printed somewhere inside the suit, and these are certainly worth following.

Don't try to remove a mark or a stain on a suit by using solvents or chemicals: they can damage the neoprene. Salt is extremely corrosive, so whenever possible rinse the suit in fresh water after each surf. UV rays will fade any colours on the suit, but more importantly will age the neoprene, drying it out and making it stiff and brittle and so more prone to tearing. So keep the suit out of direct sunlight; dry it (inside-out) in the shade. Some wetsuit manufacturers invalidate the warranty if the wetsuit has ever been dried in the sun.

Seams are difficult to repair. Don't initially try to re-stitch a seam yourself; this is more than likely a manufacturing fault and should be sorted out via your retailer and the manufacturer's warranty. Blind-stitching a seam requires specialist machinery, but an effective emergency repair can be achieved with a needle and thread. Water will seep through the needle holes, but the emergency repair will be strong and is probably better than leaving the whole seam to unravel. A good trick is to use waxed dental floss as your thread – it's more resistant to salt water.

Tears in the rubber, and seams that are ungluing, can be fixed with a proprietary wetsuit glue. Again, follow the instructions carefully, but most of all make sure that the suit is absolutely bone dry. If you aren't in a situation where you can obtain the proper wetsuit glue, then an emergency repair can be effected using the vulcanised rubber solution found in cycle puncture repair kits.

At some stage during a long surf session you'll inevitably be desperate for a pee. Some recoil in disgust at the prospect of peeing in their suit and will desperately hang on or will cut their session short. Others find it strangely comforting, and relish the sudden release of warm fluid; but bear in mind how well modern wetsuits are sealed – they won't readily flush through. So make extra efforts to wash your suit out after your session; it might not smell too much in the cold, but as the suit warms up in the back of the car the stench will be horrendous. Contrary to popular belief, urine doesn't rot the stitching or the neoprene, and if peeing in your wetsuit makes you more likely to rinse it in cold freshwater after, then it's not a bad thing. Don't use hot water, though, as this ages the neoprene, reducing its flexibility.

⬆ **Shortie.**

⬆ **Spring suit.**

⬆ **Short arm full suit.**

⬆ **Summer steamer.**

⬆ **Back zip winter steamer.**

TYPE OF SUIT

A 'full suit' used to be called a 'steamer', and that's what you'll probably need in water less than 18°C. A full suit covers the whole of your body down to your wrists and ankles. The only variable is whether you choose a high rolled neck (snug under the chin) or a low neck. A high neck will be resistant to flushing when you paddle out, but some find it uncomfortably restricting. For colder conditions some full suits will have an inbuilt or attachable hood to protect the head and ears. If the hood is non-detachable then pay particular attention to the fit of the suit lengthwise: stretch with the hood up to test it.

When the water gets a little warmer you can lose some of the rubber around your limbs. Some opt for a short-arm suit that keeps the legs covered but is cut off above the elbows; this optimises your paddling power and is ideal for a 'Californian' climate where the water is cold but the air is relatively warm. Or you could go for a 'spring suit' that has short legs cut off above the knee but full-length arms: this enables maximum mobility in the legs. A spring suit is suitable for a climate where the air might be chilly, but the sea is relatively warm – perhaps like a UK summer. Conditions would have to be pretty balmy before you can lose the legs and arms and just wear a 'shortie'.

Bear in mind that the effectiveness of all these suits depends largely on the type of stitching and the thickness of the neoprene: a 5mm full suit that's blind-stitched, glued and taped will see you through an English winter, whereas a flatlocked 2mm shortie has little more insulating property than a T-shirt and shorts.

Whatever panelling options you choose for the outside, suits are invariably lined on the inside. To increase warmth (and sales), manufacturers have experimented with a range of linings, from Merino wool to reflective copper and titanium impregnated materials, via plain old plastic bottles recycled as polypropylene fleece. Some are more effective than others, but a thicker lining will add more weight to the suit.

You can increase your warmth by wearing a stretchy Lycra rash vest that has a polypropylene fleece lining – this option can extend the usability of a suit deep into the coldest winter months. A shorts version is also a good option. Layering works, but there will come a stage where you'll lose so much mobility that you won't be able to get to your feet and will be spending more time underwater, so wiping out the benefits.

⬆ **Fleecy linings and a hooded and lined rash vest.**

⬆ **For the ultimate in warmth…**

⬆ **…get a front zip winter steamer…**

⬆ **…with an integral hood.**

⬆ **It keeps your neck free of drips and permits full movement of the back.**

BOOTS, GLOVES AND HOODS

Your extremities lose heat quicker than the rest of your body, so protecting your feet, hands and head from the cold will help extend your winter sessions. Boots do more than keep your feet warm, they ease the walk across the car park and protect you from rocky entry and exits. High top boots will fit snugly under your wetsuit leg, and a sole that's firm but not too rigid will enable you to cross rocks but still allow you to feel the board. Boots provide grip on your board; some surfers enjoy this solid 'planted' sensation, others dislike boots because they prefer to be able to shuffle their feet around a little easier. Split-toe boots aid in the 'feel' but aren't quite as warm, and do have a tendency to catch the leash when you jump up – most split-toe boots now have a rubber web to prevent this happening. The Frankenstein feet that you get when your boots are so full of water that they flop around and trip you up when you try to stand can only be avoided by buying a very snug fit. Roll boots off, and don't forget to rinse them out.

Hardly anyone wears wetsuit gloves by choice, but your fingers are precious and need protection. Mittens have fewer seams and huddle your fingers together, so they are the best for warmth. But they offer greater resistance when paddling: although you might move through the water a little faster, you'll tire much more easily, so they've fallen out of favour in all but the coldest waters. If your gloves are even the tiniest bit too large, then water will run down and pool at your fingertips, quickly freezing them. The cold can be most intense when walking back to your car from low tide in the wind; hands kept warm with well-fitting gloves will help you unlock your car door – otherwise you could be wandering around with the dreaded 'car-park claw-hand' looking for someone to work your keys for you.

In winter a hood is vital, because 50% of body-heat loss occurs through your head, cruelly exposed when paddling out and sitting wet in the wind. Repeated winter duck-dives induce an 'ice-cream headache' fierce enough to leave you vomiting with pain in the shore break.

A hood can be the full balaclava or the simple skull-cap. Some winter wetsuits come with an integral or attachable hood; this will be the balaclava type that offers most protection to your neck, but do ensure that you don't find this sort too restricting or confining. Covering the ears disorients the senses a little. If you buy a non-adjustable hood ensure it's a firm fit, as it's surprisingly easy for waves to pluck off your hood and sink it. A small peak is a good idea – hoods are used primarily in the winter, and that's when glare from a low sun can make it difficult to see.

Another way of protecting your ears is to wear plugs. These are a sensible precaution, as you aren't immediately aware of the long-term damage that wind and cold can do. There are many different types of plugs, and some of the custom-made pairs can be fairly expensive. The curse of the stuck earplug has been addressed by types that have a lip that remains proud of your ear canal.

Waxing-up is one of the great rituals of surfing: the motion and the scent can be very evocative. Perhaps this goes some way to explaining why there is as yet no satisfactory substitute for something that was developed in a garden shed back in the late 1950s.

Wax feels tacky, but it doesn't stick you to your board. It works by affecting the surface tension of the water so that it's forced to form small droplets that then roll off the board – the oily feathers on a duck's back work in the same way. Essentially, wax prevents the water from forming a slippery film between you and the polished surface of your board. That's why we scratch the surface of the wax with a wax comb – not to create grippy ridges, but to expose the clean fresh wax to the water.

⬇ **When your board looks like this, its high time to de-wax.**

Dirt and impurities prevent the wax from working effectively. You don't need to have a proper wax comb – a fork, your fingernails or a seashell can all be effective in a bind, but don't be too vigorous and scratch the board beneath. Wax picks up impurities from your suit, your feet and the water, so de-wax and re-wax regularly. Some surfers take a perverse pride in the amount of wax they have on their board, but over a couple of years you can end up with a kilo of grubby wax on your deck – and dirty wax actually absorbs water, adding even more weight.

How do you de-wax? Leaving the board in the sun for the wax to soften and then be scraped off works very well if you don't mind the ageing effects of the sun on your stick. If there's no sun then boiling a kettle of water to pour on the wax certainly works, but the hotspots can damage the glass. This method is potentially very messy, not to say hazardous. Neither of these

⬆⬇ **Wax cleaners will save you from cooking your board in the sun to remove old wax.**

two old-fashioned methods is much recommended. The best answer is to buy a proprietary wax cleaning fluid or gel from a surf shop, and do the job properly in accordance with the instructions.

How do you re-wax? Remember that you don't need to wax the entire deck – just where you lie, place your hands and stand. Some advocate systematic waxing starting with small circular movements and then progressing to longer straight sweeps, but really as long as you get the wax on the board then the job's done. Make sure you buy the right grade wax for your climate.

DECK GRIP

In the 1980s wax was facing its demise because of the advent of the deck grip – thin foam pads that offered hassle-free grip in an infinite variety of DayGlo colours and patterns. Was this to be the end of laboriously de-waxing grubby boards during a flat spell, and then cadging half a bar off surly strangers in the car-park when you realise a few days later that you've forgotten to re-wax? Nothing dates a used board more certainly than finding it covered with neon deck grip; in the 1980s surfers plastered it all over their boards. But once applied, it quickly lost its grippiness but proved almost impossible to remove. And people simply just liked waxing their boards.

Deck grip has now found its true calling not as an all-over application but just as a tail-pad, and not so much for improved grip as to supply the raised section against which you can brace to execute powerful back-foot manoeuvres. If buying and applying, again follow the instructions and get the board super-clean; then position with care, because once it's on, it's on.

⬆ **Get the right wax grade for your application**

ADDING A DECK GRIP

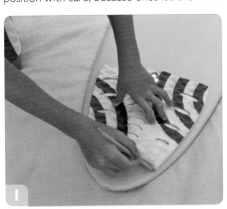

⬆ **Draw an outline around the deck grip.**

⬆ **Sand the board for a key…**

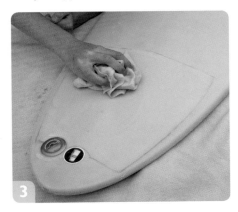

⬆ **…then wipe clean with some solvent.**

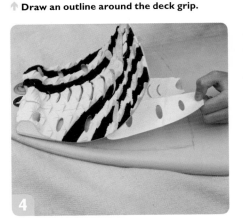

⬆ **Position the deck grip and remove the backing.**

⬆ **Press down firmly all over to ensure a good bond.**

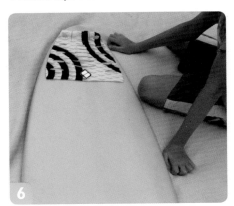

⬆ **Sit back and admire your work.**

LEASH

On 25 May 2005, in the French prefecture of Landes, an order by the Prefect made it obligatory for all surfers to use a leash, whatever the conditions. This was the first law of its type in the world. A leash isn't yet obligatory in the UK, despite calls from certain sectors of the industry for it to be made so.

There are pros and cons to having a hard missile with three sharp fins and a pointy nose tied to you with a cord of springy urethane. With a leash you're more likely to injure yourself; without one you're more likely to injure others and to exhaust yourself in a long swim.

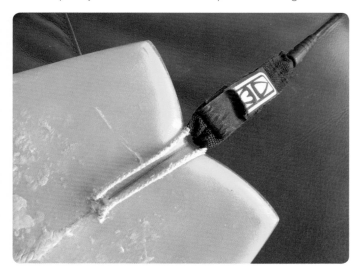

So far, then, a leash falls somewhere between a necessity and an accessory. You don't *need* it to ride a wave, but it'll make the whole process of learning less hassle, that's for sure. Strap it firmly *under* your wetsuit on the ankle of your back foot. Ensure that the other end is tied firmly to the leash plug with a thick string, short enough that the rail-saver can do its job. Many leashes now come with an integral attachment piece sewn firmly on to the rail-saver, which is a boon.

A leash dragging in the water behind you will slow you down ever so slightly. A superlight leash will slow you down less, but will more easily break in heavy conditions. It'll also offer less padding around the ankle, and the repeated action of an unpadded ankle strap digging into your softened skin will soon create a sea ulcer that may be hard to heal. Alternate different gauge leashes for different conditions.

If you forget or break a leash, it seems shameful to simply head back home defeated. The advocates of no-leash surfing point to the incontestable fact that there are now thousands of surfers who won't hold on to their boards, yet who can barely swim should they lose them. Eventually you should aim to acquire the discipline of surfing ably without the safety net of a leash – it heightens your sense of responsibility. But be sensible and practise only when your local break is deserted and you're confident you have the capability to swim in. With or without a leash, the golden rule is always to hold on to your board – and without a leash you've *got* to hold on to it.

← **Make sure the rail-saver can do its job. This one needs adjusting.**

↑ **Leashes can be a pain, but less so than swimming in and collecting your busted board from the rocks.**

NOSE GUARD

This simple rubber cone is a neat and practical method of minimising board-related injuries, and affixing one is probably the single most cost-effective safety measure you can take. Carefully follow the simple fixing instructions.

← **A noseguard is a type of cheap medical insurance.**

→ **Board socks offer only basic protection but can double as a towel.**

PROTECTING YOUR BOARD

Boards devalue readily so are worth protecting. A cloth sock is cheap, lightweight and stretchy and will protect your board from UV rays and from scratches, plus it can double as a towel to lie on and dry yourself. Heavier-duty protection costs more, but is worth it. A sturdy padded, zippered, coffin-type travel-bag will prevent dings and impacts, short of someone driving over your board. But it'll be bulky and weigh more than the board it's protecting so is often not really practical for everyday use.

→ **Padded travel bags are essential on longer trips.**

RACKS

If you've got a car you can get yourself, your friends and all your boards to the beach. Straps are invaluable and will shuck down a number of boards on to conventional car luggage racks, but soft racks are a great idea for securing boards to a rack-less car. They just fold away neatly into a small bag when not in use and are ideal for travelling when you're picking up a rental car. Often you can persuade a taxi driver to accept them as well.

← **Thread the straps through the open doorways.**

← **Remove or lash the leg-rope firmly.**

← **A towel betwen the boards prevents wax transfer.**

← **Avoid the rail with the buckle, snug down and hit the road.**

'WITH SKIING, I'M USUALLY ENCOURAGED BY THE FEELING THAT THE MOUNTAIN WANTS ME TO GO DOWN IT. IF ON AN ALP I DO NOTHING, AND RELAX, THAT'S WHAT WILL PROBABLY HAPPEN. I'M NOT SO SURE THE WAVE WANTS ME ON IT. IF I DO NOTHING AND RELAX, I WILL DROWN.'

Richard Beard, *Manly Pursuits: Beating the Australians at Sport,* 2003

CHAPTER 4

BASIC SKILLS

So, now that you've got everything you need to go surfing, how do you go about putting it all to use?

LEARNING

There used to be just one way to learn to surf: pick up a board and have a bash. There was little concept of how to systematically progress – people just tried and tried until they got better or gave up.

The surfing success rate and demographic has changed radically. Now there are younger learners, older learners, and everyone is using better gear.

Surfing has never been made to look more seductive, it's never been easier to get to the beach, and, when the hordes arrive, the industry has never been more ready to capitalise on their enthusiasm.

Of course, you *can* still just cadge some gear and get out there. With a lot of determination you'll eventually succeed, but it'll be a longer, harder slog than it need be. It's fun, but fun with gritted teeth. Enrolling for a lesson with an accredited surf school is money well spent. A good surf school can quickly get you standing, and give you the foundational skills on which to base a lifetime of surfing.

SURF SCHOOLS

Surf schools in Great Britain are currently regulated under the auspices of Surfing GB, which is the governing body for surf sport. Surfing GB is a member of the International Surfing Association (ISA), the organisation that provides the most widely recognised teaching qualification for surf instructors, the ISA Surf Coaching Award. Also highly regarded is the Academy of Surf Instructors (ASI), a large private company that accredits many instructors in the UK, France and Australia. It's highly recommended that you ensure your coaches are qualified within one of the two schemes, the ISA or the ASI.

Reputable surf schools provide the appropriate board and a well-fitted wetsuit, and their qualified instructors take you to a beach with manageable conditions. The surf coach is dedicated to ensuring your safety first and foremost; he or she is trained to spot your strengths and relative weaknesses in the water and tailor a session to enable you to get the most out of it. That's already a good head-start on what most learners can manage going it alone.

Almost invariably, surf schools have a fleet of the soft boards known as 'foamies' or 'Swellies'. These are wide, buoyant and – most importantly of all – they don't hurt when they clonk you on the head. Their design brief can be summed up in two words: safety and stability. They provide a comfortable platform for you to clamber to your feet knowing that once you get there you'll be hooked. After that, performance-wise, Swellies are extremely limited, to say the least, but who cares, they've done their job.

The aim of a surf school is to get you progressing in small, easy stages, so that your enthusiasm doesn't outrun your firm grasp of technique.

All good surf schools have a written syllabus with which the instructors will be familiar, so all lessons – conditions permitting – will more or less closely follow this pattern. It's known simply as the ABC structure: Section A provides information on equipment and the ocean environment, highlighting the potential dangers and hazards, with the focus on safety procedures; Section B is the theory and practice of catching waves just in the prone position; and Section C focuses on getting learners to their feet. A lesson following this plan will last around two hours.

Part A

▢ The instructor welcomes you, and, by way of introduction, provides a little of his or her background in the sport.

▢ All class members will have the chance to give their names and say whether or not they have any previous experience in board sports.

▢ The format of the lesson is explained.

▢ Participants are then sized up for wetsuits, and as you prepare to get changed you're shown how best to climb into them.

▢ Once in your wetsuits you're ready to be sized up for boards, depending on age, height, weight, experience and the day's conditions.

▢ You'll be teamed with a partner to double-up and carry two boards down to the water's edge, nose to nose and tail to tail.

Part B

▢ Sitting down at the water's edge, you'll be arranged in a semi-circle, backs to the sun, and preferably backs to the water also. This keeps you comfortable and not too distracted.

▢ The instructor will give a briefing on the location, explaining what makes this beach favourable for learning to surf.

▢ The locations of the lifeguard station and lifeguard patrols will be pointed out.

▢ You'll be given important information on general beach safety including the use of patrol flags, the dangers of rip currents and the potential hazards of white water and unbroken waves.

▢ You'll be shown how to recognise and respond to the hand signals and whistle signals that may be used by the instructor to keep you in the right part of the beach and to request that you return to shore.

▢ The action to take in the event of any emergency is demonstrated.

▢ You'll be shown what action to take should you find yourself separated from your group.

▢ Now comes the warm-up – a light jog, a few dynamic stretches and exercises for joint mobility.

▢ The various parts of the board (deck, tail, fin, rails etc) are pointed out, and you're shown how to properly put on a leash.

▢ Safe entry into the sea with a board is explained.

▢ Now the instructor tells you how to go about catching a wave in the prone position, paying attention to the following aspects:

 ❱ Body position.
 ❱ Trim.
 ❱ Wave selection.
 ❱ Toboggan take-off.
 ❱ Hand position, back arched, high elbows.
 ❱ Stopping the board.

▢ On land, the instructor demonstrates the prone position, and you all have a dry practice of the technique.

▢ Action in the case of a wipeout is explained, showing how best to protect your head.

▢ There's a quick recap on signals, as they must be thoroughly understood before you're allowed in the water.

BASIC SKILLS

■ You watch whilst the instructor gives a short in-water demonstration of the prone technique.

■ Leashes on: you now have supervised practice for 10–15 minutes.

■ Back on the beach, absorb the feedback provided by the instructor and ask any questions you may have.

Part C

Now you're told how to catch a wave by paddling, with emphasis on several key points:

■ Cupping the hands.

■ Paddling with alternate arms.

■ Good wave selection.

■ Efficient paddle strokes.

■ Putting in two power strokes just before take-off.

■ Pausing before the pop-up.

■ Foot positioning: back foot parallel, front foot at 45°.

■ Stopping the board.

■ The instructor will demonstrate on land, and you have a dry practice.

■ Action on a wipeout is recapped.

■ Signals and action on leaving the group are reviewed.

■ The instructor will nip into the water to demonstrate selecting and paddling into a wave, then popping up to his feet in the water.

■ Leashes on: it's time for you to put all this into one hour of supervised practise.

■ If any of the group are struggling to jump straight to their feet, the instructor may get you all out of the water to show how you can break down the pop-up into an easily achievable sequence by using your knees.

■ At the end of the lesson you'll be led in a few cool-down exercises.

■ After handing in your rash vest and wetsuit, the instructor will take a few moments to provide feedback and to get you thinking about future aims: where would you like to take your surfing from here, and what goals could you set to make that a reality?

Surf schools are now everywhere for everyone – for the under nines, for women only, for the disabled, for inner city kids with behavioural problems. Yet until the 1980s virtually everyone was self-taught, and there has never yet been a world champion who began surfing at a surf school. So does instruction actually work?

Research has been undertaken at university level in an effort to discover just how instruction compares with trial and error in acquiring basic surfing skills.

The research involved two similar groups of complete novices. One group was given the full ABC surf lesson; the other was provided with identical equipment but told just to get on with it on their own. Results were acquired both by self-rated perceived performance (questions such as 'how do you feel you did?'), and by competitive surf judges trained in the rating of beginners. Judging criteria included trimming in the prone position, getting to the feet, stance, and degree of control during the ride.

The self-rating questionnaire results showed 100% enjoyment for the taught group, but only 60% for the others. 80% of the taught group felt safe; only 30% of the self-taught group did. The taught group felt they achieved more and felt that they could go on to better things. The others had serious misconceptions and knowledge gaps – for example, not understanding that the speed of the board has an effect on stability, and not knowing what the lifeguards' black and white flags mean. For the judges, the taught group was superior, being awarded a mean wave score of 2.32 out of five versus 1.17. The highest individual scores were also given to the taught group (up to a 4.5!).

Why should there be such an obvious difference? The major factors seem to be that the taught group was at ease in the new environment: dangers were clearly pointed out and they knew a trained instructor was always watching over them. Rather than struggling to take on too much at once and becoming disheartened, the aims of the taught group were broken up into a series of discrete attainable goals.

Despite these results, lessons don't suit everybody. Personality plays a big part in how you progress. Some thrive on their own, and after a shaky start will quickly progress to a level way beyond that of taught students.

⬆ **Up and riding in your first lesson.**

⬈ **Surf lessons have been shown to be therapeutic for people with a wide range of debilitations.**

OPEN SPORT

Sporting and athletic skills can be either 'open' or 'closed'. Because surfing is so directly influenced by the environment in which it's performed, it's a prime example of an 'open' sport. Taking a free throw in basketball is a 'closed' skill – the environment is controlled and there are no outside influences, therefore you can rely totally on motor skills alone to perform precisely the same task every time: the same size ball through the same size hoop from the same distance. But nothing in surfing is ever the same, so on top of the learned motor skills the surfer needs to be able to apply judgement, perception, anticipation, knowledge and experience. It's a tall order for a learner; so the ABC structure of the surf school lesson uses what closed environment is available – the sand of the beach – to engender some skills before taking learners into the ultimate open environment of the sea.

SURF ETIQUETTE

THE TEN COMMANDMENTS OF SURFING ETIQUETTE

1–3 RIGHT OF WAY

The surfer who has priority is the one who's either –

- Furthest out or has waited the longest.
- Furthest inside or closest to the peak.
- First to feet, or first up on the wave.

4–6 COURTESY

As a courtesy to other surfers, make sure you –

- Communicate: call 'Left' or 'Right' to indicate which way you want to ride.
- Don't drop in: if another surfer has caught the wave, leave them to it. It is off-putting and impolite to keep paddling in the hope they stuff up.
- Don't snake. Wait your turn. Snaking is queue-jumping.

7–9 SAFETY

To minimise the risk of collisions, make sure you –

- Paddle wide – around and away from riding surfers if possible.
- Head for the white water if caught inside: don't paddle into the path of riders.
- Keep your board. For your own safety and that of others, don't throw away boards.
- Respect the beauty of Nature's playground and give the same respect to those who share her. Don't pollute the ocean with foul language and bad vibes.

You'll be too busy having fun to notice, but when you're in a surf school you're in your own little protected bubble. You have your coloured rash vest on in a flock of other learners in coloured rash vests; you're watched over and herded around by your instructors; you might even have your own little section of the beach allocated to you by the lifeguards. Other surfers will avoid you like the plague – you're an unpredictable menace, who'll be allowed a certain dispensation as a learner (we all had to learn once).

But as soon as that vest comes off, you're on your own. You have to take your chances with the rest of the beach, scrapping for the limited resource that is clean waves. This is when you have to learn the more or less formal rules of the road – surf etiquette. The sooner you learn, the fewer people you'll upset. Lack of surf etiquette is one certain pretext for aggressive localism; don't give anyone that justification.

Surfing etiquette has long enjoyed being based on a single surfer gaining 'priority' and then riding the wave alone. This expectation really only began in the 1960s when the first boom in surfing participation brought unbearable crowds to popular waves like Malibu. Until then surfers were happy to share and would tailor manoeuvres to accommodate other surfers on the wave, the 'go-behind' being one example. When local enforcers such as Miki Dora at Malibu eventually got the hump with others on 'their' waves they'd deliberately crash into them to teach them a 'lesson' – the lesson being that surfing was becoming a sport of individualistic male macho posturing.

Many waves are so critical that only a single surfer at a time can safely ride them, but at most of the breaks you're likely to be surfing riding alone is really just a luxury, not an inalienable right. With the exponential increase of the surfing population the whole concept of surfing solo will surely have to be revised eventually. Until then, don't get in people's way if you can help it, but don't let more experienced surfers bully and intimidate you into coming home from a session with a zero wave count.

'I THOUGHT I UNDERSTOOD WHAT ANDY HAD SAID ABOUT THE PEAK AND THE SURFER WITH PRIORITY, BUT WHEN I FINALLY GOT OUT PAST THE BREAK I COULDN'T FIGURE OUT WHERE THE PEAK WAS. I DIDN'T KNOW HOW FAR AWAY FROM THE OTHER SURFERS WAS SAFE TO SIT, AND I MUST HAVE GOTTEN IT WRONG, BECAUSE ANOTHER DUDE COLLIDED WITH ME AND ASKED ME IF I WAS BORN ON PLANET KOOK.'

Peter Heller

DEALING WITH DROP-INS

⬆ If you are nearest the peak...

⬆ ...no matter how small you are...

⬆ ...give a polite shout.

⬆ The dropper-in...

⬆ ...should get off the wave.

⬆ Leaving you to ride alone.

BEING A DROP-IN

⬆ If you have been seen to drop in on someone...

⬆ ...then you can expect the same treatment.

⬆ It's poetic justice, and most people learn quickly.

BASIC SKILLS 81

BOARD CONTROL

ventually a surfboard will become almost a natural extension of your body, but when you're learning on a longer, thicker board that sense of union is pretty hard to achieve. It's a big, awkward great lump of foam that just seems to want to damage everything it comes near and destroy itself in the process.

Control of the board is the most important aspect of preventing injury. Get the feel of the board under your arm. Heft it. Notice how easy it is for the wind to catch it and dash it against something hard. Consider that if air can do that, then how much easier it is for water to do it.

Put your leash on before you get to the water. Even when you have your own little shortboard, never let your board out of your control in the shallows. When chatting to a friend in waist-deep water pick up the board and keep the nose pointing into the waves. This is the most crucial point – always, *always* keep the nose pointing into the waves until the very moment you decide to turn to take a wave.

When practising in the shallows, lift the nose of the board over the foam of each oncoming wave, brace your weight on the board with your arms and jump up off the bottom. Use your weight to force the nose down over the back of the wave.

⬆ **Put the leash on.**

⬆ **Hold the cord…**

⬆ **…then walk out to the shallows.**

'EACH HEATHEN WOULD PADDLE THREE OR FOUR HUNDRED YARDS OUT TO SEA (TAKING A SHORT BOARD WITH HIM), THEN FACE THE SHORE AND WAIT FOR A PARTICULARLY PRODIGIOUS BILLOW TO COME ALONG; AT THE RIGHT MOMENT HE WOULD FLING HIS BOARD UPON ITS FOAMY CREST AND HIMSELF UPON THE BOARD, AND HERE HE WOULD COME WHIZZING BY LIKE A BOMBSHELL... I TRIED SURF-BATHING ONCE, SUBSEQUENTLY, BUT MADE A FAILURE OF IT. I GOT THE BOARD PLACED RIGHT, AND AT THE RIGHT MOMENT, TOO; BUT MISSED THE CONNECTION MYSELF... THE BOARD STRUCK THE SHORE IN THREE QUARTERS OF A SECOND, WITHOUT ANY CARGO, AND I STRUCK THE BOTTOM ABOUT THE SAME TIME, WITH A COUPLE OF BARRELS OF WATER IN ME. NONE BUT THE NATIVES EVER MASTER THE ART OF SURF-BATHING THOROUGHLY.'

Mark Twain, *Roughing It,* 1871

⬆ **Always keep control of the board, and listen to your instructor (even if it's your Dad)**

⬆ **Don't let the board come between you and the wave.**

⬆ **Lift the board and use it to hoist yourself over the whitewater.**

⬆ **This is the one – quickly lift and turn the board around**

⬆ **Set the board down facing the shore.**

⬆ **Push off and paddle.**

⬆ **Hands on the rail, ready to get to your feet.**

A board presented broadside to any little lump of water is simply asking for trouble. When turning to catch a wave, turn as swiftly as you can. If you're in waist-deep water use both hands to pluck the board a foot out of the water, swizzle it round rapidly, then plonk it down facing the shore. Trying to navigate it around like a ship takes too long; the fins are doing their job of offering lateral resistance. You want those fins clear of the water before you get caught broadside and blasted.

If you sense that you've taken too long and you're going to get caught broadside, then don't try to ride it out or rectify the situation by a last-second grab – just forget the board and duck smartly under the water, covering your head with your arms. Come up only once the wave has passed. This is a principle of self-preservation, but don't forget your responsibility to other beach-users who may be just behind you – this isn't a technique you should come to rely on, just a quick fix in an emergency.

Take the board out on a flat day when there are no waves – this is the best way to get the feel of it. Paddle it around, lie in different positions, then try sitting up. You need to be able to sit up, not only to see what's around you and what sets might be stacking up on the horizon, but also in order to turn the thing around. You can't use the technique you were using in the shallows, yet you still don't want to be steering it around like a supertanker – by the time you're in position the wave you wanted will have passed you by and you'll be stuck facing the beach as the next one you really didn't fancy bears down on you.

The way to turn in deep water is to pivot. Offer as little of the board's resistance to the water as possible by grabbing one rail, leaning back and pulling the board to near vertical. By shifting your body weight and sculling with your feet and one hand you can swing the board round pretty smartly. Then force the nose down with your body weight and get paddling. It sounds tricky but you can become quickly very adept at it, and you'll need to be, particularly if you're in competition for waves on a busy beach.

PADDLING

If you've borrowed a board, look for the chest-sized patch of grubby wax — that's where you should lie. If you don't have that to help you then just get on the thing and lie roughly in the middle, then check the trim of the board — how it lies in the water. Paddling's one technique that will benefit from a bit of flat-water practice. You want the nose of the board to be a couple of inches out of the surface, maybe just digging through a bit of chop now and then. If it's too low you'll soon know it — water will continually splash into your face, and should any kind of wave pick the tail up further you'll somersault forwards.

Shuffle back a little and try it now — but not so far back that you look like a sack of potatoes on the tail, with the nose pointing to the sky; that way you'll be pushing water, it'll be really difficult to get any kind of speed up and there's no chance of you catching a wave, it'll just pass beneath you. Paddling a surfboard is tiring enough; without the board in trim it's a lesson in frustration.

You'll notice that most competent surfers paddle around with a pronounced bow in the back. This 'heads up' position isn't just to enable better vision: it's a means of giving yourself some margin for shifting your body weight without actually sliding up or down the board. If your back is arched, then you have the option of lowering your head and neck to give just a little extra shunt of weight towards the nose. This helps get you over the edge and into the wave. Conversely, if you've caught a wave just a little too late, at the critical moment you can arch your back a bit further to shift your centre of gravity rearwards and pull the front of the board up out of a nosedive.

Good paddling is vital for several reasons, but the primary one is safety. Wherever there's surf, there will be currents, and they won't always be taking you where you want to go. Currents may be sweeping you straight out to sea, or around a point, or just frustratingly a little away from the peak. If you can't paddle yourself out of trouble then you're relying on someone else to fetch you back, and that can be humiliating and/or very expensive, depending on where you are in the world.

If you get into trouble, then use your knowledge of rip currents to work out whether this one's likely to let go of you any time soon, or whether this is a major tidal current. Either way, try to work out where you're best headed then paddle to safety at an angle to the current, never directly against it. Don't get off the board and swim, nor lie broadside across it and kick your legs: the most efficient way is the way you've been taught, just get your head down and keep the board in trim.

If you're not a good paddler then you'll be condemned always to be a whitewater surfer, because nothing other than a broken wave will ever carry you to the beach. There's nothing wrong with that if that's where your ambitions rest, but it's a bit like remaining on the nursery slopes doing snowplough turns in the Alps. Being a good paddler enables you to catch good waves; being an excellent paddler enables you to catch loads of good waves even when there are lots of other good paddlers around.

Some may be tempted to compensate for weak arms by getting a bigger board. The logic of that argument is seductive and does have some merit — not catching waves is no fun — but taken too far it becomes counter-productive. Get a board too big and you may be catching loads of waves but you won't be able to do much on them, because your board is too big to turn! You should be riding the wave, not the board. On a very big board you'll progress rapidly up to a point, then just stay there. Always add fitness before adding thickness. Get paddling.

⬆ **Keep the arm extension long and strong.**

⬆ **Keep the body centred in the flow line. There is no need to kick.**

⬆ **Finish off the pull all the way through.**

⬆ **With a balanced, even stroke, the board stays in trim even when you are looking around for a wave.**

⬆ **A good arch of the back.**

⬆ **Nice high elbows.**

⬆ **Powerful pull through.**

⬆ **No splash on entry.**

⬆ **The board in perfect trim.**

⬆ **Fast arm recovery without chucking water backwards, and no kicking.**

SMALL WAVES

⬆ **When a small wave approaches…**

⬆ **…stop paddling; place hands on the rails…**

⬆ **…and push the nose down.**

⬆ **Push yourself up and let the whitewater pass between you and the board.**

⬆ **Settle back into trim – paddle to the next one.**

THE PADDLE OUT

Particularly at beach breaks, most of your paddling will be aimed not at catching waves but heading the other way, trying to get out through the white water. When a ton of white water is heading your way, if you merely stop paddling and do nothing except hang on grimly you'll get battered.

In very small surf you can avoid most of the power of the white water by extending your arms fully and pushing your chest and hips up off the board. This has the effect of pushing the board down slightly (enough so the wave won't catch under the nose and flick it over) as you rise up over the white water – it passes beneath you between yourself and the partly sunken board. This method works only with a small broken wave; try it on anything over a foot or so and it'll be like head-butting a mattress.

When the waves are bigger you need a different tactic: the turtle roll or 'T' roll. Just as the wave approaches you, get a good firm grip of the rails and turn yourself and the board over so that your board, now upside down, hides you. The wave should wash cleanly over the bottom of the board, and when it has, you simply roll back up and resume paddling. Remember to ensure that you weight the nose down with your body and keep a good grip on the rails. The impact can still be significant, so be ready for it, and of course do your best to keep hold of your board.

BACK POSTURE

The next time you check a surf spot, watch the backs of the surfers: arched when paddling to get a good view of what's around, flat when accelerating to the edge, arched again just as the nose drops down the face, then into the standing position. As a sequence, it comes naturally enough, but as a physical exercise it may not – your back muscles will be screaming anyway with all that paddling, and you might not have the strength or flexibility as yet, but it will come, and it's an important factor in efficient paddling.

⬆ **Flattening the back to get weight forwards.**

THE TURTLE ROLL

⬆ When a bigger wave is heading your way...

⬆ ...if you can't duck-dive your board, you need to firmly grab the rails and turn the board over.

⬆ This 'turtle roll' allows the white water to sweep over the board with you safely underneath.

⬆ Once the wave has passed...

⬆ ...you roll back up.

⬆ Climb back onto the board...

⬆ ...and paddle off.

⬆ One last stroke as the wave steepens, and the head can come up.

⬆ The wave is caught; now arch the back to bring the nose of the board up a little.

THE DUCK-DIVE

Shortboarders can exploit the comparative lack of buoyancy and the sharper nose of the smaller board to sink it under the wave, and then direct it up out the back of the wave still in perfect paddling position. Duck-diving is a vital technique to learn; it takes a few tries but you can practise in flat water until you get the hang of it.

As the wave approaches, push up with your arms and at the same time lurch forward with your weight. This gets the nose of the board under the water and the board angled towards the bottom at 45°.

Use the knee, or even the foot, of your back leg to push the board down and under the wave. Pushing on the tail has the effect of taking the board down and under the wave in an arc; the flotation brings you to the surface out the back of the wave. It's simple once you have the timing right: too late and you'll still be on top of the water when the wave hits; too early and you'll surface just in time to get dragged over the falls backwards. Efficient duck-diving will get you out the back through almost any regular conditions.

↑ **Get your weight up and forwards.**

↑ **Sink the nose...**

↑ **...and get one knee or foot on the tail.**

↑ **The board arcs underwater...**

↑ **...you pop out on the other side...**

↑ **...ready to paddle.**

'THEY DO NOT ATTEMPT TO GO OVER THE BILLOWS WHICH ROLL TOWARD THE SHORE, BUT WATCH THEIR APPROACH, AND DIVE UNDER THE WATER, ALLOWING THE BILLOW TO PASS OVER THEIR HEADS.'

William Ellis, *Polynesian Researches*, 1831.

THE BAIL

⬆ **The easiest paddle out…**

⬆ **…is to head straight for the rip…**

⬆ **…and get a free ride out the back.**

The last resort for surfers facing a wall of white water is to bail. Chuck the board away and head for the bottom – things down there are a lot calmer. All surfers do this occasionally; *when* you do it simply depends on your tolerance for facing oncoming walls of white water. You're more likely to have to bail with a bigger board, for the bigger the board the bigger the battering.

Bailing is a kind of controlled panic move – you want to be well under the wave where the turbulence can't get you. If you're convinced that the board is going to stop you getting there, then get rid of the board and swim or sink down as far as your leash will allow you. Let the leash do the work of looking after the board, that's why you paid so much for it.

Leashes, however, are not infallible, and the sudden yank of tons of white water can tear the leash through the rail of the board. Some people try to cushion the tug on the leash by holding on to the railsaver as they sink and let the board go only at the very moment they feel the impact. But if you mistime this release the tail spins round and the fins can gouge a hole in your fingers.

The problem with bailing is you cannot be sure where the board is.

Once you've let it out of your control, a board has a nasty habit of coming back to you from an unexpected angle and at speed. That's any number of sharp fins and a pointy nose heading straight for your unprotected head. The least you can do is keep your head covered with your arms until you know the danger has passed – though this isn't easy to do when you're thrashing around trying desperately to get to the surface to breathe.

Bailing is a last resort, not something to indulge in lightly whenever you're feeling a little too tired to duck-dive. Injuring yourself is unfortunate; injuring someone else is unforgivable. If you're going to bail you must ensure you have a clear area behind and around you. If you're six feet tall, your leash eight feet long and your board an eight-footer, well that's already a twenty-two feet radius injury zone around you whenever you thoughtlessly bail your board. Unnecessary bailing is the sign of a kook, someone far worse than just a harmless novice.

Once you have the kind of board control that enables you to get out the back to the peak, then you can start to think about standing up and carving across some green waves.

THE POP-UP

Attempting to get to your feet on a clean wave is different in several ways to riding in waist-deep white water. It's easier in that the water is smooth and you aren't being bounced around on a churning mass of aerated foam; the board will be steadier beneath you. On the other hand, you're now dropping down a slope, which may be quite steep.

You'll need to try to perfect the smooth jump-up because now you have less time to waste struggling to your knees and then to two feet. By the time you've managed all that the green part of the wave has swept on down the line and left you just riding white water straight to the beach.

Practise your jump-up technique out of the water – you can do it at home on a rug, or place your board in the sand and try it there. If you can't manage it straight away – perhaps because your arms are relatively weak, or your back doesn't yet have the flexibility – keep training and it'll come. You cannot surf steep fast waves without it.

Jump up but land in a shallow crouch with legs bent to act like springs in absorbing the bumps of the ride. The bent legs enable you to shift your weight front to back as necessary – back to take the drop, forwards to accelerate down the line. Look where you're headed: thanks to the mechanics of your body the board will tend to follow your eyes.

The drop actually offers an advantage: think back to how hard it was in the shallows to hoist your knees up under your chest and drag your feet into position beneath you. Well, now that the board's actually falling away from underneath you there's more room between your chest and the board – in some ways the steeper the wave, the easier is the single smooth movement of the jump-up take-off.

⬆ **Arch the back, hands on the rail.**

⬆ **Press your torso up.**

⬆ **Swing the legs through, and sight down the line.**

⬆ **Spread the arms for balance, and look for your bottom turn.**

⬆ **Shift your weight forwards, and compress to gather momentum for the turn.**

KEY POINTS

- **Arch your back as soon as you're committed to the drop.**
- **Place your hands on the deck or rail at shoulder level.**
- **Press your torso up and swing your legs through underneath your chest.**
- **Spread your arms for balance.**
- **Adopt a slight crouch, but don't squat.**
- **Look to where you want to go.**

WAVE SELECTION

Wave selection is the vital ability to judge which waves are going to close out and which are going to peel. This ability to read a wave comes with experience, but you can give yourself a head start before you paddle out by sitting and watching the break for a few sets. To what degree are the waves predictable? Is there a clearly defined peak and channel? This will be less easy to define at a beach break than a point or a reef, but you still might be able to distinguish a pattern.

Once you've paddled out, carry on scouring the break for a makeable peak. Don't just paddle for the first thing that comes your way – that's the quickest way to waste all the effort of getting there. A close-out will be cresting along the wave in unmakeable sections, too fast for you to surf along past the pitching lip. A peeling wave will unwind smoothly from the peak on one side to the shoulder further down the line. That's the one you want.

Now, if nobody's already up and riding that wave, spin the board around, settle into your arched-back paddling position and get paddling. Not straight towards the beach, though – angle the board so that it's heading along the wave in the direction it's peeling. Paddle paddle paddle; now shift the weight of your head and shoulders forward by flattening your back, feel the wave lift the tail of your board. Once over the edge, arch back to get the nose up a little, grip the rails with your hands and spring up to your feet. In your crouch, you'll feel the fins bite in the face of the wave, the board sets in trim across the face and you're surfing!

↑ **Choosing the right wave…**

↑ **…is more important…**

↑ **…than being able to jump straight to your feet.**

↑ **You can practise jumping up on land.**

↑ **But wave selection…**

↑ **…is only developed by surfing**

STANCE

NATURAL- (REGULAR) FOOT

GOOFY-FOOT

You surf in one of two basic stances: natural-foot (also known as 'regular') or goofy-foot. Natural-footers have their left foot planted forwards; goofy-footers surf with their right foot forwards.

Most people can naturally tell which foot should be the rearwards one, but some people find it quite hard to work out. The simplest way to find out is to stand still on the beach and, without thinking too much about it, just set off on a run. The foot you leave planted on the sand on your first stride is your back foot for surfing. Or get someone you trust to shove you in the back – the foot you plant in front of you to stop yourself falling is your front foot.

Whichever stance you adopt, when you're paddling for a peak the wave can break two ways: left or right, as you're facing shore. This means that when surfing you'll be standing either face to the wave/back to shore ('forehand' or 'frontside') or face to the shore/back to the wave ('backhand' or 'backside').

Beginners usually find that surfing frontside comes easier: naturally facing the way you're going, leaning into the wave, with your weight more squarely on your toes. Backhand surfing often comes less easily; you need to twist the upper body more deliberately to keep the eyes facing the wave, and the pressure on the board is applied through your clunky heels more than the flexible toes.

To be a complete surfer you must work at mastering your backhand surfing as well as your frontside, if only because any full turn will involve shifting from one orientation to the other.

➔ **Natural -footer going frontside.**

← **Goofy-footer going frontside.**

➔ **Natural-footer going backside.**

← **Goofy-footer going backside.**

'THE ONLY THING BETTER THAN SURFING
IS SURFING WELL.'

Taj Burrow, ASP Tour competitor and author of *Taj Burrow's Book of Hot Surfing*, 2003

CHAPTER 5

ADVANCED SKILLS

Advanced surfing is not necessarily flashy surfing; it is learning the subtle rail-to-rail shifts of weight that enable you find and tap into the pockets of power of any wave. Only once you have that power at your feet can you pull the big moves that impress.

PUMPING

Once you can angle your take-off, you can explore the wave. Tracking across the unbroken face of a wave is the first sign of competence, but don't just stand there and let the wave do all the work. By pumping up and down, weighting and un-weighting, the surfer can load and release pressure on the board to gather and apply speed.

This action is particularly important for a shortboard as it lacks the pure momentum of a longer board, but driving down the line like this also gives you the *feel* for how your board works in synch with your body movements.

So far you've learned to adopt a slightly crouched position – bent at the knees, hands at shoulder height. Now, rather than standing like a statue, you'll naturally want to loosen up a little.

If you do this by extending your knees you'll stand up slightly taller, but also transmit some of the force downwards to the board. The buoyant board is pushed downwards into the surface of the water, the water resists by pressing up. The result is that the board squirts away forwards, projected by the fins.

Every time you apply a little extra force by pressing your feet and extending your knees, the board will accelerate. To climb up a little, lift the board by un-weighting: lift your feet up by flexing at the knees. Take the pressure off the board; even lift your arms a little skyward. With the downward pressure off, the board will respond by being drawn up the face of the wave. Here you can redirect and angle back down the face, regain some speed and get ready to press with your feet again and repeat the process.

⬆ **Pick a nice one and pop to your feet.**

⬆ **Extend out of the bottom turn by lifting your arms forward and up.**

⬆ **Draw the board up by lifting your knees.**

⬆ **Begin to compress again, hands down.**

⬆ **Unweight, and lift the trailing arm.**

⬆ **Push the board down into another S-turn.**

⬆ **Look for a bigger manoeuvre if the wave demands it.**

This is the pump, or driving S-turn. Try it – on a larger less responsive board your efforts will have to be that much more exaggerated, but that's not a bad thing when you're learning. You may find yourself just shooting off the back of the wave if you can't redirect, but as long as you learn the feeling of weighting and un-weighting, then you've learned the fundamentals of good surfing.

Learning how and *where* to efficiently weight/un-weight (or compress/extend) is the start of putting some 'flow' into your surfing. You're doing the work, but let the wave lead your moves; apply pressure to the board only at the very moment that you need to. Weighting the board when surfing is like changing gear when driving a car: if you try to take a sharp uphill corner in fifth gear you'll stall horribly; the same will happen if you try to gouge a huge hack on the wrong part of a wave.

OPEN STANCE

Rather than have both feet square-on to the stringer, if you try to orient your feet closer to an angle of 45° your stance will be more open. This opens your hips, tucks in the back knee and allows easier body rotation. It also gives greater control when shifting weight front to back.

⬆ The same principles of flexing the knees and lifting the trailing arm apply on your backhand, but have to be exaggerated to gain the same speed.

⬆ The weight is applied down through the heels.　　⬆ Make an extra effort to get the trailing arm forwards.

⬆ Once you have enough speed you can look for a bigger manoeuvre.

TURNS

Once you've got some speed, you can turn. But why turn at all? Shortboards are designed to work best when put on the rail, set on an edge. The best way to generate speed is to keep loading up power through the rails by turning, and the best way to turn is to have speed – it's a positive feedback loop in which the best surfers can generate more speed than they know what to do with. The pros can use that speed to gouge a massive hack, carve a monster cutback or boost a crazy air; but even at the level of the beginner, turns are important for several reasons.

→ **Turns give you a chance to make a statement on the wave.**

SAFETY

The first reason to learn to turn is nothing to do with being radical, but with being responsible. To avoid hazards, and to avoid being a danger to others, you have to be able to manoeuvre your board. The hazard could be a falling lip, a surfer dropping in on you or a learner wallowing in your path. You have a *duty* to be able to turn; if you can't do it then you put the onus on others to avoid you and assume the initiative for your safety.

SPEED

Turning helps you to maintain and generate speed by keeping in touch with the pocket of the wave, where the power is. If you outrun the pocket and cannot turn back to it, your board is dead in the water.

SENSATIONS

Sometimes you might be content to enjoy the relaxation of just cruising along a wave. On other occasions you'll want to crank a huge turn simply to really feel the g-forces generated using the power that the wave is offering you.

STYLE

The turn is the first chance to make some kind of statement on the wave. How you turn and where you turn are marks of individuality, almost like a signature. You'll learn a few fundamentals to effective turning, but there's really no right or wrong way: your body language when you turn is entirely yours.

REACTION

Surfing is responding: the wave comes first, and you respond to what the wave demands. For learners, the difficulty is that these demands will rarely be the same from one wave to the next. Increasing your repertoire enables you to accommodate the irregularities, the peculiarities and unexpected sections of the wave – these will all become opportunities for you to practise and show off different manoeuvres. Experienced surfers can instantly spot a misplaced and mistimed manoeuvre: it will look forced and unnatural. The best surf photos look good because the wave seems to have invited the surfer to perform a particular turn or punt.

↖ **A perfectly placed lip bash.**

⬆ **If you don't like the look of a looming section…**

⬆ **If the wave is closing out…**

⬆ **…take evasive action.**

⬆ **…do a shallow bottom turn.**

⬆ **Do a quick check around you…**

⬆ **If you can't lift the board over the lip…**

⬆ **…and straighten out.**

⬆ **…try to punch through it.**

THE 'STRAIGHTEN-OUT'

If you see an unmakeable section looming then you must take steps to avoid it before it swipes you and your board sideways. Straightening out is easy: you need to gently turn the board so it's heading to the beach (a gentle backhand turn if you're riding frontside, a forehand turn if you're angling on your backhand).

THE 'OUT OVER THE TOP'

The problem with straightening out is that you've escaped a bashing but you haven't escaped the white water: you're being forced back to the beach. So instead of straightening out, you can turn into the wave and go over the top. This is easy to do so long as you don't leave it too late to avoid the lip. If surfing forehand just continue the lean, do a gentle forehand turn then out. Vice versa if you're going backside. This way you're still out the back, ready to try your luck on another wave.

THE BACK FOOT

In all turns, the back foot is always the power foot; but applying too much weight here will sink the tail. This results in lifting the nose and shortening the effective length of the board: you may find it easier to pivot, but, as less hull length means less speed, you'll turn at the expense of speed. Remember: turn with the rail, not the tail. The more rail you have biting the water, the more speed you generate. On the best modern boards the improved forward curves and entry rocker mean that the front foot can do much of the work of redirecting.

THE BOTTOM TURN

Angling your take-off gets you into a peeling wave and racing away down the line, and on a fast-breaking wave this is sometimes all you can do to get away from the curl. But it's a shame not to maximise the potential of the drop and head straight down to the trough of the wave, compress into a crouch to coil up energy, then extend and lean into a proper bottom turn. It's the foundation of good surfing.

With a good bottom turn you can begin to surf *vertically*. The bottom turn is fundamental for a couple of reasons: it enables you to load up the vertical energy of the drop before releasing and projecting it into lateral motion; and it's your first opportunity to make a statement on the wave, to signal your ownership of it, to *style*.

A solid bottom turn requires commitment: the later the drop then the more speed you'll have to play with. But remember that the ability to commit to a steep drop can only come as a result of you having worked hard on your paddling power and the quick pop-up.

Delay the actual turn until *just before* you lose speed on the flat – easy to say, but this is something that can only come with experience. Begin the turn by leaning your weight to the two o'clock position (on your forehand) and lifting your eyes from the nose of the board. With your forward (outside) hand *look and point* to where you intend to go.

Lean and plant your inside hand in front of you on the water to act as a virtual pivot. Load up the weight in the inside rail, keeping your weight in and forwards: you should feel your toes pressing into the deck of the board. Lean forward and over the inside rail, but keep a good part of your weight on the back foot.

At the point of maximum compression, explode out of the turn by un-weighting and throwing yourself up at the oncoming face of the wave. Once you've redirected you need to re-centre your weight over the board and make a decision as to where you want to be next.

The bottom turn has subtle variants. If you need distance you can gain it by doing a couple of pumps to gain speed before you crank the turn. If you need to stay near the pocket, you fade the bottom turn so that you actually run a little back towards the curl before you turn to race on to the face.

THE FOREHAND BOTTOM TURN

⬆ **Begine the turn before you lose speed.**

⬆ **Crouch to gather energy.**

⬆ **Weight through the toes on to the inside rail.**

⬆ **Inside hand down to act as a pivot.**

⬆ **Look where you want to go.**

⬆ **Drive through the turn with a nice straight back.**

⬆ **Un-weight and bring the board on to the flat.**

KEY POINTS

- Turn before you lose speed on the flat.
- Crouch to compress energy.
- Look and lean.
- Outside hand forwards to project, inside hand forwards and down to pivot.
- Inside rail evenly and fully weighted.
- Un-weight and re-centre at the end of the turn.

THE BACKHAND BOTTOM TURN

⬆ **Look over your inside shoulder.**

⬆ **Lower your butt to the water.**

⬆ **Get the inside hand down to pivot.**

⬆ **Rotate the shoulders...**

⬆ **...to bring the outside arm around.**

⬆ **Pick up the inside hand.**

⬆ **Get the board off the inside rail and planing.**

KEY POINTS

☐ **Turn your head early to look.**
☐ **Crouch, and lower your butt.**
☐ **Rotate the shoulders. Pivot on inside hand.**
☐ **Bring the rear arm around and forwards.**
☐ **Turn the feet slightly and apply pressure through the heels.**
☐ **Weight on the rail, not the tail.**

The bottom turn comes more naturally, however, if you're *facing* the wave. Turning is leaning, and it's easy to lean in the direction you're facing, where your moveable counterbalancing weights (your arms) are in front of you.

So what about when you want to execute a nice bottom turn on your backhand? This is tricky – the body mechanics are different – but it's worth learning because it's a mark of real competence.

Backhand surfing comes less naturally for several reasons:

- Because you're always looking over your shoulder at the wave, vision is restricted.
- The rear arm tends to trail, and this affects weight distribution.
- Pressure is applied to the board through the heels instead of the toes.

Firstly, as the term 'backhand' implies, one of your arms isn't where it should be: it's behind you, away from the direction of travel. Getting that arm around to the front is the key. The rear arm holds the weight over the tail instead of the inside rail – if that arm trails behind then you'll never have the speed to drive *into* a backhand turn and *through* the turn with any momentum. You get it forward by twisting your body and rotating the shoulders.

Start with the eyes – you'll go where you're looking. You'll never have quite the range of vision that you have when facing the wave on your forehand, but it's nevertheless too easy to lapse and look shoreward. Make a special effort to turn your head and fix your eyes high on the face of the wave.

Turning the head to *look* begins to bring your shoulders around; drop your inside shoulder a little to help you look over it. Throwing the back arm around and forwards completes the transfer of weight: now your inside arm moves the weight on to your inside rail to turn, and the outside arm shifts momentum forwards to maintain your drive.

In the backhand bottom turn, if you lean too much you'll fall over – your knees simply don't bend the right way. You get the weight over the inside rail by crouching lower to get your butt closer to the water, and by rotating more. Thinking about getting your inside hand on the water to pivot will help you to get lower and rotate your shoulders. Keep your weight evenly on both heels.

The only weight you need on the tail is your back foot – that's plenty, but it needs to be applied with the heel. This is the tricky bit: in rotating your shoulders around your weight twists away from your back foot, but you still need to keep some power down here through

REARWARD ARM

Bringing your rearward arm around is the sure way to swing your momentum through any manoeuvre. It pays to exaggerate the effects by imagining your rear hand holding on to a two-kilo dumbbell – if you leave that weight behind you the tail will sink and you'll stall; hold it out forwards and over the inside rail and you can pivot around it; keep it in front and you're going to pick up speed; swing it around following your eyes and you'll shift your weight smoothly from one rail to another.

the heel. It helps if you twist your feet slightly so that that they're less perpendicular to the stringer and more oriented towards the nose, just by a few degrees – the 'open stance'. Then push with the back leg. Unweight to get high – swing that outside arm around and up.

Backside surfing seems more difficult but does have advantages – not least that it makes a cutback easier because you'll be cutting back onto your frontside – but that's for later.

THE TOP TURN AND THE SNAP

Once you've learnt how to bottom turn on your forehand and your backhand you're basically home and dry. The top turn uses the same body mechanics – the weight forwards and on the inside rail, the loading and unloading of pressure, the use of the moving weights that are your hands and arms. But now the body mechanics are transferred to the top of the wave, the lip, instead of the bottom, the trough. Hence the common terms 'off the lip' or 'lip bash'.

In the bottom turn you're utilising the speed gained from the drop to carve through the dead spot of the trough. The difference with the top turn is that your speed is diminishing because you're climbing *up* the face of the wave. So on a weak wave don't let yourself run too far out on the flat, because you'll be unable to get back up the lip with any power. Be less vertical, and draw it out a little.

THE FOREHAND TOP TURN

⬆ **Pick a spot to hit.**

⬆ **Get your weight forwards.**

⬆ **Swing the trailing arm through.**

⬆ **Punch the tail of the board into the lip.**

⬆ **Ride through the turn...**

⬆ **...and get your weight re-centred over the board.**

THE BACKHAND TOP TURN

⬆ The trailing arm has to come forwards.

⬆ Look high up to where you want to hit.

⬆ Lift the nose of the board on to the lip.

⬆ Begin your rotation.

⬆ Punch the tail through the turn.

⬆ You are leaning into the turn so should be able to bring the board around fairly simply.

KEY POINTS

- ☐ Load power on to the inside rail.
- ☐ Pick a spot to hit.
- ☐ Un-weight to climb the face.
- ☐ Rotation is key: lead with the arms and the upper body.
- ☐ Re-centre body weight over the board.
- ☐ Use the knees, reapply pressure on the opposite rail to inject speed and momentum out of the turn.

⬆ Re-centre over the board and ride out the manoeuvre.

THE SNAP

⬆ **A gouging variation of the top turn...**

⬆ **...requires more body torque.**

⬆ **Lower your whole torso to act as a pivot.**

⬆ **The trailing arm can come higher because you are looking to bury the opposite rail.**

⬆ **Shove your butt into the lip to stall.**

⬆ **Jam the tail around with your back foot...**

⬆ **...to begin to bring the board back under your body.**

⬆ **Re-centre and absorb the drop with your knees.**

Take into account what you're going to hit. A soft foam ball flopping over in an onshore breeze will demand more power from you to whip the board around than will a clean pitching lip.

Body rotation is the key. You must swing your shoulders around to keep the weight over the rail. As you're transferring your weight from one rail to the other, you cannot forget about your trailing arm just because you can't see it. This is the arm that has to be most active. Trailing is stalling.

Good judgement comes in picking the right spot on the top of the wave to hit. Start the pivot early otherwise you may find yourself drifting over the back. You can decide to pivot around the top of the wall or hit the lip as it spills over. A lip bounce injects a bit of extra rotational force into your turn just at the pivot point where the manoeuvre is most likely to stall out, helping you bring the board around and finishing the turn.

Always finish the manoeuvre by picking an angle of attack out of the turn. Staying low helps cushion the drop, ready to reapply power into the next turn.

On the backhand top turn, rotation is key to climbing the face. The turn is easier because it happens under your body — you're on top of it. Once at the top of the wave your weight is already pulling you back down around: you don't need to rotate so much, just make sure you get your weight re-centred over your board.

You can practise the top turn at the end of every wave without worrying about wasting a ride with a botched manoeuvre. If you want to go fins-out, wait a fraction longer before redirecting and then extend your back leg further. For the occasional session, make a plan to end every close-out with a big gouging top turn re-entry.

RAIL TO RAIL

The top turn is a real milestone in your surfing because now you can shift your weight from one rail to another. A cranking bottom turn is great, but you're only taking the board from flat in the water over on to one rail — only half the story in surfing. Being able to go rail to rail opens the whole wave face to you: up, down, backwards, forwards, the wave becomes a blank page for you to scribble all over, instead of a ruled page where you can only go from left to right.

The trick in rail-to-rail surfing is to keep the power on through the turn. There may be occasions when you do want to stall and stop on the face of the wave — to tuck into a barrel, or to reset your fins after a slide — but generally the weight shift is a continuum. Keep the weight going forwards by always looking for the next manoeuvre.

Don't aim just to complete manoeuvres, aim to complete a ride. One problem with a surfing manual such as this is that by its very nature the manoeuvres are compartmentalised for ease of instruction, an approach that's antithetical to good surfing. Think 'connection' — the 'end' of one move is merely the beginning of another. Thinking ahead is the best way to keeping your body weight and impetus forward. You'll gain speed and flow.

All other things being equal, it's more difficult to take a 23in-wide board from one rail to another than it is an 18in board. If you want to work on your rail-to-rail transition and you're getting frustrated on a wider, learner-style board, then now may be the time to jump on a shortboard and give it a go. It's always a trade-off — a shorter narrower board will lack momentum on a slacker wave, but then it's easier to turn and put near the pocket of the wave where the power is. A wider, longer board will retain its momentum, but by the time you crank it around you might be nowhere near where you ought to be.

CASUAL AND COMMITTED

Can you be casual and committed at the same time? They might seem mutually exclusive qualities, but to surf well is to combine the two.

A relaxed body posture allows for feedback. Your ankles, knees and hips have to be free of tension in order to feel what the wave is doing and to respond with fine adjustments in trim. Some surf coaches recommend getting a big old board and consciously letting your shoulders, hands and fingers relax and hang down. The twitchiness of a shortboard invites tension because you think you have to fight to control it. With a tank of a board you have to go with the flow — the result is smoothness, less upper body tension.

A committed attitude with weight on the front foot gets you in to the wave, up to speed, and out of trouble. It's safer to commit, because hesitating and pulling your weight back on the tail leaves you planted in the lip. Get weight forwards and rely on the curve and rocker of the front rail to get you in and pull you around on track.

CUTBACK AND ROUNDHOUSE

nce you've learned to trim well – climbing and dropping to gain speed – you'll find that you occasionally outrun the wave. You have too much speed for the face of the wave and you've raced ahead of the pocket: now you need to cut back to the power source. This requires timing. Cut back too soon and you'll run out of room; too late and you'll run out of juice.

Cutting back means making your outside edge your inside edge. You shift your weight from rail to rail, going from surfing forehand to momentarily riding backhand. You're using techniques that you've already practised, but instead of deploying them vertically you're projecting in a more horizontal (or lateral) trajectory.

To carve a lateral arc:

- Start high: you need more room on the wave because the arc of a cutback is likely to be greater than that of a vertical bottom or top turn.
- Start fast: turning laterally implies a loss of speed because you have less assistance from gravity.

Going into the cutback, look for a slightly sloping shoulder and track as high on the face as you can without losing speed. Not having enough height means that you'll end up too low on the face at the end of your turn, out of speed in the trough.

Widen your stance slightly by moving your back foot to feel the heel of your tail pad. Un-weight to climb a little, without sacrificing speed. Swing your shoulders to bring your rear arm around to the front, rotate and look over your lowered leading shoulder in the direction you want to head. Don't let your rear hand come too high – keep it at shoulder level otherwise it'll force your weight down instead of around.

Apply the power evenly through your back foot by keeping the knee flexed: this prevents you from jamming in the tail too firmly, which will make you turn smartly but puts the brakes on. Straightening the front leg as you turn whilst the back leg is flexed keeps forward weight poised – like hovering your foot over the pedal ready to accelerate out of a corner in a car.

Drop the outside shoulder a little as you rotate. The outside hand can drop down to touch the face of the wave, giving you a point around which to pivot. This encourages you to keep driving the trailing arm around with the nose of the board until it becomes the leading arm, by which point you'll be facing the way you just came and hopefully no further than halfway down the face of the wave.

Don't relinquish your speed. The best surfers stand out by seeming to actually go faster as they go through the turn. That's asking a lot of you, but with practice it's possible to *find* some speed at all points in the roundhouse – pressure on the rail to crank into the turn, then shift your weight quickly to get the board back on the flat planing surface, then pressure on the opposite rail.

At the end of the cutback, instead of pulling up short you can rebound off the white water. To turn your cutback into a roundhouse you have all the speed you need to hit the foam and bounce back, shifting your weight and going rail-to-rail again to head back down the line.

As for the backhand cutback, for once, the backhand manoeuvre is the easier, because you're turning on your toes with your eyes facing the wave. Don't look down. Don't look at the bottom of the wave, or at the board – keep your head up, looking at where you want to go, which is *always* high on the wave.

FOREHAND ROUNDHOUSE CUTBACK

1

⬆ **Start high and fast.**

2

⬆ **Weight on the inside rail.**

3

⬆ **Rotate the head and shoulders.**

4

⬆ **Pick a target spot.**

5

⬆ **Swing the trailing arm through.**

6

⬆ **Keep the power on through a bent rear leg.**

7

⬆ **Lift the board on to the oncoming lip as for a lip bash.**

8

⬆ **Begin to transfer power from one rail to the other.**

9

⬆ **Hit the white water.**

10

⬆ **Rotate.**

11

⬆ **Punch the tail through the turn.**

12

⬆ **Your weight over the board will help you bring it around.**

13

⬆ **Re-centre and ride out.**

KEY POINTS

- ☐ **Start high and start fast.**
- ☐ **Widen your stance.**
- ☐ **Rear hand swings forwards no higher than the shoulder in rotation.**
- ☐ **Outside arm drops to use hand as a pivot.**
- ☐ **Rear knee stays flexed for an even application of power.**
- ☐ **Turn the head by keeping the eyes high.**

BACKHAND ROUNDHOUSE CUTBACK

⬆ Start high and fast.

⬆ Get your body low and compact.

⬆ Pivot around your hand.

⬆ Don't straighten your back leg – keep the power loaded on through the turn.

⬆ Keep as much of the inside rail in the water as possible – this will help maintain your speed.

⬆ Bring the front arm around and up to point at your target spot.

⬆ Legs still bent and loaded with power – you do not want to stall here.

⬆ Gather more speed as you head back from the foam.

⬆ Start to climb to hit a spot high up.

⬆ Hit the white water and begin your turn back to the face.

⬆ Rotate.

⬆ Re-centre over the board and head back down the line.

FLOATER

A lip bash or top turn is usually executed more or less as vertically as you can – partly for the heck of it, but partly because the free power that the pitching lip's offering you is heading that way, straight down. But what if you don't want to go straight back down the face? What if there's an extended section of lip pitching ahead of you, presenting an obstacle to you getting back to the clean face of the wave? Usually you'll use the speed of the re-entry to execute a long driving bottom turn and try to race around the section, but another option is the 'floater'.

Maintain your speed on the approach to the lip by taking a slightly less vertical line. Lift the nose on to the pitching lip, flatten the board, keep your weight evenly distributed, and float across the upside of the lip. You're weightless for a few moments, so enjoy the sensation. But before all your speed is gone, dip the inside rail to catch an edge, and drop back in.

KEY POINTS

- A fast, less-than-vertical approach.
- Lift the nose on to the lip.
- Quickly flatten the board to maintain speed.
- Arms high to keep weight off the board.
- Dip the inside rail to drop back in before loss of momentum.
- Knees braced for impact on the drop.

FOREHAND FLOATER

1

↑ Hit the lip with a less-than-vertical aspect.

2

↑ Flatten the board on the top of the lip.

3

↑ Centre your weight.

4

↑ When you start to slow...

5

↑ ...pick a landing spot...

6

↑ ...dip the inside rail...

7

↑ ...and get ready for the drop.

8

↑ It's hard on your knees...

9

↑ ...and on the board so expect a few knocks.

BACKHAND FLOATER

1

↑ Again, a less-than-vertical approach.

2

↑ Weight over the centre of the board.

3

↑ Turn out before all your speed is gone.

4

↑ Dip the inside rail...

5

↑ ...and drop back in.

6

↑ Absorb the impact with the knees flexed.

TUBE RIDING

The most photogenic of surfing manoeuvres is perhaps the most intimidating. The tube-ride is the image that most non-surfers associate with surfing, but to get there you'll have to paddle harder and get to your feet quicker than ever before. The barrel is difficult to master for a couple of reasons:

■ Most waves don't barrel. You generally don't get much opportunity to practise; and anyway, as a beginner, most waves you ride shouldn't tube.

■ Tubing waves are scary. The first reaction of most novices is to panic and shut their eyes. Keeping relaxed enough to keep your eyes open is the single most important trick.

There are basically two ways of pulling into a barrel. With each method there are advantages and disadvantages:

■ You can take off very deep on the peak – almost behind it – and duck under the curtain as it comes down ahead over your front shoulder.

■ Or you can get ahead of the peak, anticipate that the wave is going to pitch over a ledgy section, and stall to let the lip catch up over your rear shoulder.

The advantage of taking off deep and racing the tube is that you're already charging at full speed, so the board is more responsive; minor adjustments (and escape) are therefore easier. The potential problem of racing the pitching lip is the natural tendency to go too low and

consequently getting pole-axed by the lip landing on your head.

The problem with stalling is that you're deliberately shedding speed at a very crucial moment, and unless you're deft with your subtle shifts of weight in a critical situation you face the prospect of drifting up the face and getting pitched over the falls. The advantage of stalling is that you're in control: you can see what's coming ahead of you, and if you lose your nerve you have a moment to press the accelerator and get the heck out of there.

At less predictable beach breaks you're unlikely to have the luxury of choice in *how* you get tubed; you'll just have to be sharp enough to take what comes. Either way, you have to give yourself the chance – stall harder than you think you need to, and take off deeper than you think you should do.

Once you've managed to put yourself in the frame to get tubed you need to cultivate a mindset of relaxed determination:

Relaxed, because you need to stay aware of what's happening around you: the barrel isn't a fixed entity, it may well demand fine adjustments of trim to successfully negotiate. And you need to enjoy the experience whilst you're in there. Look around, check the view, listen to the roar, see if time really does expand in the tube!

Determined, because you can ride deeper than you imagined and still come out: don't give up – plant your feet firmly on the board and keep looking, looking for the exit.

Getting tubed frontside might seem easier at first. You're facing the wave and can see the lip pitching over; it's also easier to keep your

FOREHAND TUBE

↑ **Take off nice and deep.**

↑ **Instead of a full bottom turn, jag your inside arm...**

↑ **...this will help get you into the wave high on the face...**

↑ **...and under the lip.**

↑ **Weight now on the front foot to gain speed.**

↑ **Duck under the curtain...**

↑ **...enjoy the view...**

↑ **...and then think about getting out of there!**

leading shoulder tucked in and driving you forwards. Subtle responsive shifts of weight and trim are applied through the flexible toes and not the heels – another advantage.

When looking for barrel on your backhand the lip pitches from the blind spot behind, which can make you uneasy. Body rotation is again key, so twist everything you can, including, of course, your head (to give you a better view of the lip) and your feet (to take some of the weight off your heels). Grabbing the outside rail is a way of ensuring that you bring the rear arm around towards the front for drive as well as aiding control of trim. But remember to open the knees to complete the rotation of the body. Most surfers will adopt a 'pig-dog' stance riding backhand in the barrel – lowering your rear knee almost to the board and grabbing the outside rail with your trailing arm gets you nicely tucked in and your shoulders squared. Pig-dogging does limit your fine tuning in the barrel, however, so the most advanced surfers will ride hands-free in a crouch.

One great advantage of backhand tube riding is the amount of fine control available. Going frontside you can plunge your inside arm in the wave to help stall in the barrel; going backhand you have your inside arm but also your whole butt to jam in the face of the wave if need be. Top surfers will virtually lie on the face when riding deep. Using this method you can ride as deep as your nerves will allow.

The crucial thing is to get *in* there; getting *out* is nice if it happens, but not a disaster if it doesn't. Bear in mind that deep in the tube is often the safest place to be. A wipeout in the eye, with the forces revolving around *you* at the centre, is usually nowhere near as bad as the alternatives, which include getting pitched full-length over the falls on to the shallow flats, or getting a ton of lip whomping straight on to your head. Just remember to stay on the board as long as you can, grab a deep breath and bail out full-length and flattish. Fall behind and away from your board if you possibly can. Only penetrate the surface if you know you can bust through the thick back of the wave. *Don't* penetrate if you're falling towards the flats where water is draining off the reef.

FUNCTIONALITY

The manoeuvres above are all fully functional – you can't ride a wave effectively without competence in this basic repertoire. Depending upon what the wave demands, you'll always *need* to pull out one or more of these fundamental manoeuvres or face losing the wave. It'll go on without you, and you'll have wasted a rare opportunity. Surfers who you beat to catch that wave will be watching you – if you stuff it up, they'll at the least groan good-naturedly, or at the worst not let you catch another wave ever again.

BACKHAND TUBE

1. ↑ Take off deep.

2. ↑ Grab the outside rail to bring the board around sharpish.

3. ↑ Plant your inside hand on the face to help control your speed.

4. ↑ You are now 'pig-dogging' to get your profile low, rear knee almost on the deck of the board.

5. ↑ The lip is pitching behind from your blind spot so make sure you rotate to fit in under the lip.

6. ↑ Now you've got to get the board flat, get some speed and chase the exit.

NEW SCHOOL / ADVANCED

The following manoeuvres belong to what's sometimes called the 'new school'. Initially they created some controversy, particularly in the realm of professional surfing. Here there was at first no real consensus on how they should be scored because they didn't neatly fit the old judging criteria.

Their controversial nature rested partly in the fact that they aren't functional manoeuvres as such but are unashamed products of the modern media age. But often the people who don't like them are simply those too old to try them.

The manoeuvres are difficult but aren't totally out of this world – they're all evidently derived from basic moves. The top turn led to the fin waft, the floater led to the aerial, and so on into the future of surfing. Once you have the fundamentals down pat, if you don't want to get left behind, have a go.

LAYBACK

The layback has significance because it's 'old school new school' – the first 'slash and tear' manoeuvre that went right against the grain of graceful and fluid '70s surfing. Going frontside, twist your body the wrong way (rotating *away* from the turn), jam your inside arm into the face of the wave, and fall back on to the face. Shove the tail of the board around underneath your back foot and let the wave pop you back up on the board as it comes around. A generation after it was invented, it's still a great 'shock move'.

LAYBACK

⬆ **Get high on the face, as you need room to bring the board back underneath you.**

⬆ **Shove the rail into the face of the wave...**

⬆ **...while falling *away* from the turn.**

⬆ **Try to land flat on the water...**

⬆ **...as you don't want to penetrate.**

⬆ **Flatten the board...**

⬆ **...so the face of the wave can support both your board and you.**

⬆ **Drag the board back to you with your knees...**

⬆ **...as the lip pushes you on to it.**

⬆ **Get yourself back over the centre of the board...**

⬆ **...and look for the next section.**

FIN WAFT

⬆ **Go up for a top turn...**

⬆ **...but delay the turn.**

⬆ **Aim for a spot high enough and your fins will pop free.**

⬆ **Be ready for the tail to slide around...**

⬆ **...and keep your weight on the front foot.**

⬆ **Fully extend the back leg...**

⬆ **...but keep your weight low for balance.**

⬆ **Shift your weight back a little to reconnect your fins.**

⬆ **Once you feel the fins bite...**

⬆ **...you can reset the rail...**

⬆ **...and set yourself up for the next manoeuvre.**

FIN WAFT

If you're pushing the limits of your top turn it won't be long before you slightly misjudge your weight distribution, pop out the fins and do an accidental tail slide. With the fins out you'll lose drive, but there'll be occasions when this is precisely what you want to achieve – a radical change of direction combined with a stall in the face of the wave.

The approach needs to be vertical and the turn slightly delayed – as if you're aiming to turn above the actual top of the wave. Rotate hard and punch your back foot through and away, then release it to get the fins out. Then let the wave and your weight bring the board back to you.

The way to control a tail slide is to get your weight back up over your fins when you want to regain drive. If you delay doing this you can turn the waft into a wafted tail slide: crouch and keep your centre of gravity low over the front of the board until you ride down into the flat, then jam the tail down and ride out of the turn.

WAFTED TAIL SLIDE

1

⬆ Go up for a top turn...

2

⬆ ...but delay the turn.

3

⬆ Aim for a spot high enough and your fins will pop free.

4

⬆ Be ready for the tail to slide around...

5

⬆ ...and keep your weight on the front foot.

6

⬆ Fully extend the back leg...

7

⬆ ...keep your weight low for balance...

8

⬆ ...but you keep your weight over the front of the board...

9

⬆ You are now riding backwards...

10

⬆ ...but you must keep your weight low and centred to prevent the rails from setting.

11

⬆ A little weight back on the tail...

12

⬆ ...will force the fins to bite...

13

⬆ ...and around you come.

14

360 SPIN

⬆ **Commit yourself to a big top turn...**

⬆ **...as if you were turning a foot or so *above* the wave.**

⬆ **You have to get the fins free early in the turn.**

⬆ **Extend the back leg and get your weight over the front of the board.**

⬆ **Try not to squat too low so that you can rotate easier.**

⬆ **Keep your weight over the front and get the tail through 180 degrees.**

⬆ **If you can keep the rotation going and keep the fins free...**

⬆ **...then when the fins bite, the nose will be facing forwards.**

⬆ **You can then reset the rail.**

360

Releasing the fins and throwing a slide brings the board around 180° – you're now effectively surfing backwards. Now, instead of getting the fins to bite back in, keep your weight centred and forward and, leading with the shoulders, continue the rotation of your body. The nose of the board will slide around further. When the fins do bite – by shifting your weight a little to the tail – the stalled tail will force the nose right around to a full 360.

The key is weight distribution and rotation. Rotation brings the board around; weight distribution stops the rail from setting and throwing you off sideways. Weight has to be kept over the centre of the board to allow the rails to freely slide around. Small fins and a board with less catchy rails will help.

CHOOSE YOUR SPOT

You've just competed a 360 spin that looked impressive and was fun to do, but you'll have lost speed. Choose carefully where on the wave you want to do a slide 360 – you don't want to be dead in the water just as a monster tubing section is about to bear down on you. Surfers will usually execute the 360 on a mellow section where there's little at stake, or even on a flattish take-off where they can quickly regain speed on the drop.

AIRS

The aerial is perhaps the ultimate new-school manoeuvre. The air began life as a floater, but flying is quicker than floating. As such, it's a functional manoeuvre, and yet it caused much controversy when introduced in the 1980s, with ASP judges initially frowning on the manoeuvre and refusing to reward it with good scores. Aerial manoeuvres implied a radical departure in the way a wave was visualised. The surfer looking to do an aerial was looking at the wave merely as a launching ramp to riding the air; in some minds this was tantamount to sacrilege.

At first something of a 'special' high-risk move reserved only for end sections or close-outs, the aerial repertoire has now become part of the down-the-line process, just as much as a cutback or off-the-top, and judges have moved to accommodate it accordingly. Not that too many aerial specialists are bothered – taking a lead from other extreme sports such as motocross and skateboarding, they now have their own showcase with big prize money available in aerial contests online.

The aerial revolution is a re-conceptualisation of the sport – most of the progression in surfing is now taking place *above* the wave. But putting aside the philosophy of aerials, how do you set about doing one of the things?

You need speed and a launch ramp. Initially, try to do a little 'chop-hop': look for a little piece of chop or a tiny section and try to boost off it. Staying high on the face and pumping the board will generate all the speed you need, and now when you see a nice section folding in front of you lift the board up and over it as you would for a floater – not too steep an angle of attack, un-weighting nice and evenly – but keep going, keep the weight off the tail as you leave the water.

Here's where the aerial reveals its Californian skating origins, because you basically need to 'ollie' up into the air. Get the board to level out in

AERIAL TIPS

BOOST AND TRY SOMETHING – if you make it, you make it. Be relaxed about the possibility. But best not try it just yet on shallow reefs.

FRONTSIDE IS EASIER – it's easier to pop, and staying over your board comes more naturally on your forehand.

BACKSIDE IS MORE DIFFICULT – it's harder to find the speed to boost. Staying over the board is tricky, so grabbing is pretty much essential. There's a real chance of the board inverting too much.

THE HIGHER YOU GO, THE HARDER YOU FALL – low airs are easier to stick, so, rather than height, start by looking for lateral distance in your airs, where the angle between your board and the wave is less.

ROTATION – your first rotating air should be the 'ally oop', on your forehand rotating out to sea, as it were. A grab isn't necessary, as more rotating torque can be provided by a taller stance, and if you land sideways the turning forces on the fins will leave you facing the beach.

ROTATION IS KEY

1 When you bust an air...

2 ↑ ...it is natural to want to squat low over your board.

3 ↑↓ But if you can stand up a little, you will find it easier to get good rotation.

FRONTSIDE AIR

⬆ **You need speed...**

⬆ **...and commitment...**

⬆ **...so get your arms high and the rest will follow.**

⬆ **Let the board come up to you by flexing the knees.**

⬆ **Widen your stance...**

⬆ **...and get in some rotation.**

⬆ **Look for a landing...**

⬆ **...on the white water rather than out on the flats.**

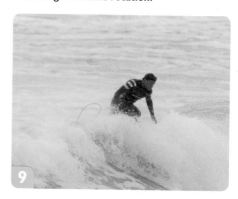

⬆ **Brace yourself for the impact.**

the air by effectively lifting the tail. The way to do that is to get a little pressure over the front – slide your front foot forwards a little just as you launch. This levers the tail into the air, and the wider stance will give you more chance of landing the aerial.

Your weight has to be central and low over the board, so encourage the board to come higher to you by pulling your knees to your chest. Grab a rail if you need more control, it doesn't matter where; someone will have invented a name for it. Now look for a landing. An aerial without a landing is just an impressive wipeout, and it's got an old-school name: its called 'falling off'.

AIR REVERSE

The back foot allows the tail to come up and pushes the tail around whilst the front foot presses the nose down. Landing tail first, the nose has to be lower. Keep the rotation going by looking over your shoulder

and, if you've managed to get the tail facing the beach, once the fins bite the nose should spin around to complete the reverse.

In the air, and while you're landing, all sorts of variations can be introduced. There's no end to the invention of new aerial manoeuvres and the terminology can be confusing. Distinctions are based on the amount of rotation, the direction of rotation, whether or not the rider holds the board, and *where* the rider holds the board:

Double grab air – both hands hold the rails.
Indy grab air – rear hand on the toe-side rail.
Mute grab air – front hand on the toe-side rail.
Stalefish grab air – rear hand on the heel-side rail.
Varial – an aerial with an invert.
Superman – two hands on the board, two feet off.
Rodeo clown – aerial with a spinning twist.

BACKSIDE AIR

⬆ Backhand it is harder to find the speed to boost...

⬆ ...so make the most of any little launch ramp that comes your way.

⬆ Arms nice and high initially...

⬆ ...but then you might want to grab a rail to stop the board from getting away from you.

⬆ Bring the board up higher by flexing the knees.

⬆ Start to flatten the board out for landing.

⬆ Land on the white water...

⬆ ...and brace for impact.

FRONTSIDE AIR REVERSE

⬆ You need commitment...

⬆ ...speed...

⬆ ...and height.

⬆⬇ Rotation has to be such that when you land the tail, you have already completed a 180 with the board nice and flat, your weight over the nose.

⬆ Now you can look to set the fins...

⬆ ...complete the turn and ride out.

BACKSIDE AIR REVERSE

⬆ Speed is essential...

⬆ ...to get the whole board airborne.

⬆ Get the rotation...

⬆ ...and get your weight forwards.

⬆ Get low on the landing...

⬆ ...ready to absorb impact and control the final part of the reverse.

⬆ Set the rail and bring the nose around.

THE BIG STUFF

It doesn't require mathematical measurement; any wave you think is big is big, simple as that. If you're a small grommet it doesn't take much for you to get bashed about like a rag doll, but you do need to keep pushing to progress. Every surfer should have a go at surfing waves bigger than they'd really like to. Anyone wanting to surf outside his or her comfort zone can start by buddying up with a mate – not someone who'll just get you into trouble through peer pressure, but someone with a bit of experience who can coax you, look after you, and get you out of trouble if need be.

Don't let the excitement go to your head and rush into ugly situations. Watch and pay close attention to the size and frequency of the sets, the position and strength of the rips, the length of the sections, the best place to paddle out. Have a plan, and set an achievable goal – maybe just to get out the back and sit there, or just to catch a single wave on the shoulder.

If you want to ride big waves frequently then you need to get serious, committed and focused – done casually it's way more dangerous. Get fit: particularly, work out with regular hypoxic sessions to improve your capacity to go without oxygen in the case of a heavy hold-down.

Get a bigger board so you can get into waves earlier and project out of your turns; ideally, though, you should still be able to duck-dive it. Having the right fitness and the right equipment will generate confidence. Psychology is a major factor; you have to get some sort of enjoyment out of it.

Even if you aren't cut out to be a full-time big-wave charger, being comfortable in bigger surf is a useful skill to have. When a massive swell does turn up at your spot, you don't want to be scuttling around the coast with everybody else to find a sheltered cove – get out and catch some bombs with just one or two others in the water.

'BE LIKE WATER MAKING ITS WAY THROUGH CRACKS. DO NOT BE ASSERTIVE, BUT ADJUST TO THE OBJECT, AND YOU SHALL FIND A WAY AROUND OR THROUGH IT... BE WATER, MY FRIEND.'
Bruce Lee

CHAPTER 6

FITNESS

If you're like most people, you surf intermittently: going for weeks without being able to get to the beach, or being at a beach for long spells with no rideable surf. When the surf does arrive, it's important to be primed and able to maximise the time you have in the water; and vital to avoid the niggling injuries that keep you out of it.

GETTING FIT

When undertaking any programme of serious physical training, first consult your doctor. Even if you've previously trained hard, after a lay-off don't assume you can just pick up where you left off. As a general guideline, if you feel a sharp pain, quit.

WHAT ARE THE DEMANDS OF AN AVERAGE SURF SESSION?

Paddling – You need dogged staying power to cope with white water and strong rips; and sprinting ability to out-manoeuvre a competitive pack and get in the right position for take-off.
Taking-off – You need strength and poise to repeatedly pop-up to your feet in one swift and controlled movement.
Riding – This requires the rhythmic application of power combined with quick reactions to respond to the wave.
Wipeouts – You need to be mentally assured, and have the physical capacity to hold your breath in stressful circumstances.

WHAT ARE THE COMPONENTS OF AN ALL-ROUND FITNESS PROGRAMME?

Flexibility – Your normal range of motion at a joint. Flexibility is vital in order to perform movements without injury, and to rehabilitate after injury.

Power – If strength is the sum force your muscles can produce, then power describes how rapidly that force can be applied: it's the *speed* of a muscle action combined with overall force applied.
Endurance – *Aerobic* endurance is the capacity to prolong physical activity at an efficient respiratory level, *ie* breathing normally. *Anaerobic* endurance is the ability to make repeated explosive lung-bursting efforts, to tolerate the lactate waste products occurring as a result of muscular respiration in the absence of oxygen.

For surfers, a training programme can only be considered sport-specific when the components of fitness are systematically matched to the demands of a surf session.

Different types of training tend to be associated with different elements of all-round fitness, the obvious examples being weight training for strength, yoga for flexibility, and swimming for aerobic endurance. But each can be adapted. Experiment with them all and go with the ones you like. It doesn't do to be too prescriptive, because you surf for fun, so why make training a chore? With a bit of thought, if you like you can adapt yoga to emphasise strength, you can swim to lengthen your muscles, and do light weights in assisted stretches. Do what's fun, but try to cover all the bases.

⬇ **With a paddleboard, flat spells become an opportunity to increse fitness.**

PADDLING

Paddling is your primary skill, because if you can't paddle you can't surf. A weak paddler will always struggle to get out the back, and once there will only be catching the leftovers that all the better paddlers don't want. Being a fast, efficient paddler maximises your wave count, and catching lots of waves is how you improve your surfing.

During a good surf session you might paddle a couple of miles catching waves and heading out the back for more. It sounds exhausting but is easy to do because the carrot is always dangling in front of you. But how can you keep your motivation to practise paddling during flat spells?

Get hold of an old longboard, a windsurf board or, even better, a racing mal and go and see what's around the corner. Get dropped off by a friend at a beach a few miles away and paddle home (after having checked the currents and weather, and notifying the coastguard, of course). A longer board will have much better planing qualities and will be an absolute joy to paddle compared with your shortboard – it's excellent for aerobic endurance.

Most of your surf paddling is in recovery mode, slogging back out after a ride. The all-out effort to catch a wave, however, makes demands on your anaerobic system. You need to be able to sprint, whether to beat the pack to the wave of the day, to get over the ledge on a juicy one, or to escape a pounding from a rogue set.

For anaerobic endurance, with any paddling craft you can make up a set of repeated 50 sprint strokes/50 recovery strokes, for example. You could set your digital watch to do 30-second interval sprints with 30 seconds of rest in between; or you could mix it up simply by sprinting between conveniently spaced fishing buoys.

If you live in the higher latitudes and are working full-time, then short of surfing in the dark your winter paddling practice will be restricted to weekends, at best. This is where dry-land training aids can come in useful. All use the principle of resistance with varying degrees of complexity. The simplest are elasticated cords affixed to a wall at waist level: you face the wall, bend at the waist and, imagining you're somewhere else, paddle. Apart from the tedium, the major disadvantage with these aids is the potential for injury. Make sure anything loaded with force is well affixed. Reduce the risk of back injury by keeping your spine in the neutral position – something that a surfboard takes care of naturally in the water.

⬅ **The narrow lines of a paddleboard help you lengthen your stroke.**

⬆⬇ **Knee paddling – an excellent means of increasing core strength and equalising shoulders, as well as paddling fitness.**

STROKE-CORD EXERCISES

Elasticated stroke cords are cheap, portable and infinitely adjustable: you can increase or decrease the resistance simply by stepping backwards or forwards. Before any session, warm up the shoulders with a few minutes of arm swings. Secure the cords firmly. Place your feet shoulder-width apart, flex the knees, and bend forwards, maintaining a flat back. Engage the core muscles by tightening your tummy. Control the cord – exercises should be completed not by bouncing and jerking, but with the cord under steady tension.

Suggested session:

Catch (or pull) – Take a step back and pull the cords from an arms-extended position back to your thighs; 3 × 25 seconds, rest interval 15 seconds.

Push – Take a step forwards and push the cord handles rearwards from your hips, elbows locked by your side, to fully extended behind; 3 × 15 seconds, rest interval 15 seconds.

Full stroke – Take a central position and combine the two previous arm movements; 3 × 20 seconds, rest interval 15 seconds.

Rest and repeat the sequence three or four times. To progress, either simply shorten the interval times or increase the repetitions.

THE SHOULDER

The shoulder is one of surfing's vulnerable joints. Increasing training loads means that you must take extra care of it. 'Prehab' exercises to strengthen the important rotator cuff muscles and scapular stabilisers will help prevent shoulder injury:

■ Standing with a weight in each hand and arms by your side, shrug your shoulders forwards, up, around and back in a controlled manner. Then reverse the movement. 20–30 repetitions.

■ Stand with elbows tucked into your sides, forearms horizontal to the floor, a stretch cord between your hands. Slowly rotate your hands out to the sides and return. 20–30 repetitions.

■ Sitting in a chair with armrests, brace your elbows and push your hips up off the seat of the chair, feet off the floor. Aim for 10 repetitions.

■ Leaning into a counter-height surface, arms on the counter at shoulder-width, do a short push-up *without* bending your elbows. Let your shoulder blades pinch together as you lower your chest just a few inches; then round your back as your shoulder blades pull you back up. 20–30 repetitions.

SWIMMING

Since the advent of the leash, too many surfers can get away with being poor swimmers. Foremost, this is a safety issue — who's to say a leash will never break? But these surfers are also missing out on the well-known benefits of swimming: it improves strength and endurance, encourages flexibility, and develops cardiovascular capacity. It's also the only readily available sporting activity that mimics paddling — but you can do it indoors in the depths of winter, and accurately measure your progress.

The resistance of water means that by swimming just one mile you gain the aerobic benefits associated with running four. The thermal conductivity of water means that you can train at high intensities before there's any real threat of dehydration or heat exhaustion. Water is kind to your muscles and — paying appropriate attention to technique — kind to your joints.

Front crawl may be a near relative to paddling but there are important distinctions. For swimmers, technique is every bit as important as fitness because they gain velocity both by increasing propulsive force and reducing drag force. On an adequately sized surfboard your drag force is always going to be minimal, so a surfer's swim programme is best aimed at developing a powerful and efficient way of grabbing water and pushing it towards the feet — maximising propulsive force. Consequently, it'll be worth going to a few coached sessions to ensure you don't develop bad habits that overload the shoulders.

One of the most important aspects of pool training is learning how to *feel* the water. As if you're gripping the rungs of a submerged ladder, hold on to the water with your hands as you slide your body past. If your hands are moving back faster than your body is moving forwards, you're slipping, not gripping.

→ **Learning to feel the water is one great benefit of pool training.**

LUNG TRAINING

Not everyone is inclined to train their lungs by diving for boulders and running along the seabed with them, but we can all use the pool to improve aerobic capacity. Incorporate these hypoxic exercises into a swim session: on a 200m (220yd) swim, once each length dive down and touch the bottom, then back up and continue. Or sprint the last 10m of each length, tumble-turn out and cruise. This type of hypoxic exercise simulates the demands of a paddle-out and improves cardiovascular efficiency.

⬆ Roll the body, to increase your effective hull length.

⬆ Not too much splash on arm entry.

⬆ Keep the stroke long and strong.

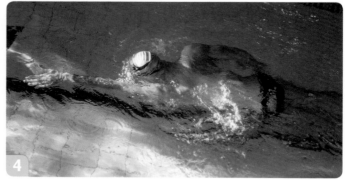

⬆ Your front hand feels for a grip on the water...

⬆ ...as your pulling arm continues to push past your hip, and you roll the body to let the hand release.

⬆ High elbow in the recovery arm, and only now does the forward hand begin its stroke.

⬆ At each stroke there should be a second when both your hands are forwards of your shoulders, in the front quadrant of the stroke.

⬆ Roll onto the opposite side to lengthen the stroke.

← Don't drop your shoulder nor your elbow in the catch.

Concentrate on your arm and hand angles when swimming (and keep that focus when back on the board).

Break the freestyle stroke into three phases –

■ **Press** – Keep the elbows and shoulders up when the hand enters the water. The press is the entry where you feel the water to find resistance and start moving your body past it. Don't push water down, you're pressing it to get a good grip instead.

■ **Follow-through** – Don't let the elbows lead at any point in the first two-thirds of the pull. The hand accelerates to full extension of the arm, from shoulder width into the centre-line of your body: a nice powerful S-pull. Keep the hand perpendicular as you sweep in well below the hip joint – you should be pushing water back to your feet, not up into the air. On the board your arm is higher above the water, but if you can see water being thrown into the air at the end of a stroke you're seeing energy wasted. Push water back, not up.

■ **Recovery** – Keep your shoulders loose so your elbow can stay high; a high elbow keeps the body movements neatly inside the flow line. The elbow leads in the recovery always, but never in the pull.

STROKE DRILLS

Stroke drills are essential to perfecting technique and improving power and efficiency. These can be done using a pull buoy or kick board, normally available poolside. The cardiovascular system doesn't know the difference between drills and regular swimming, so if you do drills rapidly you get every heart/lung benefit at the same time as improving your stroke.

■ **'Catch-up':** leave the front hand outstretched until the recovery hand meets it, then begin your arm-stroke. This improves stroke length, glide and hand position.
■ **'Feathering':** trail the fingers of your recovery arm along the surface of the water. This evens your stroke and improves body alignment.
■ **'Chicken-wing':** the thumb of the recovery arm has to touch your armpit before extending forwards. This keeps the elbows high and helps with body rotation.
■ **Doggie-paddle** and **sculling** are good exercises for getting the feel of the hands pulling back, not down, nor up.

If swimming is your best training option between visits to the surf, then do as much as you can to make it interesting. No two surf sessions are the same, but pool sessions do require some element

POOL SESSION

[50 minutes – 2,000m]

■ **400M WARM-UP:** 50m front crawl kick, 50m catch-up, 50m chicken-wing, 50m full-stroke, x 2.
■ **200M:** 50m backstroke, 50m front crawl, x 2. Lengthen and count your strokes: try to achieve as few on your front as on your back.
■ **500M HYPOXIC PYRAMID:** 50m breathing every three strokes, 50m breathing every five strokes, 25m breathing on seven, 50m breathing on five, 50m breathing on three, 25m backstroke, x 2, with one-minute rest interval.
■ **8 X 75M:** cruise for the first 50m breathing every three strokes, sprint the last 25m taking only two breaths. Descending rest intervals: 30 seconds for two, 25 for next two, etc, down to 15 seconds.
■ **300M COOL-DOWN:** 50m backstroke, 50m breast-stroke, 50m front crawl x 2.

↓ A high elbow keeps the shoulder loose and your stroke nicely inside the flow line.

of consistency and repetition to make your progress measurable: make your programmes imaginative as well as rigorous, however. Generally speaking, it's best to put training for middle distance swims at the heart of your pool programme, as it incorporates elements of sprint and distance, speed and endurance.

STRENGTH

Front plank – hold for 30 seconds.

Swimming and paddling do only so much for your muscular-skeletal strength, so specific strength training is a valuable extra weapon in the armoury. This is particularly true for older surfers when you consider that, without training, we lose 10% of our body strength for each decade that goes by.

When training for strength always focus first on the engine before the propellers: the abdominals, spinal rotators and erectors, hip flexors and glutes are all essential core muscles that enable your torso to transmit power cleanly through to your arms and legs. These are the stabilising muscles that help you balance and are foundational for many surfing movements.

In a few simple exercises, the core muscles can be trained anywhere, any time, cost-free.

Plyometric exercises (what used to be known simply as 'jumping and bouncing') are an excellent way of using just your body weight to develop explosive power and speed of movement. Making

⬆ **Side plank** – hold for 30 seconds each side.

⬆ **Leg raise** – raise slowly and hold for 20 seconds; lower even slower.

⬆➡ **Slow crunch** – 30 repetitions. Add the twist if you like.

⬇ **Standing jump** (× 10).   ⬆➔ **Squat thrust** (× 4) into pop-up (× 1).

your maximum explosive effort for each repetition, plyometrics should be intense, so it's essential to warm up properly and to rest alternate days. Always try to work out on a forgiving surface – grass or sand is ideal.

Repeat sequences then rest for one minute. Aim to achieve three or four sets.

STABILITY BALL

If you feel inclined to buy strength-training equipment, then don't be ashamed to make your first gym purchase a giant pink blow-up rubber ball, known also as a fit ball, stability ball or Swiss ball. Cheap and cheerful, they can nevertheless cause injury if you don't pay special attention to technique. Get a good quality ball, the right size for your height and weight.

⬆ **Walk out to press-up and twist** (× 8).

← **Leg raise.** Slowly raise and hold for five seconds (x 5).

← **Tricep extension** (x 8).

← **Scissor plank** (x 12 each side).

← **Squat** (x 12).

Back extension. Raise and hold for 10 seconds × 2.

The added dimension of instability that the Swiss ball brings to exercises means that you automatically recruit bands of muscles radiating out from your core to stabilise your extremities – exactly what you need for poised and dynamic surfing. The control and precision of Swiss ball exercises enhance muscle balance, develop posture awareness and help stabilise the back.

There are aspects of surfing that require explosive effort, bursts of energy that, if prolonged, produce lactic acid. Strength training can develop your fast twitch fibres and condition your muscles to increase tolerance to lactic acid build-up. Training can be intensified by using machines or free weights – and here it's *always* advisable to seek expert coaching, though the principles of strength training with weights are fairly simple:

Resistance (overload) – Choose the load that stresses your muscles whilst permitting proper form, training over the muscles' full range of motion. Muscle adaptation is forced by exceeding your body's normal threshold.

Repetitions (progression) – Lower repetitions with a higher weight build power; lower weight with more reps promotes muscular endurance. Adaptation means constant reassessment and adjustment of your programme.

WEIGHT TRAINING FOR STRENGTH

To train for strength without large gains in weight or bulk use the simple formula of 'one set of 8–12 max'. Find a weight you can lift 8 times and train until you can lift it 12 times. Then add weight and repeat the process. Timing and control is important with weights – raise in two seconds, lower in four.

Recovery (frequency) – Within a session, more rest allows for more intensity. Give serious thought to how often and how much to train. Ideally, alternate muscle-group exercises to allow a 48-hour recovery for stressed fibres.

Press (× 8).

FLEXIBILITY

When muscles are tight, motion is restricted and action requires more effort. Proper relaxation during effort gives better resilience against fatigue and injury. A programme of stretching is the best way of enabling muscles to work repeatedly and correctly through their whole range of motion with least risk of injury. Flexibility will also confer poise and grace to your movements when surfing.

TYPES OF STRETCH

Static – Attain a pose and hold.
Ballistic – Use the momentum of body weight to go beyond normal range.
Passive – Hold a limb in position using another part of the body.
Assisted – Use a partner to achieve and hold a position.

Stretching is less beneficial when you're cold, so pre-surf mobility exercises do need to have some element of dynamism in them; but this requires more thought than just bouncing around on one leg chatting to your mates as you struggle to zip up your wetsuit. As a general principle, start slowly, gradually adding more dynamism. Simple dynamic or ballistic stretches are neck rotations, torso twists, leg swings, ankle rotations and single and double arm swings.

YOGA

Flexibility trainers are often advocates of exercises and techniques derived from yoga. The integrated *asanas* (postures) of Hatha Yoga are beneficial for many sports but are particularly suited to surfing.

Yoga is based on natural movements of the body and is suitable for anyone at any age in any condition, but it's recommended that you initially consult a qualified teacher to receive instruction in the

⬆ **Neck rotation.**

⬆ **Shoulder stretch – 1.**

⬆ **Shoulder stretch – 2.**

⬆ **Tricep stretch.**

⬆ **Quad stretch.**

⬆ **Hamstring stretch.**

correct manner of adopting the poses. Once you have a good grasp of technique you can practise alone wherever and whenever you like.

Morning practice energises you and sets you up for the day; evening practice unwinds you and finds you more naturally flexible. Don't feel you have to stick to one or the other, but always try to practise on an empty stomach with empty bladder and bowels. Cold draughty conditions are best avoided, but neither should you practise in the hot sun; find somewhere warm and calm if possible.

Movements should be slow, fluid, harmonious and controlled. Coordinated with breathing, concentration and body awareness, the *asanas* can benefit the surfer on several levels.

Not only are *asanas* effective for developing correct body posture and increasing flexibility in joints and the spinal column, the postures can equally stimulate the cardiovascular system and pulmonary organs. They can also increase strength, endurance and the ability to relax completely, and they promote concentration. Benefits are also claimed for the nervous and endocrine systems.

YOGA TIPS

Assume the posture slowly and smoothly, with concentration and full awareness of your body. When stretching and balancing, listen to your body, and accept your flexibility, balance and strength as it is now. Don't confuse push with rush: the position you can readily achieve is the one that provides most benefit. Don't force or compete. Just hold each posture long enough to relax into it. Pay attention to your breathing.

As a general rule you breathe out as you contract your front, and breathe in as you contract your back. For example, bending forwards you exhale, leaning back you inhale. When maintaining the posture, breathe regularly, feeling your belly moving.

THE EXERCISE SPECTRUM

SUPPLEMENTARY EXERCISES – **Surfing tends to develop only certain muscles, or muscles that are moved in a limited range of motion. If you're doing a lot of surfing, supplementary exercises are a kind of active rest for the body.**

COMPENSATION EXERCISES – **These counter the imbalances in the body that are a result of one-sided sports, partial loading, weakening of one side and the over-strengthening of the other.**

REGENERATION EXERCISES – **Important exercises for regaining strength and preventing injuries by relaxing the loaded, stiff and shortened muscles that are a product of hard surfing.**

Yoga is time-friendly because it affects the mind and body simultaneously. You practise attention-concentration focus (a mental skill) while simultaneously stretching and warming up (or down) your body, increasing flexibility and body awareness. Regular practice is the key: a little yoga integrated naturally into your lifestyle will benefit you more than hammering out a few postures only when there's a run of surf.

⬆ **Mighty pose.**

⬆ **Warrior.**

⬆ **Triangle.**

⬆ **Chest to leg extension – 1.**

⬆ **Chest to leg extension – 2.**

⬆ **Forward bend.**

⬆ **Wide leg stretch – 1.**

⬆ **Wide leg stretch – 2.**

⬆ **Plank.**

⬆ **Eagle.**

⬆ **Upwards dog.**

⬆ **Downwards dog.**

⬆ **Rear foot square on.**

⬆ **Knee aligned with the front foot and making an angle of 90 degrees**

BALANCE TRAINING

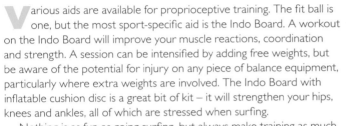

Various aids are available for proprioceptive training. The fit ball is one, but the most sport-specific aid is the Indo Board. A workout on the Indo Board will improve your muscle reactions, coordination and strength. A session can be intensified by adding free weights, but be aware of the potential for injury on any piece of balance equipment, particularly where extra weights are involved. The Indo Board with inflatable cushion disc is a great bit of kit – it will strengthen your hips, knees and ankles, all of which are stressed when surfing.

Nothing is as fun as going surfing, but always make training as much fun as possible. Do what you enjoy – all training methods work if you apply them. It's not so much the method but the everyday practice that brings progressively evident results. You're most likely to stick at a system that's uncomplicated and time-efficient. In the long run, the fewer the gadgets the better.

AEROBICS

Aerobic training covers anything that directly affects the efficiency of your cardiovascular system. Running and cycling are the classic outdoor examples; swimming and indoor 'step' aerobics would be good indoor winter options.

For best results you need to set measurable rates of effort. Training at about 80–85% of your maximum heart rate would bring good results. If you haven't got the means to measure your heart rate accurately, then 80% effort roughly equates to you being able to carry on a somewhat breathless conversation when training.

← **If you are running barefoot, make sure you ease and warm up your achilles tendons before setting off.**

→ ↗ **Sand dunes are nature's way of making you do interval training.**

DIET

Pomegranate juice also boosts your antioxidant levels, which makes it excellent for a post-exercise drink.

Figs – Used by sportsmen in Rome and ancient Greece, figs are high in carbohydrates, rich in potassium and fibre. The potassium and fibre help to reduce blood pressure. Their high levels of magnesium and calcium mean that figs are also very good for replacing salts lost to exercise.

Blueberries – Packed full of antioxidants, and with high levels of potassium and vitamin C. Blueberries also have anti-inflammatory properties, useful if you're working your muscles very hard.

VEGETABLES

Beetroot – A daily glass of beetroot juice with its high nitrate levels has been shown to boost stamina and endurance.

Onion and garlic – This vegetable family has anti-inflammatory properties, is very good for circulation and can help reduce high blood cholesterol levels.

Broccoli – Sky-high in minerals, vitamin C and the B complex of vitamins.

FATS

Not all fats are bad fats. The high levels of Omega 3 fats found in fish, walnuts, flax and pumpkin seeds are important for good joint health and have anti-inflammatory properties. Two servings of fish per week or a handful of walnuts a day will provide the recommended daily 3–6g of good fats.

PROTEINS

Protein is essential for recovery, muscle retention and tone. If you're a vegetarian or have intolerance to dairy foods or nuts, then hemp offers a convenient 'complete' protein. Rich in iron and vitamin E, hemp will also boost your immune system. It's high in magnesium so reduces cramps if you're sweating a lot. It contains lots of good fats too. Add hemp to soups, casseroles and cereals; a finely ground flavoured hemp powder can also be used in smoothies.

Quinoa is a gluten-free grain. Rich in magnesium (which help relax tired muscles), it also happens to be a complete protein containing all eight essential amino acids.

If the rest of your diet is junk then you're wasting your money buying superfoods. They don't work on their own. Leave off the crisps and burgers if you don't want to gain weight, as superfoods can contribute a lot of calories. They can also add a few pounds to your grocery bill, because of the premium the market places on the commodity that's 'health.'

So what is there for the surfer who doesn't want to spend a day's wages on a goji berry and manuka honey smoothie for brunch? If you're on a budget then your superfoods are oats, bananas, potatoes, onions, milk, rice, eggs, broccoli/spinach, mackerel/sardines and lentils. They're flexible, cheap and nutritious, and, with a few judicious spices or sweeteners, can do wonders for your nutrition levels without costing the earth.

Surfers tend to binge: when there are waves, they'll surf till they drop. But if you carry this binge mentality over into your eating habits, you're storing up trouble. Surfing does place great demands upon your metabolism, and it certainly makes you hungry, but using up loads of calories in the water should never be an excuse for refuelling with poor quality foods.

If you're serious about improving your sporting performance, it pays to do some thinking about nutrition. Over and above the widely recognised general advice about a healthy diet – high fibre, low saturated fats, low refined sugars, plenty of fruit and vegetables etc – there are changes you can make to your nutrition that'll keep you in better shape for surfing. The closer a food is to its natural state, the better it is for you: an orange is better than orange-flavoured soda; oats are better than granola; baked potato and fresh salad is better than mushy peas and chips.

Foods that are believed to have higher levels of health benefits are often termed 'superfoods'. The health food industry is a big business with sophisticated marketing strategies, so always seek independent reputable information where you can. Amongst an ever-expanding list of so-called 'superfoods', benefits can be substantiated for at least the following:

FRUIT

Pomegranates – Juice from the crown of the fruit is effective in fighting the free-radical damage brought on by increased exercise levels.

SURF-FOOD IDEAS

Breakfast – A cup of porridge oats; two cups of goat's milk; and a banana. Mix and bring to boil, stirring as you go. Add cinnamon or honey to taste. Or, to aid digestion, soak oats overnight in apple juice, water or milk. In the morning add live yogurt. Add a little sliced fruit (maybe apple, kiwi, dates or raisins). Top with wheatgerm and seeds (pumpkin, sesame).

Power sandwich – If too much carbohydrate for lunch leaves you sleepy, then try this: mix a tin of tuna with cottage cheese or low fat mayo; finely dice red onion, peppers and spring onions. Season with a choice of soy sauce, Tabasco, lemon, salt and pepper or olive oil to taste. Put on a slice of wholemeal or rye bread, toasted if you like.

Peanut energy balls – One cup peanut butter; one cup of oats; one cup of maple syrup or honey; one cup of sesame or sunflower seeds; four tablespoons desiccated coconut; a pinch of cinnamon. Mix it all together using hands or a wooden spoon. Roll handful into a ball, dab in coconut and leave in the fridge overnight.

Winter-warmer soup – One pound of sweet potato, peeled and diced; one onion finely chopped; one crushed garlic clove; one tablespoon medium curry powder; a pint and a half of vegetable stock; two ounces of red split lentils; a little coriander. Place all in a pan and bring to the boil. Reduce heat, cover and simmer for 30 minutes or more.

Mussels and rice – Mussels can be foraged from the shore during any month with an 'r' in it: but check that the area doesn't have persistent sea pollution problems. 500g mussels; tablespoon of butter; one finely diced onion; three cloves of garlic; one sliced chilli; splash of white wine if required; 150g quick-cook long-grain rice; handful of spinach or rocket; squeeze of lemon; sea salt and pepper to taste. De-beard and check the mussels (discard any open ones). Heat the butter in a large open pan, chuck in the onion and garlic and sauté until golden. Add the chilli. Tip in the mussels, and add wine if required. Cook with a lid on high heat for five minutes. Once the mussels have opened, lift them out and keep on a tray. Add 200ml of water to the pan and tip in the rice. Stir, put the lid back on, bring to the boil, then simmer on low heat for about 12 minutes until the rice is cooked. Meanwhile, pick the mussels from their shells, and then tip them back into the pan. Once the rice is cooked and the mussels have warmed through, turn off the heat, and stir in the spinach along with the lemon and any seasoning. Serves two.

Summer smoothies – If you spend any money at all in your kitchen, spend it on a blender. Blending fruit and vegetables helps streamline the digestion process and makes nutrients easier to absorb. *Green Genius* – This smoothie is packed full of vitamins, and plenty of calories all from good fats. Juice two apples, half a celery stick, a handful of spinach, several slices of cucumber, half an avocado, quarter of a pineapple and half a lime. Blend with ice. Celery is great for the B vitamin complex and for potassium; cucumber is good for antioxidant vitamins A and C.

Protein Plus – Good fats and high protein that'll satisfy any after-surf hunger pangs without bloating you up before another session. Blend four brazil nuts, four almonds, two dates, two bananas, sesame seeds, blueberries, 300g natural live yoghurt, half a teaspoon of vanilla essence and ice. Zinc is provided by the sesames seeds and brazils; high fibre and carbohydrates by the dates. The probiotic content of the yoghurt helps balance the good and bad bacteria in the gut, another essential aspect of good nutrition.

SNACKS

If the thought of preparing a fancy meal between or after surfs is too much for you in your exhausted state, don't just reach for a junk snack. Make sure you keep healthy snacks around you. Apple and cheese. A hard-boiled egg and an orange. Mixed nuts and raisins. Pumpkin seeds and dates. A banana and cream cheese. You can keep this kind of snack in a sealed container at home, in the car, at work, without it going off. It will reboot your energy levels and take the edge off the hunger that drives you into the local corner-shop with the sugar, salt and fat craving that makes you spend a small fortune on crisps, cake and chocolate.

Drink at least a couple of litres of water per day – more if you indulge in diuretics such as coffee and tea. Sip some water just before and after exercise, as it helps muscles work and recover without cramping up.

You don't need to be a risk-taker to enjoy surfing. Although the ocean is by nature unpredictable, there are certain precautions you can take to minimise the risk of injury.

Cultivate a sense of the way things are going: gauge the conditions by using your own meteorological knowledge, visiting websites, talking to locals. Simple things make a big difference:

- **The state of the tide** – How will tidal movement affect the waves, your entry and exit, the depth of water?
- **The wind** – Is it due to start howling; from which direction would cause you problems?
- **The weather** – Are you well enough protected from the elements?

This kind of preparation should begin before you even head to the beach.

Once you get there, get the feel of the place: use your warm-up time in the car park to keep a critical eye on the way the waves are breaking. Who's out there already, how are the surfers coping? Ask someone about local hazards – is there anything you should look out for? Are there any rocks under the water that you cannot see?

Extra precautions are obviously necessary at a break you're surfing for the first time, but don't get complacent about your home break. What about that storm last night – has it thrown up some new banks, created new powerful rips that are going to cause you problems? Has the wind that's been blowing cross-shore all night created a lateral drift that's going to sweep you around the headland? Has sand been shifted to expose boulders or a rock shelf that you've never had to deal with before? All this kind of preparation will lessen the risk of getting into trouble. If a place spooks you, turn around and try somewhere else.

Once you're in the water you're largely at the mercy of forces you cannot hope to control, but you can fit yourself into them. If you try to 'take on' the ocean you'll come off badly. You'll get hurt, demoralised, or perhaps be put off surfing forever. Don't fight a rip to the point of exhaustion, and never abandon your board. The surf will always be trying to push you to the shore somewhere: if you're not having a good time, get out before you get hurt.

Surfing is inherently safe in many respects: for example, wearing a 5mm wetsuit, it would take an added 25lb (11.3kg) of lead to actually sink you. Being already equipped with superb life-saving devices (a board and wetsuit), the good news is that you aren't going to drown unless you knock yourself unconscious. The bad news is that you're tied to the very object that's most likely to do just that.

Sixty per cent of surfing injuries are caused by the surfer's own board. That's why it's always best to keep hold of it if you can – the

HITTING THE BOTTOM

Don't try to shrug off a hard whack on the head; the risk of permanent spinal damage is real. Surfers tend to have strong muscles around the neck and top of the shoulders, and this can mask an injury to the spinal column that will manifest later, possibly with devastating consequences. If you suspect any neck injury, keep your head as neutrally aligned as possible and seek further assistance. Even with a minor blow to the head, get medical attention should you experience headaches later. Any concussion or alteration in your level of consciousness should spur you to get out of the water until you're certain you're fully recovered.

⬆ **If you botch a turn...**

⬆ **...and know you are going to fall...**

⬆ **...get your hands in front of you and fall seawards off the board.**

⬆ **This is a better top turn...**

⬆ **...but potentially a worse wipeout.**

⬆ **Falling flat on the back, with the board about to follow on.**

thing is at least under some kind of control. Always cover your head with your arms or at least block your face with your hand when surfacing after a wipeout – you really never do know for sure where the board is.

Get into the habit of thinking defensively – if the leash feels fully taut then the board is about to fly back to your head like a javelin; if there's no tension on the leash, then it's already on the way.

Basically, when you fall get out of the way of your board. This doesn't necessarily mean dive as deep as you can, but try to fall off seawards of your board. When wiping out, never lead with your head – sometimes you want to penetrate the water to get away from a heavy lip, but do it with your hands – the bottom can be nearer than you imagine. It's better to break a wrist than a neck. Most of the time it's safer to 'starfish' – spread your arms and legs and land flat on the surface.

RESPONSIBILITY IN THE WATER

Being well equipped with a board, leash and wetsuit means that you can be the first to offer others assistance when required. If you do see someone in trouble then assess the likely dangers to yourself before paddling over. If it's safe to approach, reassure the casualty, then preferably tow him or her out of trouble using your leash, or haul the casualty on to the front of your board and paddle to safety. Always let others know you're taking rescue action so they can monitor your efforts, and call for back-up if need be.

SURFING INJURIES AND DISORDERS

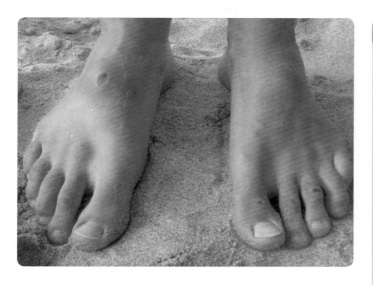

↑ **Keep small cuts clean and dry.**

Skin is softened in water, so seemingly innocuous scrapes can produce wounds easily. Water dilutes blood; exercise makes it flow faster, so any cut whilst surfing often looks like a catastrophic bleed. Wipe the area clean and inspect the wound before you jump to any conclusions. Most small cuts and abrasions will require nothing more than the salt and UV treatment they'll receive naturally. If the wound reddens and angers, then clean it with peroxide and antibiotics.

With persistent immersion, even a tiny scrape can turn into something more sinister and serious – a sea ulcer. Never getting the chance to heal, ulcers get deeper and deeper. The build-up of scar tissue around the edge of the wound makes healing more difficult and makes it easier for you to keep knocking it, so opening it up all over again. Keep ulcers scrupulously clean: a good drying antibiotic powder will help. Only several days out of the water will sort it out properly.

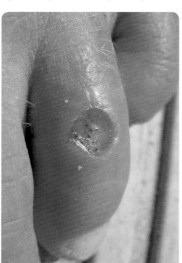

← **Angry red ulcerated cuts spell trouble, and need attention.**

DEEP CUTS

With the force of a wave behind them, fins can slice through 5mm of neoprene with little problem, so it's useful to know the procedure for treating deep cuts: if not your own, you might well one day have to deal with a surfing casualty on the beach.

Deep cuts can be difficult to assess because of the apparent quantities of blood caused by water dilution, but keep calm, and make a rational assessment of the injury site. Is this a life-threatening bleed? Arterial bleeding is characterised by bright red oxygenated blood spurting from a wound, not merely oozing. Large quantities of blood can be absorbed by the dark lining of a wetsuit, hiding crucial evidence of a serious bleed: be thorough in your assessment.

The treatment for any serious cut is direct pressure and elevation: press something absorbent on to the cut and raise the injured limb above the level of the heart. This should slow the bleeding. If it bleeds through, tie something else on top. You can use indirect pressure by clamping down on one of the arterial pressure points – the brachial point just down the upper arm from the armpit, or the femoral point just down the thigh from the crotch. If only a tourniquet will stop the bleeding then improvise one by using a leash or twisted strip of cloth. Remember, you **MUST** note the time the tourniquet was applied.

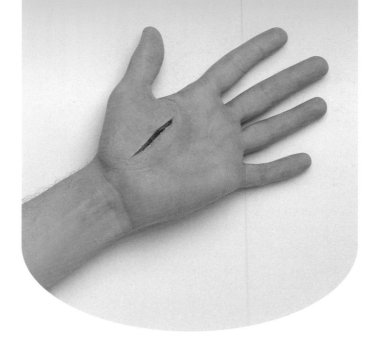

↑ **A purple puncture wound surrounded by an inflamed region of skin suggests a weever fish sting if you've been stomping around the shallows.**

↑ **Treatment for a weever sting is immersion in water as hot as you can stand.**

MARINE STINGS

Weever fish are a hazard in European coastal waters; they lie buried in the shallows at low tide with just their poisonous dorsal spines protruding above the sand. You're more likely to be stung when learning, as you spend more of your surfing time shuffling around the shallows. The pain from a sting asserts itself gradually but is most intense after about 15 minutes. Thereafter it should ease naturally. Pain can be alleviated by rapid immersion in hot water, but beware the potential for scalding, particularly if you've already taken painkillers. Intense pain, some swelling and redness are to be expected, but be wary of the hyper-allergic reaction known as anaphylaxis: redness and swelling around the face or difficulty in breathing demands immediate emergency medical attention.

The Portuguese man of war is an occasional visitor to UK shores in the warmer months. Distinguished by a bright blue air-sac up to 6in (15cm) long, the creature's stinging cells are loaded in a singled coiled tentacle that may be extended to a couple of metres in length. Victims will display a bright raised welt on the skin showing a prominent beading effect, with redness surrounding. Pain can be severe. Wash off remaining tentacles with seawater; but don't try to rub off stuck tentacles, as this will encourage more stinging cells to discharge. Pick them off with a gloved hand. A cold pack can be applied.

With regards to marine stings, UK waters are relatively benign; if going abroad do your research regarding local dangers and prepare accordingly.

↓ **The tentacles of a Portuguese Man-o-War can still sting when high and dry, so take care.**

SURFER'S EAR

The medical terms are exostosis (hyperostosis if it's larger) or osteoma. These are bony growths in the ear canal that develop over several years as a result of exposure to cold, wet and wind. Blockage of 90% is by no means uncommon in hardy regular surfers. It often occurs to a greater degree in one ear or the other; usually you find that it's your windward ear that suffers if you surf on a beach that has persistent cross-shore winds.

The problem is not so much hearing loss as the risk of persistent painful bacterial infections that develop in water trapped in the ear. The prevention is hoods and plugs. The cure is the drill. The bony growths regress if the adverse conditions are removed – but regress only over a long period of time.

The drill is to be avoided for two reasons: one is that it seems to spur the growth to come back even faster (so you have to be extra diligent with further preventative measures); and two, because the risks of complications include accidental piercing of the ear drum, and damaging the facial nerve that runs near the exostosis, so causing Bell's Palsy or facial paralysis.

If surgery is a must, then the surgeon's chisel is less invasive and is quicker to heal. Recovery takes three to four weeks rather than the several months after the drill.

Keep the ear clear of wax (which has a tendency to build up behind the exostosis) by using warm olive oil. Never jam anything into your ear.

STOMACH BUGS AND ENT INFECTIONS

Unfortunately the pressures of population growth mean that in many places the sea has to take more effluent than it can deal with. Various directives have forced councils to measure and make public the levels of pollution in the sea – testing mainly for the E. Coli bacteria that indicate the presence of human faecal matter.

If there's a beach information board do check it out, but be a sceptic. Check other sources of information such as local papers and news reports. Ask lifeguards if any sewerage discharges have been reported. Use your senses – if it smells dodgy it probably is; if it tastes of detergent then other contaminants are probably present; if you can see sanitary waste on the tide line and in the water then things are bad. It's hard to keep your mouth closed for a whole surf session, and in any case microbes can also enter your bloodstream through the small cuts that surfers inevitably have on their feet or hands. So take as few chances as possible with water quality. There are also two proactive measures you can take: have your jabs and join an environmental pressure group.

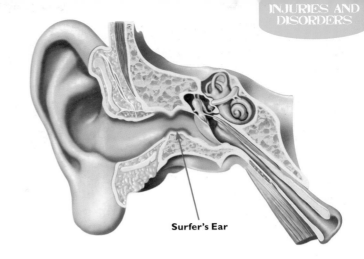

Surfer's Ear

How are these results measured?
The tests are done to check compliance with standards set in the Bathing Water Directive. The Directive sets limits for a number of substances, and all countries in the EU have to ensure their popular beaches meet these standards.
Two thumbs up': Water quality in the sample met the Directive's most stringent Guideline standards
Thumbs up': Water quality in the sample met the Directive's main Mandatory standards
2010 RESULTS

DATE	RESULT	DATE	RESULT	DATE	RESULT	DATE	RESULT
.06.10	👍	1.07.10	👍	26.7.10	👍	25.8.10	👍
.06.10	👍	9.7.10	👍	2.08.10	👍	3.09.10	👍
7.6.10	👍	14.7.10	👍	10.8.10	👍	10.09.10	👍
5.6.10	👍	18.7.10	👍	20.8.10	👍		

To find out how water quality is tested contact the Regional Office of the Environment Agency at Manley House, Kestral Way, Exeter.
EX2 7LQ. Telephone 01392 352489
Or visit the Agency website at www.environment-agency.gov.uk

←⬇⬆ **Which of these sources of information would you rely on?**

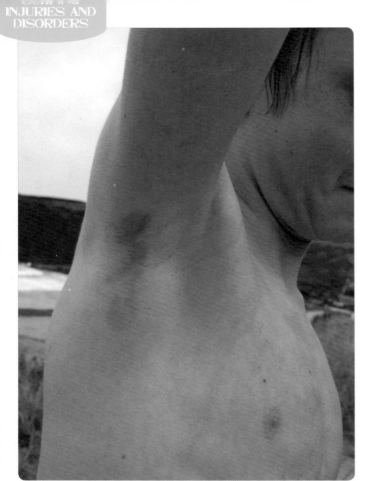

↑ **This boy needs a rash vest!**

WETSUIT RASH

This can look like nothing at all but it can feel like hell, and force you out of the water. Avoid it by diligent use of a rash vest or the application of a lubricant such as petroleum jelly. For temporary relief try putting on a T-shirt; it might help briefly, but will probably bring on a new rash somewhere else. Sun cream, margarine from your sandwiches, *anything* that gets rid of the friction between your chafed skin and the lining of your suit will help when you're desperate. The underlying problem will eventually have to be addressed: get a better-fitting suit.

COLD INJURY

Surfers in the higher latitudes expect to get cold. This isn't altogether a bad thing: cold boosts circulation, so where it doesn't prevent injury it promotes recovery; cold also strengthens your immune system. But when surfing, cold injury is always a threat because water is 20 times better than air at taking heat away from the body. Most experienced surfers hate feeling cold so will suit up appropriately, but learners are constricted by two things – they may not have the luxury of choosing from a wardrobe of wetsuits, and their enthusiasm can get the better of them, keeping them chasing waves even as their core temperature slides towards the danger zone. Avoid cold injury by getting the best wetsuit you can afford.

It's stimulating and a bit of a rush to feel the cold. But remember, shivering is one of the first signs of cold injury, and the sinister aspect of cold injury is the vicious spiral downwards – the further it progresses, the harder it is to make a rational decision to escape the conditions that are causing it.

Cold shock is especially a threat in waters below 10°C, but can occur when the sea is anything below 25°C – a level that's never exceeded by the coastal waters of the UK. Cold shock occurs within the first three minutes of immersion: the patient will involuntarily take an initial huge gasp and could inhale water. There will be a rapid rise in respiration rate (up to tenfold), the patient cannot hold his breath voluntarily, and limb coordination is lost. Massive vasoconstriction as the blood is rushed to the body core weakens the limbs. It also increases heart rate and blood pressure, which can lead to a stroke. Don't jump into cold water unprepared.

Most winter surfers will have experienced extremity cooling, where the extremities are cooled rapidly to the low 30s. Muscle function and nerve action are affected, so simple tasks – like turning the key in your car door – become a torturous impossibility. In bad cases a

HELPING OTHERS

As a surfer, you may well be first on the scene at all kinds of accidents, so you have something of a moral obligation to familiarise yourself with a few basic but effective rescue and first aid techniques.

↑ **Provide shelter and insulation.**

↑ **A warm sweet drink can be given in the case
of mild cold injury, but not for hypothermia.**

patient might lose the ability to coordinate a swim stroke. The core temperature of the patient, however, is still above 35°C, so he's not yet hypothermic.

When the core body temperature falls from the normal 37.5°C to below 35°C, then the patient is considered hypothermic. In UK coastal waters this would take 30 minutes to occur even without a wetsuit, so it's relatively uncommon amongst sensible surfers.

It's important to be able to distinguish between the cold casualty and the hypothermic casualty, because treatment is different. A cold casualty can be actively re-warmed, whereas a hypothermic casualty cannot. Actively re-warming a hypothermic casualty can lead to problems with heart rhythm and subsequent cardiac arrest.

Cold casualties will be alert, lucid, flexible and shivering. They can be safely warmed by sitting or laying them down, wrapping them up, covering the head, and giving them a warm drink. Recovery should be evident within a short while. Hypothermic casualties will have a lowered level of consciousness, will be confused and will be mumbling incoherently. The body will be more rigid and will no longer be shivering. Such casualties should also be laid down and wrapped up, but *not* actively re-warmed. They must be evacuated to hospital immediately.

HEAT INJURY

At the other end of the scale is heat injury. This might not seem a problem in the higher latitudes, but the human body actually deals much better with cold than it does with heat. The body can lose 10°C in core temperature before death occurs, but a rise of only 4°C would prove fatal for most of us.

Avoid heat stress initially by ensuring good hydration. Being surrounded and suspended by water can affect your thirst mechanism. In the sea, you can't see how much you're sweating. If you're surfing hard in warm conditions, come in every now and then for a pre-emptive drink.

With a body temperature of around 38–39°C the patient is suffering from heat exhaustion. Symptoms may include sweating, thirst, weakness, cramps, headache and nausea. The casualty needs to be removed to a cool area, laid down, have clothing loosened, and be cooled by means of a damp cloth on the torso, forehead or back of the neck. They should show a marked improvement within 30 minutes.

If not treated, heat exhaustion will progress to heat stroke, a life-threatening condition. If the casualty has a body temperature above

40°C his skin will be hot but dry to the touch – he's no longer able to sweat. If conscious, he'll be confused and may have a fit. Rapid treatment is essential – cool him any way you can (pouring water over his head, applying cold soaked blankets over the torso) and evacuate to hospital.

SUN DAMAGE

Minimise your exposure to the sun's rays between the hours of 10:00 and 14:00. Buy and apply a good waterproof high factor sunscreen, paying special attention to areas like the top of the head, ears, under the eyes and chin.

Allow for the reflection off the sea surface – it can double exposure to harmful UV rays. A good tan is no real protection, it's just a sign of skin damage. A suntan is worth no more than SPF 2–4.

IMMERSION/SUBMERSION CASUALTIES

A near-drowned casualty is anyone who may have inhaled water into the lungs. The casualty will present with shortness of breath, coughing, vomiting, chest pain and a reduced level of consciousness. This patient must be advised to attend hospital because of the risk of late-onset near drowning (otherwise known as secondary drowning).

Late-onset near drowning usually occurs within the first 12 hours of immersion, but may be delayed for up to 72 hours. The casualty will initially appear well, but saltwater inhalation causes inflammation of the lung tissue, and fluids are subsequently released to counter the salt imbalance in the lungs. The casualty deteriorates rapidly when oxygen uptake is inhibited and he effectively drowns in his own fluids. Intensive care is required immediately.

A submersed drowning casualty is someone who's been underwater long enough for all breathing effort to cease – usually this takes only a minute or so. The result will be cardiac arrest. The casualty may be found floating face down. He needs to be removed from the water and CPR commenced whilst the emergency services are summoned without delay. Your primary role is to get help – the patient is unlikely to recover without definitive care.

CARDIO-PULMONARY RESUSCITATION

This resuscitation technique is a last resort for the first-aider. If a casualty isn't breathing then CPR is required for several reasons, not least for you to feel that you did everything possible to help. Statistically, CPR is unlikely to bring back a casualty who isn't breathing and lacks a pulse, but what it does achieve is to keep the organs viable until definitive care is available. You can act as the heart and lungs of the patient until help arrives, but your primary responsibility is always to ensure that the emergency services are immediately alerted.

ADULT CPR FOR A DROWNED CASUALTY

Tilt the patient's head back to clear the tongue from the airway, then give five initial breaths. Using two hands one on top of the other, with stiff arms apply 30 chest compressions in the centre of the chest to depth of 5–6cm at a rate of 100–120 per minute. Continue to give two breaths after every 30 compressions. The technique is not difficult but is best taught by a qualified instructor.

Be prepared for the unpleasantness of the patient voiding and vomiting. Chest compressions alone have been shown to be fairly effective at providing the patient's lungs with air, so if the patient has severe facial trauma just do the compressions. If you fear contamination from body fluids such as saliva and don't have anything to act as a barrier mask, then just do the compressions. If you suspect spinal trauma and are fearful of tilting the head back, then remember that oxygen trumps spinal integrity – the airway has to be opened even if you're only going to administer the chest compressions.

Broken bones and blood aren't really common on the beach, but they do get your heart racing when you're presented with them. However, if you're called upon to act in any emergency situation related to the water, the easiest way to remember how to prioritise your treatment is to think 'breathing over bleeding over bones'. *Make sure the airway is open and stable* before you tackle any bleeding, and only after any catastrophic bleeding is subsequently stopped should you then check for fractures.

ONCE COMMENCED, STOP CPR ONLY:

- [ ] **To check for recovery if signs present.**
- [ ] **To hand over the patient to a qualified crew.**
- [ ] **If a doctor declares the patient dead.**
- [ ] **If you are in danger.**
- [ ] **If you become exhausted.**

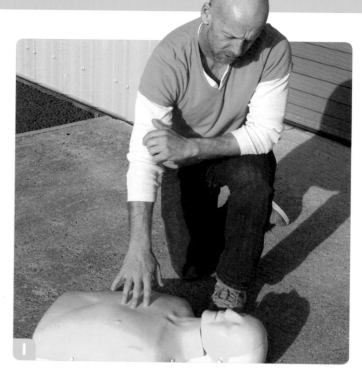

↑ **Make sure it is safe to approach the casualty, and assess the level of response.**

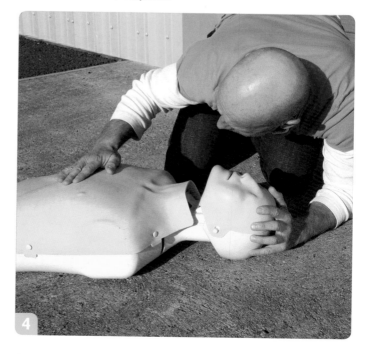

↑ **Look listen and feel for signs of breathing.**

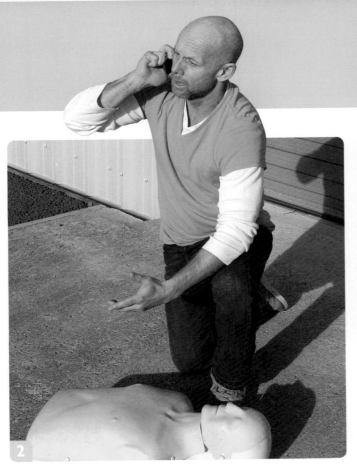

⬆ If the casualty is unresponsive, call emergency services.

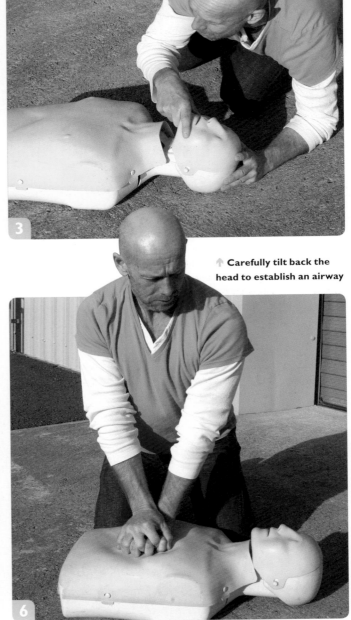

⬆ Carefully tilt back the head to establish an airway

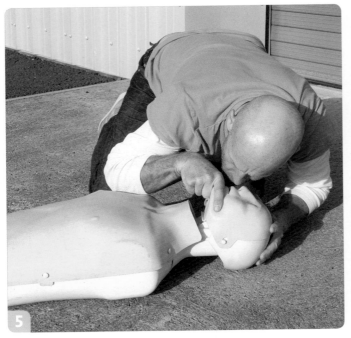

⬆ Give five intial inflations for a suspected drowning. Mouth-to-mouth with a good seal to prevent air leakage.

⬆ Arms rigid, the chest compressions centre on the patient's sternum. If you hand over your patient, make absolutely sure it is to someone qualified.

'OUR TALES FROM A LOST HORIZON WERE A WAKE-UP CALL TO FELLOW SURFERS THAT IT'S BETTER TO HAVE YOUR PASSPORT IN SOME THIEF'S POCKET IN A FOREIGN LAND THAN SITTING IN A DRAWER AT HOME.'

Kevin Naughton, *surf journalist and film-maker*

CHAPTER 7

TRAVELLING

At some point during your surf career you'll become good enough to get restless. The waves at your local beach are too crowded, too inconsistent; winter is too cold, and friends have brought home tales of great waves abroad. So you decide to take a trip. There are four main points to consider: how to go, where to go, when to go, and what to take.

HOW TO GO

Whether you book as an individual or block-book as a 12-person group, the simplest way to surf abroad is a trip where most of the logistics are handled for you: a surf camp.

SURF CAMPS

The upside

The surf camp has become almost the default trip for two main groups of surfers: those lacking the experience or confidence to organise their own trip, and those with time pressures at home who cannot afford to leave anything to chance. Surf camps are designed to maximise your wave count and minimise your hassles. Accommodation, food and transport to the waves will be included; tuition and equipment is provided for learner surfers. Extras might include a souvenir DVD of footage from your sessions. You might even have exclusive access to certain breaks. The undoubted attraction of such a deal is that the everyday complications of finding the right conditions in a new environment are taken away from you.

Surf camps filter your travel experience: you know the water will be safe to drink, the food well-cooked, the mosquitoes screened, and the locals more or less happy to see you and your dollars. In a sport where so little is predictable, there's a lot to be said for nailing down the peripheries and focusing on the thing that counts – the waves.

The downside

Surf camps maximise your wave opportunities, there's no doubt about it, but you'll always be carrying your own small crowd around with you. An exclusive crowd is still a crowd. Do you want to rock up at a beach in a minibus piled high with boards and spend 24 hours a day with the same bunch of people? For some, the very qualities that make a surf camp – the organisation – can feel like regimentation.

There can be a certain vibe with a surf camp that doesn't sit well with the less goal-driven freewheeling adventurer. People *demand* more from surfing when they've paid for it like a ride at a theme park. They want a return; there may be a level of expectation that permeates and compromises your interaction with the local environment and culture.

'WHAT DISTINGUISHED TRAVELLERS IN THOSE DAYS WAS THAT THEY HAD PLENTY OF TIME ON THEIR HANDS. TRIPS LASTED FOR MONTHS ON END. SURFERS WERE ALL OVER THE MAP, EXCHANGING NOTES VIA THE COCONUT WIRELESS ON WHAT SPOTS WERE HAPPENING. IT WAS ALL ONE GREAT ADVENTURE AND THE POSSIBILITIES WERE AS WIDE OPEN AS THE WORLD AT LARGE. IT ALL SOUNDS PRETTY ODD WHEN COMPARED TO THE "SURGICAL STRIKE" SURF TRIPS COMMON TODAY, WHERE YOU FLY IN, GET IT, AND FLY BACK BEFORE ANYONE KNOWS YOU WENT SOMEWHERE (DID YOU?).'

Kevin Naughton, surf journalist and film-maker

↑ **The sanitised surf camp experience isn't for everyone.**

Your choice is basically one of two types of surf camp — the land camp or the boat trip. The land camp is the simplest surf camp experience; the boat trip can be rather more intense.

Land camp
■ On the coast near a single break or variety of breaks; if you're lucky all are within walking distance, and not too much driving is involved.
■ Staying right on the break, you can get in early when conditions are good and the crowd is thin.
■ There will often be a boat laid on to taxi you out to the local reef if you haven't got the arms for the paddle.
■ You're free to leave the camp whenever you fancy a change of scene.
■ You're rather dependent on your local breaks working well for the duration of your stay.

⬇ **A boat trip will get you access to the best reef passes.**

Boat trip
■ There's the flexibility of being able to rock up at any break or reef pass to get the optimum conditions for whatever the swell is doing.
■ No matter how swanky the onboard accommodation, you're confined to a boat: you have to like boats.
■ Cooped up in a tropical climate, sea conditions can be rough and accommodation can be tight.
■ Some sort of rotation has to be put in place when you get to a reef because you'll all be arriving at the same time — it's difficult to slope off for an early session unannounced.
■ The reef might already be crowded by the time your boatload rocks up there; and this can lead to tensions.

Centred on issues of privatisation and saturation of surf spots, the rise of the surf camp phenomenon in recent years hasn't been without controversy, but there's little doubt that surf camp culture is here to stay.

INDEPENDENT SMALL GROUP

If you hesitate to accept foreign waves as a packaged commodity, then you might want to consider an independent trip. Going along with a friend or two is ideal because the costs of accommodation and transport are shared, as are the memories. Make sure you all surf at roughly the same level and are looking for the same kind of waves.

Independence means flexibility. If conditions aren't good where you happen to be, then you can up-sticks and go search for somewhere better. If the dynamic of your group turns out to be less than ideal, then you can adjust your plans to better fit the differing personalities. You can go your separate ways for a few days, then meet up again later; or take another independent traveller on board for a while.

Travelling in a small independent group means that you have a mutual support system but without being insular: you're still able to make connections with the locals, one of the rewards of foreign travel.

SOLO

Going solo is the most adventurous way to travel. Alone, the local surfers – and hence the local waves – are more likely to be open towards you.

For this type of surf trip you have to be able to invest the time and effort to sort out everything for yourself. You have total freedom but the responsibility is all yours too. Every item on the itinerary, every ticket, every night's accommodation is entirely up to you to arrange. Every setback is yours to put right; but then all the rewards are yours to enjoy to the maximum when you do strike it lucky.

If you're anxious about going solo, remember that the major advantage of travelling alone is that it makes it easier to share: alone you're less of a threat, more vulnerable, more open to meeting new people, less insular.

IMPACT

Responsible surf camp operators will have undertaken an assessment of their impact on the local community and environment. Enquire before you book, and go only with those outfits that seem to have some empathy with the culture and environment in which they're embedded. Do they employ local staff, or are they all blow-ins? Do they contribute anything directly to the local scene, or are they just out to cream off what they can?

Going solo might make you feel a little more Lonely Planet than Thomas Cook, but travelling independently doesn't necessarily mean travelling responsibly.

There are simple ways of minimising your footprint:

Free camping – Use a previous site if possible. You found the old site because it's a scar on the landscape, so don't create another. Scorch marks, tyre marks, cut trees, litter, dead grass, compacted soil, trails – if they've already been created then don't blunder off and make new ones. Try to take pride in improving an area rather than degrading it. Take pride also in working out how to make the least possible impact: camp on the intertidal zone of the beach, above the regular high tides but where a spring tide will sweep away any traces.

Trash – You packed it in; you pack it out. Rusty metal and broken glass can cause the cuts and infections that ruin a trip – yours or some other unfortunate who comes after you. To minimise waste, unwrap and repack stuff before you set out. Separate and compact the wrapping waste that you do end up with. Paper and cardboard can be used in your fires. Organic matter such as peelings take a while to break down, so if you bury it bury it deep to prevent scavenging animals digging it up.

Proofing – Rodent-proof all your dried goods – use Tupperware or cheap margarine tubs. Food scraps will attract animals that could be dangerously diseased or dangerously large. Sun-proof all your perishables and keep them boxed but ventilated to prolong life.

Toilet – Is it OK to crap on the beach? Well, yes if the tide will wash it away: organisms, UV and wave action will rapidly break it down. But bear in mind the issue of concentration: if you all take a dump in one place at the same time of day then the risk of faecal-borne diseases like dysentery, cholera and hepatitis are increased, not to mention stomach ailments caused by the E. Coli bacteria. Make sure you're always at least 200m away from any water source – it may not be yours but it could be someone else's. Or dig a hole, not too deep but within the organic layer of the soil to help breakdown; mix soil and faeces and bury. Burn the loo paper.

Campfires – A cosy fire is one of the nicest things about camping, but equally the one with the worst potential consequences. If in doubt then don't burn anything. Sparks can leap in an offshore breeze that might flare up at night as you sleep. Fire can smoulder out of sight and spread within turf. Just because there's a used fire pit at your site doesn't necessarily mean that conditions are still safe. Think. If it's safe, then get your fuel from downed wood, or best of all from driftwood.

Cleansing – Scouring with natural elements is best. Scrub and scour and leave in the UV; soaps leave ph traces. Remove scraps.

Wildlife – Is your presence disturbing it? Are you blocking a trail, monopolising a water source? Is your dog having great fun terrorising native fauna for miles around?

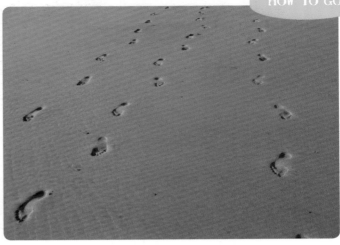

⬆ **Minimise your impact.**

Foraging – Find out what the season is for the food you intend to harvest, and don't deplete populations. Always gather local knowledge before your gather local foods. Assess likely environmental contaminants, particularly before harvesting seafood.

Vehicles – Should your trip demand the flexibility and speed of movement that only a 4x4 can provide, then rationalise your movements, economise on fuel – don't abuse the fact that fuel may be cheaper than at home. Don't strike off into the bush, gouging new tracks that might take decades to disappear. Don't think scrub or desert is empty – nesting sites are hard to spot but easy to disturb.

Drinks – Electrolyte powders can be useful to replace minerals and to flavour local water that might be unpalatable. Always drink from sealed containers and beware of the provenance of ice cubes.

However you travel, do your research. Trips used to be very hit and miss, based largely on rumours and tall tales. Now, the grapevine is online. There are so many resources available to minimise the element of chance that there's really little excuse for missing waves. Guidebooks, websites, magazine articles all provide the information you need.

First, deal with the fundamentals. When it comes to surf, almost everywhere has an in-season and out-of-season. If you want the near-certainty of in-season swells, be prepared for crowds. You might be content to trust to luck in getting waves out-of-season if you want to surf somewhere quiet.

Learn what you can about the factors that affect local winds. Find out whether the local climate is influenced mostly by predictable and stable trade winds, or regular fast-moving depressions and frontal systems. If you can predict wind shifts you might score a good session where other travellers miss out.

Closer to your departure get the swell forecast. Such is the modern availability and reliability of swell forecasting websites that many trips nowadays are of the 'surgical strike'. variety. The swell forecast comes first; everything else is hastily slotted into place around it. Even if your plans are less precise, a swell prediction can help you plan roughly where along a stretch of coastline you need to be.

Finally, find out about events that could affect your enjoyment of the waves – local holidays, for example, can affect the crowds in the water as well as the availability of services and health care.

THE INTERNET

So pervasive is the Internet in modern surf culture that a popular forecasting site in the UK will get 500,000 unique visitors per year. Swell predictions, surf reports, discussion forums and users photos all create a virtual surf community online. This vast resource can help you plan a successful trip to a familiar spot, but the Internet can equally be a tool to discover entirely new waves. Satellite imagery and aerial surveillance mapping enables us to zoom in on virtually any part of the world's 860,000 miles of coastline and perhaps see a swell wrapping around a headland, marching down a point, or exploding on to a reef pass. For many parts of the globe the image resolution might presently be poor, but this will only get better with time.

Satellite imagery available online is the modern equivalent of the original surf explorers digging out Admiralty charts and crude local maps and trying to identify remote areas that just might have waves.

Whatever you may think it does to the 'soul' of surfing, the Internet is a reality and you need to learn how to use it to your advantage – whether that's by catching a swell early at your local break or catching a plane to escape the crowds to some newly-discovered magic spot.

'THE ACTUAL SURF SPOTS – THOSE TINY DOTS ON THE MAP – WERE TREASURED SECRETS OCCASIONALLY REVEALED TO FELLOW SEEKERS AROUND REMOTE CAMPFIRES.'
Kevin Naughton, surf journalist and film-maker

WHERE TO GO

The days of genuine pioneering surf adventure are drawing to a close. Wherever you decide to go, the chances are that someone surfed there before you. But that does mean there are so many more documented surf destinations from which to choose.

So much of the globe is now open to you that deciding where to go is often your biggest problem. Apart from the waves, your major considerations are the same as for any other tourists: language, culture and climate. You might also want to take into account the reputation of the local surfers, but don't let this type of hearsay blinker you to other possible realities.

Sometimes it is easier to begin by eliminating – for one reason or another – the places you really *don't* fancy.

THREATS

Read the broadsheets, keep abreast of the news. Some surf magazines publish regular updates on the global situation and any impacts developments might have on travelling surfers. Problems can be:

- **Political** – Terrorist threats, internal security issues, kidnappings, instability.
- **Environmental** – Epidemics, extreme weather, forest fires, parasites, wildlife.
- **Social** – Chronic issues of race, poverty, gender, religion, poor communications.

Be acutely aware of the international situation, but also try to work out what is largely propaganda. Some marginal political groups just want to scare you away, some airlines and tourist bureaus just want to sell you tickets – the real picture might lie somewhere in between. You must try to make an informed decision: is the risk worth it for a few waves? Don't just blunder into a sticky situation that could easily have been anticipated with a simple bit of research, and don't expect to be able to wave your Western passport like a magic 'get-out-of-jail-free' card if you do get into trouble.

Insurance – get some. But first check the small print to see whether surfing is an excluded activity. Some insurers class it as an extreme sport, which may require an added premium.

What type of waves can you expect? Certainly you're planning to go somewhere where the waves are in some way 'better' – but does that mean bigger and faster, or just warmer and less crowded?

Need you rethink your quiver? Or are you going to be able to stick with what you know and not have to make the awkward adjustment to a new board in a new environment? If you're taking a board unfamiliar to you, make sure you give it a few tries at home first. You might not be able to test it under optimum conditions, but you'll at least get the way it feels underneath you.

If you're going somewhere where the waves have a *lot* more power, then gear up accordingly. You'll be grateful for a more gunny board in bigger faster waves, and a narrower tail for suckier waves.

If you can't stretch to a brand new board, just taking a different set of fins might change the performance of your trusty old board enough to give you confidence in more challenging conditions. A lot more drive and a lot more hold can be bought for a tenth of the price of a new board. This is where fin systems really come into their own – a couple of sets of fins are a lot cheaper to buy and easier to carry along than another board. They can have a comparable effect on performance.

FLYING

Removing the fins also makes a big difference to peace of mind when you're packing the board for air travel. Glassed-in fins invite damage and are easily knocked and broken even when protected in a board bag. And although repair isn't that difficult, it's an unwanted hassle just out of the airport. With empty fin plugs, the board presents less of a target for baggage handlers. Two finless boards can easily fit in the space taken up by a single board with glassed-in fins, so bear that in mind when you're gathering up a travel quiver.

Flying is an age-old bone of contention with travelling surfers as airlines usually slap on a surcharge even if this is the only item of luggage that you're checking in. Make sure you have a written printed copy of any surcharge imposed upon booking and take that with you to the check-in desk. Booking agents and the check-in clerks don't always confer or agree on charges – this is usually to your disadvantage if you have no documentation to argue otherwise.

On the plus side, check-in clerks seldom have much of an idea of how big a surfboard actually is, so as long as you turn up with a single bag that's under the weight restriction there's little stopping you from cramming four boards in there, even though you've declared just the one 'windsurfer' or 'paddleboard' on the booking form.

Many budget airlines charge you per checked item of luggage, so pack a cabin bag with all your dense, heavy items (books, hardware, etc) and chuck everything else in the board bag: clothes, towel, wetsuit, anything that offers a bit more protection.

A travel bag should be well padded, with a sturdy zip. A reflective silver covering on at least one side helps prevent boards overheating – melted wax on the inside of the bag is a messy inconvenience. You

← Make sure your board bag has clear symbols for international travel.

→ A ding kit in the middle of nowhere is worth its weight in gold.

↓ Your first glimpse of a foreign surf coast is always a thrill.

may have to sign a form that effectively says that the airline can do what they like with the board once they've got their hands on it, so even with a good bag it pays to pack the board as well as you can. Polystyrene blocks around fixed fins are a good idea, as is foam pipe-lagging around the rails – all cheap, lightweight and effective protection.

Rigid travel cases are available but are inconveniently bulky if you're travelling onwards after arrival. The most effective board bag on the market at the moment is the inflatable type. You need a good pair of lungs, but the boards get unmatched protection and it doubles as a sleeping mat when times, and the ground, are hard. It even comes with a puncture repair kit.

But you need to pay for this type of protection, so much so that the bag can sometimes be worth more than the boards you're trying to safeguard. What then? There's no regulation that says you have to travel with a board bag. If you're caught abroad facing a flight home with a favourite board and no bag, there's no reason to despair: there's a school of thought that says just giving the airline an unpacked board will shame them into being careful with it. It might just work.

ACCESSORIES

Wax, leashes, repair kits and fins might be unavailable or prohibitively expensive at your destination, so take extras with you. Unused items are great tender and you'll quickly make friends if you're the only surfer for 50 miles with any resin for repairs.

Opting for the UV-curing small repair kit will enable you to patch minor dings rapidly but will leave you struggling to fix a major hole. A full kit with cloth, resin and catalyst will cope with most breakages but takes up more space and will have to be checked in the hold.

If you use fin systems, then a spare plug or two will take up no space at all but might be invaluable, as these tend to suffer on shallow reefs. Weigh it up, taking into account the waves you're expecting. A good metal adhesive tape is handy for cracks and creases in the glass that can be fixed temporarily without using up precious resin.

Expecting the waves on your trip to have more power, pay extra attention to your leashes. Check all your old ones for nicks on the urethane, chafe on the string, and wear on the swivels. New leashes aren't cheap, but a longer, stronger spare or two might be good insurance on the trip, especially if you don't rate your board repair skills.

De-wax your boards before you go – get a nice solid base coat on and then finish waxing up when you get to the destination. Use wax designed for your new environment – a harder wax for warmer conditions, softer if you've gone to higher latitudes. Wax is cheap, so

take plenty; at the end of your trip it's nice to donate stuff to those who might be short.

As regards wetsuits, take into account the variability of the climate. April in Samoa might have a temperature variation of 2°–3° so is very predictable; April in the Canaries could see a differential of 15°C should a front come through.

Remember, your aim is to bag as much surf as you can: that means surfing early mornings before the sun is up, and surfing cold onshores in the afternoon. Therefore it might be sensible to have a wetsuit one notch up from what the guidebooks say you can get away with. Better to have too much rubber than not enough. Neoprene will do a good job of protecting your board on the flight over and it'll also protect you from reefs, rocks and the sun.

If too much wetsuit rubber really is driving you mad, then don't be afraid to get your knife out and customise it. Chop it off above the elbows (if the water is cold but the air is warm) or at the knees (if the air is cold but the water is warm). Once back home, a replacement wetsuit is relatively easy to find; quality waves aren't.

BOOTIES

If you surf the reefs at home, you'll know how valuable boots are for protecting your feet. This is even more the case on a trip where an infected cut can spell the end of your surfing. In a tropical climate you'll obviously not want to be wearing your 5mm winter booties from home; the alternative is a pair of a reef boots that are thinner (for better feel) and cut lower at the ankle. Make sure they're a good fit

↑ **Reef booties.**

If you have a preferred brand at home then take as much sunscreen as you're likely to need. Remember how much stronger the sun can be abroad in an aquatic environment, and how you're likely to sweat more in a hot humid climate – is your home brand up to it? Regularly reapplying zinc cream on the lips, cheeks, ears and bald spots just before a session is sound strategy.

Although dermatologists would never advise sunbathing, it is occasionally suggested that a moderate tan is healthy for your skin. Melanin is an antioxidant with anti-ageing properties, but never skimp on sunscreen, as even a good tan is equivalent only to an SPF of 2–4. SPF numbers are based on values obtained by plastering a generous 2mg of cream on every square centimetre of skin – not something we achieve with most creams. Lightweight wide-brim surf hats are available too; they fit with a clip-on chinstrap and save your head from the glaring tropical sun.

and preferably have some kind of adjustable strap to keep them on in the surf, as you won't necessarily have the leg cuffs of your wetsuit to protect them. The boots-and-boardshorts combination might seem an odd fashion statement, but it's functional.

SUNSCREEN

Don't let sunburn keep you from the surf. There are two types of radiation that will damage your skin: UVB causes sunburn; UVA won't burn you but it'll age your skin, and could lead to melanoma. It might seem fine to be out there all day wearing a high-SPF (sun protection factor) gel and not getting burnt, but consequently you're staying out exposing yourself to more of the cumulative damaging effects of UVA rays.

Strong sunlight will damage both you and your board. Use protection wisely.

SUNSCREEN

So what's the good stuff? Look in the ingredients for micronised titanium dioxide or micronised zinc oxide. They tend to spread effectively. Whatever the active ingredients, they need to comprise a minimum of 4%. If a product irritates you it's because the skin is absorbing it too readily, an indication that the polymer size is too small to be very effective anyway. It's likely to wash off easily too – not a good thing for a surfer. Always go for a long-lasting product – this is likely to be the least irritating for that reason. Apply it early – at least half an hour before you think you need it.

TRAVELLING WELL

With careful preparation most travelling illnesses and infections are preventable. Seek medical advice at least eight weeks in advance of departure; but even if you're leaving at short notice, it's never too late to get informed.

Requirements are constantly updated, but will vary in any case depending upon your past health and medical history, what part of a country you'll be visiting, and what activities you'll be taking part in. So it's a good idea to consult a doctor experienced in travel medicine to get further up-to-date information for your particular trip.

Even if you're told that no jabs are compulsory for your trip, you'd be highly recommended to have certain vaccinations and medications. 'Compulsory' requirements are made to protect the local inhabitants, not the visitor; you'll likely need greater protection. Although developing countries usually pose the greater risk, you may need to think about such things as tetanus and diphtheria boosters and hepatitis jabs even if travelling only to a 'developed' region.

You cannot fill home prescriptions overseas so take what you know you'll need. You don't want to be scrounging medications off unreliable strangers. Drug names are often different abroad; drugs are sometimes repackaged and mislabelled. If you must purchase drugs, buy only from a large store in a major city.

Don't share your medications with other travellers – they may have allergies of which you're not aware. You might also need those drugs later on yourself. Know your blood group.

TRAVELLERS' MEDICAL KIT

General
- ☐ Travel insurance with good emergency medical cover.
- ☐ Vaccination certificates.
- ☐ Sterile needles.
- ☐ Scissors and tweezers.
- ☐ Digital thermometer.
- ☐ Any regular medication that you use, however sparingly, at home.

Mosquito diease
- ☐ Insect repellent.
- ☐ Long-sleeved, light-coloured clothing for evenings.
- ☐ Nets treated with Permethrin.
- ☐ Knock-down spray.
- ☐ Mosquito coils.
- ☐ Prescribed malaria tablets.

Water
- ☐ Clean straws.
- ☐ Clean sturdy plastic bottle.
- ☐ Purification tablets.

Stomach
- ☐ Electrolyte powders.
- ☐ Imodium (stops diarrhoea symptoms).
- ☐ Antibiotics.
- ☐ Laxative.

Wounds
- ☐ Dressings – plasters, non-stick dressings, gauze, crepe bandage, closure strips, tape, triangular bandage.
- ☐ Suture kit.
- ☐ Antiseptic cream.
- ☐ Antibiotic powder.
- ☐ Hydrogen peroxide.
- ☐ New clean toothbrush for scrubbing cuts.

Allergies and bites
- ☐ Antihistamine tablets.
- ☐ Steroid cream.
- ☐ Anti-sting gel.

Dental
- ☐ Oil of cloves.
- ☐ Temporary filling.

Sexual
- ☐ Condoms.
- ☐ Water soluble lubricant.

Feminine
- ☐ Tampons and sanitary pads.
- ☐ Period pain medication.
- ☐ Treatments for vaginal thrush and cystitis.
- ☐ Emergency contraception.

Any medications carried overseas should be accompanied by a covering letter from a doctor. This is also useful for needles and syringes. All your medications should be packed in a single container, labelled, and with a medical symbol displayed – a white cross on a green background is universally recognised. Protect your kit from extremes of temperature and damp.

TUMMY BUGS

Food

If you can't cook it, boil it or peel it, then forget it. It's better to miss a meal through caution than through illness. Eat food immediately once it's been cooked thoroughly; don't leave it to cool. Especially avoid raw seafood and unrefrigerated unpasteurised dairy products. Always clean your hands, and inspect cutlery and crockery. Eat only at restaurants with a good reputation, or where you can see the food being prepared in a hygienic manner.

Water

Use only reliably sourced bottled water for drinking, cleaning your teeth, washing wounds and washing food. Water boiled for one minute can be considered safe. On a longer trip, you might want to carry a proprietary water purifier. If bottled water isn't available, stick to cans or sealed bottles of local soda.

Ocean

Use your eyes and nose. What's being chucked into rivers, what's being flushed out of boats, what's being washed up? Are there rats on the beach at sunset? Be particularly wary when paddling out through river mouths and harbours.

MALARIA

Follow this three-point plan:

Avoid mosquitoes – It's the female mosquito that carries malaria, feeding between dusk and dawn. Limit your exposure during these times by avoiding rural areas and watercourses. Cover up by wearing full-length light-coloured clothing. Mosquitoes are attracted to powerful scents, so don't use strong perfume or body sprays. Regularly use mosquito repellent. Sleep in air-conditioned or screened rooms where you can, having first used a 'knock-down' spray to clear the air. Where there's no screening, a sleeping net is essential – check it for holes, and tuck it in well. Most effective is a net recently treated with Permethrin.

Take malaria tablets regularly – Which ones you take depends upon your medical history, your destination, duration of stay and your desire to avoid various side effects. Start your course before you go, then any undesirable side effects can be discussed with your doctor. You'll suffer from fewer side effects if you take your tablets with food and drink. If you forget a dose on the prescribed day, take it as soon as you remember, but don't take extra doses to make up. Always finish the course – if you don't, you may well come down with the disease. If the risk of malaria is very low, you're more likely to get sick from your tablets than malaria, so decide whether the medication is worth it.

Treat fevers immediately – Even taking the tablets diligently, you can still catch malaria. Be alert for fever, anything that takes your temperature above 37°C. Carry a digital thermometer. Treat any fever as malaria until proven otherwise – positive diagnosis is by a finger-prick blood test. Malaria can be completely cured if treated early, but left untreated for only *three days* it can prove fatal.

IF YOU GET SICK

A reliable doctor can be located using your medical insurance hotline. If you have no insurance, try at an upmarket hotel. Your embassy will usually be able to recommend a doctor. Until you can get to a reliable doctor, treat yourself. There are several ways to speed recovery:

- **Rest** – Stress interferes with the workings of the immune system.
- **Eat well** – The body needs the nutrients available in healthy foods to manufacture new tissues.
- **Hydrate** – Plenty of water helps flush out toxins and replace fluid lost in sweating.
- **Record** – Note the times and dates of any major symptoms.
- **Trust your body** – Give yourself a chance to heal before you take medication that might cause complicating side effects.

CUTS

Cuts are unlikely to heal on a surf trip; you'll be too keen to stay in the water for that. But don't ignore minor cuts as you might at home.

Preventing reef cuts from becoming sea ulcers is the big challenge; once established, tropical ulcers can be hard to cure. Infection delays healing, so prevent infection by touching the wound as little as possible. Clean cuts vigorously as soon as you can; a little pain early on can save you lots later. Irrigate the wound with sterile water or salt solution. If available, pour dilute hydrogen peroxide solution on the wound. If the wound has been contaminated with coral or marine slime, then it needs to be scrubbed. Using sharp scissors, cut away any obviously dead tissue.

Deep cuts or large abrasions will probably need further medical attention – again, the rule is to clean it and close it. Steri-strips are a handy way of pulling the edges of wounds together, and you might be well advised to carry a suture kit too. Head wounds can sometimes be closed by the simple method of tying strands of hair together. When closing a wound, make sure you don't leave an air space beneath the surface. For best healing, keep closed wounds dry and open wounds moist.

Monitor the wound for signs of infection. Antibiotics will likely be required if:

- Pain increases.
- Redness increases and spreads.
- There's smelly greenish discharge.
- The wound bleeds easily.
- You experience fever and increased pulse rate.

MARINE STINGS AND BITES

It's always best to seek local advice, as treatment will vary widely depending on the cause, and the causes are numerous – sea wasps, bluebottles, stonefish, fire coral, jellyfish, etc.

Never rub a wound with bare hands nor with sand, as it causes the stinging cells to discharge more poison. Adherent tentacles should be removed only with poured water, or by scraping with a knife or flat piece of wood. If the pain is very severe seek further medical advice. If breathing becomes compromised or level of consciousness is altered then urgent medical attention is needed – closely monitor the patient and be ready to administer CPR.

Sea urchin spines need to be dug out immediately after surfing, whilst your skin is still soft. Once your skin dries and hardens it can be very difficult to remove spines, but the alternative is having them work their way deeper and then fester. Sterilise the knife or needle over a flame.

FOOD POISONING

There are two types of food poisoning, and knowing which type you have helps you treat it. The key is working out how much time has elapsed between eating the suspect food and getting sick.

- If symptoms develop within 2–12 hours of eating dodgy food then you probably have the 'toxin' type of poisoning. This is the result of eating food contaminated for some time with germs that have released bacterial toxins as waste products. You'll experience little diarrhoea but a lot of vomiting, which is to be encouraged. Treatment is rest, hydration and wait for 12–24 hours. Vomiting out the poison is the best way to recover.
- If symptoms develop 12–24 hours or more after a suspect meal then your illness is probably a result of having ingested food contaminated with a few germs that have then multiplied inside your gut. 'Germ' poisoning will take longer to run its course and will involve more diarrhoea. Treatment is rest, and regular small amounts of fluid supplemented by electrolytic solutions. Eat starchy foods to encourage the 'good' bacteria in your bowel.

Note that fever with diarrhoea, or blood and/or mucous in the motions, indicates a serious intestinal infection and should be treated with antibiotics.

HEAT STRESS

The young, the slim and the physically fit are less prone to heat stress, so most travelling surfers should be lower risk. But don't be complacent: if it's hot enough, no one is immune.

It can take two weeks to fully adapt to a new climate. In the meantime, drink more, eat lightly with a little extra salt, avoid caffeine and alcohol, and cover up. Tiredness and profuse sweating due to the heat is known as 'heat exhaustion'; but if the sweating stops, body temperature rises and behaviour becomes erratic, this has progressed to the more serious 'heat stroke'. Cool the patient immediately and restrict activity; seek further medical attention.

HOME

Should you find yourself suffering from any of the following once you return home, then you need a post-travel check-up:

- Fevers.
- Persistent diarrhoea.
- Stomach pain.
- Dark urine.
- Skin rashes or lumps.
- Persistent cough.
- Headaches or joint pains.

LOCALISM

'LIKE KING CANUTE ORDERING THE TIDE TO STOP, THE HARD-CORE LOCALS OF YESTERDAY ARE BEING SWEPT INTO SUBMISSION BY A CONSTANT TIDE OF RECREATIONAL SURFERS SPREADING AROUND THE GLOBE.'
Glen Hening, surfing journalist, quoted in Nat Young's *Surf Rage*, 2000

Although not confined to locals, 'localism' describes any aggressive territorial behaviour aimed at deterring strangers from surfing a particular spot.

It has been suggested that the heyday of violent locals was in the 1980s and that it has since gradually abated; there are now so many more surfers that it's almost impossible to tell who supposedly *belongs* to a break and who doesn't. It's simply too much work and hassle, too difficult for the old-time enforcers to keep enforcing. If this seems to be the case at your destination, it still doesn't mean you can rock up anywhere and act like a kook or a prima donna. More than likely the reality still is that if you travel, you're a target.

Surfing is an individual elitist sport. You surf alone on the wave and there's no limit to how many waves you can catch. This often translates into no limit to how many you want, then 'have a right to', then 'deserve'. Almost anywhere you surf you'll find someone who thinks he has more right to surf at that spot than you do. This can happen 10,000 miles from home or 200 yards from your door. Whatever the reason, the outcome is pretty much the same: you won't get your share of waves.

There are various strategies for dealing with localism, and none of them involve appealing to a referee. The lack of regulations may be what makes surfing so liberating, but it also makes things difficult when you need an umpire and a few cast-iron rules to abide by. Violently aggressive surfers *have* been arrested and sentenced to fines and exclusion orders, but this is after the fact; police generally don't like to get their feet wet.

How you respond might depend on increments in the level of intimidation:

■ **Eyeball.** ■ **Verbal.** ■ **Physical.**

'THE RULES OF SURFING ARE COMPLEX AND FLUID. THEY CHANGE TO SUIT THE AMOUNT OF TIME A SURFER HAS SPENT AT A SURF SPOT, AND HOW WELL HE SURFS, THUS CONFUSING THE COCKLES OUT OF THE BEGINNER AND PUTTING THEM IN A POSITION THEY HAVE NO IDEA HOW TO GET OUT OF AND CAUSING FLASHES OF TEMPERS FROM SURFERS WHO EXPECT ORDER AT THEIR BREAK.'
Derek Reilly, surfer, quoted in Nat Young's *Surf Rage*, 2000

EYEBALL

Eyeball intimidation is usually just a demand for a certain level of respect to which locals somehow feel they're entitled. If you're getting mean glares, or 'stink-eye' in the car park, then you should assess whether the level of intimidation will remain low or is likely to escalate. Surf passively and don't impose yourself on the break until you feel you've been accepted.

VERBAL INTIMIDATION

If you're repeatedly yelled at, take a moment to consider whether you're at fault. Have you been getting in everyone's way? Have you been taking more than your fair share of waves? Have you been acting like a loud and obnoxious tourist? Even if you feel you're blameless, the least confrontational response to adopt is to paddle away from the instigator and surf somewhere else; that might mean 50 yards down the line or it might mean another beach entirely. It's not your job to teach anyone a lesson, and the 'local' hasn't gone surfing to be given one. The only problem with this strategy is that his aggressive behaviour tends to be reinforced by what he perceives as 'successful' intimidation.

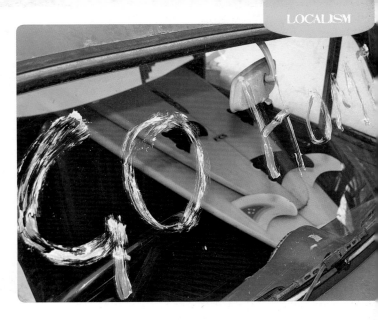

> **'LOCALISM IS A TOXIC SPILL THAT HAS CONTAMINATED A LOT OF SURF SPOTS, AND SOMETIMES YOU HAVE TO HELP IN THE CLEAN-UP.'**
> **Glen Hening,** surfing journalist, quoted in Nat Young's *Surf Rage*, 2000

> **'I HAVE PERSONALLY THROWN ROCKS, STOLEN BOARDS OFF UNKNOWN CARS, WAXED WINDOWS AND LET AIR OUT OF THE TYRES OF COUNTLESS UNLUCKY STRANGERS, ALL BEFORE I WAS 16 YEARS OLD.'**
> **John Philbin,** a contrite local from Palos Verdes, California

If you feel you *should* be the one to teach him a lesson, think carefully about the implications. You could try to reason with him, or you could square up to him, but you don't know the outcome of either of these scenarios. Really, how likely is it you'll achieve your optimal result – shutting him up and surfing wherever the heck you want? You must be very sure of your reasoning skills and your physical capacity to defend yourself if the confrontation escalates.

Is there anything to be said for localism? Can you argue that the old enforcers were some of the most effective 'monkey-wrench environmentalists', keeping a spot 'from being overrun and trashed by the devouring herd', as Steve Barilotti puts it? That's not much of an argument if you're one of the herd, as we all really are. Treat other surfers the way you'd like to be treated at an unfamiliar location.

PHYSICAL INTIMIDATION

Violence is unacceptable. If someone assaults you in or out of the water, defend yourself, obtain willing witnesses, then alert the authorities. Provide as much detail about the incident and perpetrator as possible. This kind of intimidation has gone on for decades at both crowded beaches and secret spots all around the world, and was long considered all part of the rough and tumble of surfing. But times have changed. In 1981 a case was heard in California concerning a deliberate spearing (when one surfer kicks his board out at another). The perpetrator was found guilty of assault with a deadly weapon. If you have no faith in the

rule of law where you're surfing, then, before somebody gets seriously injured, be the bigger person and withdraw from the scene to surf another day.

It is not impossible to imagine that the rule of law might eventually come to some of the more crowded spots. The idea of an aquatic force of 'surf cops' empowered to give warnings and even issue tickets was seriously outlined to a prominent newspaper by a State Representative from Australia's Gold Coast in 2004. Again, the idea was eventually dismissed as unworkable. Unworkable, but no longer unthinkable: that it itself is a sign of the times.

CALIFORNIA OPEN WAVES ACT

In 1998 San Diego's lifeguard chief Chris Brewster proposed legislation to be known as the California Open Waves Act. The wording stipulated that the coastline and waves were 'owned by no person and available to equal use by all' and that 'no person, regardless of residence, lineage, social status or other reason may lawfully claim the right to a wave, waves or wave break area.' Strong factions opposing the regulation of any aspect of surfing meant that the legislation was never proceeded. The lack of support led a disappointed Brewster to suggest that 'some who do not openly practise localism nevertheless perceive a benefit from its existence. Namely, there is less congestion at their local spot.'

> **'RESPECT IS ONE OF THE MOST OVER-USED WORDS IN THE ENGLISH LANGUAGE. IT USUALLY MEANS ONE PERSON OR GROUP IMPOSING A DUBIOUS SET OF STANDARDS ON SOMEONE ELSE, USUALLY AT THEIR EXPENSE. I DON'T GO SURFING TO SHOW RESPECT TO ANYONE. I GO OUT TO ENJOY MYSELF, AND AM PREPARED TO DO IT WHILE CAUSING MY FELLOW SURFERS THE LEAST AMOUNT OF GRIEF.'**
> **Fred Pawle,** surfer, quoted in Nat Young's *Surf Rage*, 2000

ETHICS OF SURF TRAVEL

Thanks largely to the surf media, it's easy to regard exotic surf travel as a right. Much has been written about the fantastic kit you can buy to take abroad with you, but be aware that if you take a conspicuously consumerist lifestyle to a region marked by poverty, injustice and chronic lack of opportunity then you're heading for trouble. Not everyone aspires to the lifestyle you might be flaunting, and attempts to export it may be resented. Surfing may be naturally conspicuous, visual, and exuberant, but you need to travel with modesty, grace and cultural sensitivity.

Surfers like to think of themselves as basically non-exploitative, but at the same time they often take a perverse pride in remaining coolly indifferent to problems of politics, race and class. But travelling without awareness of the potential impact of the western surfing lifestyle is little more than casual imperialism.

Are you looking for nothing other than cheap beer, good waves and submissive locals? Do you think that fun for dollars is a simple straightforward trade? Your dollars *might* be part of a wave of foreign influence drowning local culture. Whether it's the tall tales of a backpacker in a pub drawing maps on beer mats, or a 60ft catamaran with camera crew and pros on board all paid for by the industry, surfers are often the advance scouts of development. It's by no means inevitable, but 'development' too often means environmental degradation, more rubbish, water pollution, resource depletion and social fragmentation.

'HOW DO WE BALANCE THE FREEDOM OF SURFING WITH LONG-TERM PRESERVATION OF THE REAL VALUES THAT WE'RE ALL AFTER, THAT INCLUDE OTHER PEOPLE TOO?'
Pierce Flynn, Surfrider Foundation former executive director

← **What impact will your presence have on the local culture?**

↑ **Scoring empty waves is one thing; burying your head in the sand is another.**

→ Exclusive
rights to
waves are
great – if you
are on the
right side of
the fence.

Go the extra mile, and get the extra rewards.

Steve Barilotti, surfing journalist, from *Surfer* magazine

What might 'ethical surf tourism' look like? What does the host culture get in return for providing an aquatic playground for rich Westerners? There are many documented cases of what sounds like crass exploitation. Travellers at some privatised breaks are happy to pay exorbitant fees to surf while local workers are paid a pittance to serve. But equally, there are cases where, in exchange for exclusive rights to an island or a particular reef, the surf tourism industry has guaranteed local villages valuable regular income and steady jobs. The results can be improved sanitation, health and dental care, and provision of electricity, raising entire communities out of grinding poverty.

The arguments in favour of the surf tourism industry (STI) are that it promotes awareness of an area, raising profiles and bringing in dollars. It also contributes to the funding of airports, infrastructure and clinics, drinking water – all worthy causes. The counter-argument centres on the issue of an implicit entry fee – the feeling that if you can't bring dollars, you're not worth having.

Find out what you can about specific surf tourism enterprises. The deepest controversy concerns the overall trend to 'exclusive access' and privatisation, often marked by heavy-handed protectionism.

Do you want to be part of this evolution to privatisation and the protection of inequality? Think about the wider, long-term implications of the type of surf trip you embark on. If you believe that the Surf Tourism Industry isn't doing enough to foster social benefits in the area you've chosen to visit, and if you have a social conscience or a spirit of discovery, travel and surf independently. If you're convinced that a steady, controlled influx of surfers in well-run camps is bringing a wealth of welcome benefits directly or indirectly to the locals, then get packing and have a great time!

'IT DAWNED ON ME HOW MUCH MORE FUN THIS WAS: SURFING WITH A MATE, YELLING AND HOOTING IN THE SURF, NO ONE AROUND FOR MILES AND GOOD ENOUGH WAVES COMING THROUGH AMONGST THE MUCK TO MAKE IT WELL WORTHWHILE. AND ALL ON OUR TERMS: WE DIDN'T BUY IT, WE DIDN'T ROPE IT OFF AND STOP ANYONE ELSE COMING – WE JUST USED OUR KNOWLEDGE OF THE COAST AND THE WEATHER AND HUNTED OUT A CHUNK OF REEF FOR OURSELVES AND GOT LUCKY.'
Mike Frood, surfer, quoted in Nat Young's *Surf Rage*, 2000

HAVING A SAY

Surfing may be an individualist sport, but surfers have been organising since the Outrigger Club was formed in Hawaii to protect access to the waves at Waikiki in the early 20th century. If you feel strongly about *any* issues concerned with the surfing world – environmental, political, legal or social – there are now powerful and influential surfer-based organisations that can represent you and help you project your opinions and values at local and international levels:

SURFERS AGAINST SEWERAGE

2 Rural Workshops
Wheal Kitty
St Agnes
Cornwall
TR5 0RD
United Kingdom
Tel 01872 553001
Email info@sas.org.uk
Website www.sas.org.uk

SURFRIDER FOUNDATION EUROPE

79 bis rue d'Espagne
64200 Biarritz
France
Tel (+33) 05 59 23 54 99
Website www.surfrider-europe.org

SURFRIDER FOUNDATION USA

122 S. EL Camino Real No67
San Clemente
California 92672
USA
Tel (+001) 949 492 8170
Website www.surfrider.org

SURF AID INTERNATIONAL

Website www.surfaidinternational.org

Surf Aid was started by NZ MD Dave Jenkins to help people like the Mentawai islanders – half of whom suffer from malaria, and who as infants have only a 50/50 chance of reaching their fifth birthday. 'We believe that everyone who partakes in the surfing culture, be it from reading, writing or advertising in a magazine, watching or producing a video or wearing a label, has a role to play in helping these people.'

FOR AN ORGANISATION DEVOTED TO GATHERING THE BEST MINDS OF SURFING FOR GOOD CAUSES VISIT:

www.groundswellsociety.org

⬇ A SurfAid group forum. www.surfaidinternational.org

'SURFERS' LIFESTYLES MANIFEST IN DISTINCTIVE TASTES, AESTHETIC AND ETHICAL DISPOSITIONS, ARGOT, DRESS, AND HUMOUR, ALL OF WHICH SEPARATE SURFERS FROM NON-SURFERS.'

Douglas Booth, Australian academic

APPENDICES

Is surfing a sport or a lifestyle? Well, there are no rules, no boundaries. You can ride groundswell, windswell, clean waves, junk waves, bore waves, standing waves, artificial waves. You can ride them on a shortboard, a longboard, wakeboard, kiteboard, ironing board, or no board at all. Research has shown that even skilful surfers spend only 8% of a session actually up and riding. That seems to answer the question: surfing is 92% lifestyle. So read on...

SURF STYLES

ave riding takes many forms, all have their own advocates and all are entirely legitimate. All come from the simple realisation that it's fun to catch waves and ride them to shore. What you ride them on is purely a matter of personal choice, and the choice is ever expanding. Some styles of surfing have been enabled only by advances in technology, some rekindled by nostalgia.

The focus of this manual has been on shortboarding, but does it matter what you ride? Pay attention to what other wave-riders are using and, if it looks like they're having fun, find a way to have a go. As a surfer, you'll find that many of the skills are readily transferable, although to really master them some styles require a manual of their own.

LONGBOARDS

What do you do when the waves at your local spot are chronically slow and gutless; or you want an extra edge in paddling for crowded waves; or limited flexibility means you can only slowly clamber to your feet? You pull out a longboard.

As the direct descendant of the Hawaiian *olo* boards, modern longboarding often lays claim to be the authentic surf experience. The greatest advantage of longboards is the power latent in their buoyancy; it makes for a graceful surfing style. Sliding through long, drawn-out manoeuvres has a certain undeniable aesthetic appeal. Longboarding

teaches you good form; manoeuvres have to be executed properly or they won't happen at all – the elements of a turn have to be spot on because the board won't respond to anything less.

But why turn anyway? Longboards have the momentum to glide gracefully through dead spots on a wave where a shortboarder would need to throw himself into a frenzy of agonised twitching and bouncing to generate adequate speed. Of course, you can turn hard if you want to: extra rocker and curve in the plan shape combined with modern lightweight construction can make a contemporary longboard

⬆⬇ **Even a grommet can throw around a modern longboard.**

capable of heavy back-foot manoeuvres as well as enabling some nifty footwork up and down the board. For many surfers this is the best of both worlds.

Many longboarders take pride in differentiating themselves from shortboarders. Robert Wingnut Weaver – star of *Endless Summer II* – thinks the styles should be distinct: 'I have a very harsh opinion of "progressive" longboarding. I just feel that longboards and shortboards should be surfed differently. You can struggle through the manoeuvres but that's what shortboards are for. I'm not nostalgic, I just believe in the music. Shortboards are rock'n'roll; longboards are classical. That's it.'

STAND-UP PADDLEBOARDS (SUPS)

Have you tried a longboard and are still struggling to get waves? Then add more foam and a paddle. The ideal antidote to flat spells, modern SUPs have gained a following amongst surfers who like a thorough workout in small waves and don't mind hostile glares and the occasional shout of ridicule. Stand-up paddleboarding gives you strong abs and a thick skin.

You can get away with thinner neoprene, though – once you acquire the basic balance skills you spend the session clear of the water, and dry, which is a great bonus in the winter. Standing up, you can spot the set waves coming long before those less evolved surfers hunkered down in the water; and you have the paddling speed necessary to quickly get into position almost anywhere in the line-up.

One thing to consider is the extra foam between you and the wave. This supplies less feedback when riding, but a lot more weight dragging you around at the end of your leash during a wipeout. In a crowded line-up, the unpopularity of learners on SUPs is due partly to the hazard their bulk presents to other surfers. But once you have the knack you'll catch an awful lot of waves, and can rapidly progress to a shorter SUP that'll be far more manoeuvrable.

TOWING IN

Tow-surfing began as a bit of a lark, wake-surfing behind rigid-hulled inflatable boats (RIBs). Once jetskis (motorised personal water craft – MPWC) became widely available, surfers soon realised this combination could unlock the door to what used to be revered as the 'Unridden Realm' – huge waves that were potentially rideable but simply couldn't be caught.

When you paddle down the face you need to reach a speed that'll unstick your board from the surface friction as the wave passes beneath. You need to do this before you get pitched over the falls. Bigger waves move faster, and the displacement of air up the onrushing face also presents a substantial opposing force. You can add length of hull and buoyancy to increase paddling speed, and that works up to a point, that point being when the board is so thick and long that it becomes unmanageable on the face.

Matching the speed of the swell by mechanical means, and using a MPWC to whip the rider on to the face of a building wave, means

If fear doesn't put you off, what might? The anti-MPWC lobby cite the noise, the smell, the cost, and the disruption to marine wildlife. A reverence for the heritage of surfing and the belief that paddling into a wave is half the skill is what keeps some people from accepting tow-surfing. But it's a new and exciting aspect of the surf experience, providing an unmatched visual spectacle.

The early years of tow-in surfing prompted a call to bar MPWCs from Mavericks: California's only world-class big wave venue happens to be part of a US National Marine Sanctuary. To the proposers of the ban, 'permitting a MPWC operation in a nature sanctuary is like permitting a motorcycle gang to overrun a playground.' (Mark Renneker). Tow-in surfers argue that the new four-stroke machines are far less polluting, and subsequent environmental damage is negligible compared with other leisure craft using the area.

BODYBOARDING

There are other waves that are, practically speaking, off-limits to most stand-up surfers. Slabs, wedges and super-sucky shore breaks are standard fare to the sponger. Also disparagingly referred to as lids, speed bumps, shark biscuits, and bath mats, no form of surfing started life in such ignominy only to garner such respect in recent times.

The modern bodyboard was developed in the late-1970s almost as a plaything to provide fun in unchallenging summer conditions. It was conceived as little more than a replacement for the old wooden belly-boards. The design brief catered for those unable or unwilling to scramble to their feet on a surfboard. Closed-cell polyethylene foam construction gave reassuring buoyancy, flexibility and safety.

Apart from tweaks in hull design, rail and tail profiles, the templates of bodyboards have changed little; what limited the performance and longevity of early boards was excess flexibility, and that issue has been addressed by a number of innovations. A range of stringer designs – tubular, multiple or structural foam beams – now provide stiffness without eliminating flex entirely.

that half the battle is won. Behind a MPWC the board can actually lose length and buoyancy such that monster waves of 60ft (18m) are being ridden using boards that are less than 6ft (1.8m) in length. The boards are so small that extra weight has to be added in order to get them down the face.

It's a sport not to be trifled with. You're part of a two-man team and have to be well-drilled enough as a unit to have absolute faith in your partner and in your machine.

You can catch a wave so early that it's not much more than a bump in the ocean, but once it rears over the ledge then you're committed, and the consequences can be very serious indeed. In a wipeout, a buoyancy vest helps you bob back to the surface (restriction is not an issue because you have no need to paddle in) but your tow partner needs to be able to come and get you out of the impact zone. Wearing a buoyancy aid, you won't be able to paddle yourself out of trouble on a short heavy board.

Differing flex properties (for heavier riders, for hollow waves, for different temperatures) are also achieved through material composition. PE (polyethylene) still makes up the core, but now a skin of high-density material known as Surlyn is bonded to the bottom; good quality skins provide projection and recoil when laminated in a process that allows tension to be built into the board. The result is a finely tuned rocker with inherent 'spring', flex that's designed to contour to your body.

All these technical advances enable the boundaries of performance to be pushed further and further. Full-rail turns, spins, massive airs, super-steep drops, deep barrels – all are on tap for the modern booger.

Now, lying down to surf is no longer to be sneered at. Bodyboarders will take on waves that would be death to a stand-up surfer. And they can more easily travel to find them, too. Bodyboarders are the pioneers of modern surfing.

BELLYBOARDING

This is perhaps the original surfing experience. A slim plywood board reminiscent of the *paipo* boards of the Hawaiians, with a slight kick up on the nose, enables you to ride until your costume is filling with sand. You'll never get the g-forces associated with a cranking turn on a shortboard, but a neat sense of speed is gained simply by being so low and close to the water. Pushing off the bottom in waist-

⬇ **Kitesurfing, or kiteboarding, demands expert tuition before you start and plenty of attention to safety.**

deep water is how the traditionalists catch waves, but add a pair of flippers and you can head out the back to catch some green ones. Watch out for digging the back of the board into your gut if you pearl; other than that it's safe, cheap, easy and great fun, whatever the conditions.

BODY SURFING

If your idea of tuning into the ocean is to minimise the amount of gear you use, or get rid of it completely, then body surf. With just a pair of flippers to help you get into the wave early, you can plane on your chest and hand, rolling on to your side when you want more bite in the face of the wave. Flexing your body adjusts your natural rocker to increase or lose speed. Use a hand-gun when you want even more planing speed. It's not standing up, but it *is* pure surfing.

KITESURFING

No more paddling out. No more staying out of the water when the wind is howling onshore. No more sitting freezing between sets. It sounds great, but the forces involved in harnessing the wind with a kite up to 16m (52ft) square are enormous, so safety is paramount.

There's a raft of important safety measures to master before you can even go near the water. Lessons are absolutely vital; it isn't really a sport that you can just pick up ad hoc.

One of the benefits of coming to kiteboarding from a surfing background is that once you've mastered the art of riding toe-in, you can pick up any of your old shortboards and get carving.

JET-SURFING

Invented, naturally enough, in California, the jet-board is touted by a few visionaries as the future of surfing. Designed to reach offshore 'bombies', to match the speed of giant waves, to eliminate the need to find a tow partner, the jet-board also allows the (wealthy) owner to eliminate even the need to check the weather – he can crank out moves when there are no waves at all.

Standing sideways and holding a throttle in your forward hand at the end of a leash, you lean over to turn on the rail just like a real surfboard, but there the similarity ends. Currently the engine makes the jet-board bulky and heavy, and seemingly unlikely ever to replace the refined modern shortboard; but it's found a niche with those who don't wish to be weather-dependent.

If you cannot deal with crowds on optimum surf days and would rather do lonely aqua-donuts in a gravel pit somewhere inland, the jet-board could be for you.

In the 1950s the movies of Bud Browne documented, and helped spread, the first boom in contemporary surf culture. Ever since, surf movies and the advancement of surfing have gone hand in hand. Many movies have achieved classic status because, for whatever reason, they help to define their era:

1953 **Hawaiian Surf Movie** by Bud Browne. The original: believed to be the first genuine surf movie.

1958 **Slippery When Wet** (also known as *Barefoot Adventure*) by Bruce Brown. The first 'corporate' movie backed by Velzy, the largest board manufacturer of the time. It created the template of vagabond surfers goofing around in exotic locations. Set to an original jazz soundtrack by Bud Shank.

1959 **Gidget** directed by Paul Wendkos. A tame Hollywood treatment, billed as an exposure of the underground subculture of dangerously rebellious youth. For all its laughable corniness (it featured surfer Mickey Muñoz in a wig and bikini, doubling for Sandra Dee) it had an almost incalculable mainstream impact.

1959 **Surf Fever** by John Severson. Severson's first movie, notable if only because it provided many of the stills that would go to comprise the pages of the first ever *Surfer Magazine* in 1960.

1960 **Surf Trek to Hawaii** by Bob Evans. Filmed in Hawaii by Australian surf entrepreneur Evans, it was the first movie to star an Australian surfer: Bernard 'Midget' Farrelly. Evans followed it up with *The Midget Goes Hawaiian*.

1964 **Endless Summer** by Bruce Brown. Gaining a 35mm release to major acclaim, the film made Brown enough money to retire. A perennially popular travelogue, it features smartly dressed men with boards under their arms jetting around the globe, patronising the locals and looking for perfect waves. Almost impossibly exotic and hugely influential, it showed for three years and inspired a whole generation of surfers. 'Anyone who can't see the beauty and thrill of it hasn't got eyes' declared the *New York Post*.

1964 **Muscle Beach Party** by William Asher. Mainstream a go-go! Featuring the non-existent surfing talents of Frankie Avalon and Annette Funicello. So corny now that it's actually quite cool, and has an undeniably infectious energy.

1964 **Ride the Wild Surf** by Don Taylor. Another Hollywood effort: woeful script and leaden acting, with little of interest other than kitsch value and stunts performed by some top Californian surfers.

1968 **The Innermost Limits of Pure Fun** by George Greenough. Greenough was the Californian transplant to Australia whose maverick wizardry embodied the sense of limitless invention of the new era. He was the first to build a water-housing for his cameras and get to the heart of where it was all happening – slow motion deep in the tube at Lennox Head. It's something of a cosmic experience, with an acid-heavy original soundtrack from Californian groovers The Farm.

1968 **The Hot Generation** by Paul Witzig. With a great contemporary soundtrack, Witzig captures the Honolua sessions that effectively announced the end of the longboard hotdogging era.

1969 **Evolution** by Paul Witzig. Featuring the futuristic surfing of Wayne Lynch, Witzig was again ahead of the game by being the first director to forgo the somewhat dated convention of using a narrator.

1969 **Pacific Vibrations** by John Severson. Closing the '60s, Severson lets his creativity splurge all over the movie. A hard-hitting environmental warning combined with indulgent artistic excess, this sums up the late '60s surf scene better than any other document. Severson says it's 'a film to remind you of your roots…A witness to the truth.'

1972 **Morning of the Earth** by Alby Falzon. Hot surfing with a country-soul ethos. Film-making of the highest quality with environmental concerns at the forefront; Fazon really captures the mood of the moment. A best-selling album soundtrack, too.

1972 **Five Summer Stories** by MacGillivray-Freeman. An epic surf tale that lays the emphasis on the brotherhood of surfing. Another great soundtrack.

1973 **Crystal Voyager** by Alby Falzon and David Elfick. This fascinating and evocative profile of George Greenough captures his unique style of being both hands-on and spaced-out. The final montage features endlessly hypnotic tube sequences soundtracked by Pink Floyd.

1974 **The Forgotten Island of Santosha** by Larry Yates. Exploring an unnamed tropical wave paradise, the film is a thinly veiled nostalgic trip bidding a final farewell to the lost innocence of the Californian '60s.

1975 **Tubular Swells** by Dick Hoole and Jack McCoy. Hot Australian and Hawaiian surfing, but also one of the first films to showcase spectacular secret spots in Bali. The stand-out sequence is the opening, soundtracked by Mike Oldfield's *Tubular Bells*.

1978 **Free Ride** by Bill Delaney. The film that lent its name to the radical generation invading the Hawaiian North Shore in the mid-'70s. It captures one of the best winters for swell in years and features the groundbreaking surfing of Southern-Hemisphere greats Shaun Tomson, Rabbit Bartholomew and Mark Richards. A great soundtrack featured genuinely stirring original music by Pablo Cruise. The film's wide distribution ensured that it was hugely influential.

1978 **Big Wednesday** by John Milius. The introduction of serious Hollywood money to surfing. Setting out to try to capture the essence of surfing as it moved from free and easy 1960s California to the nemesis that was Vietnam, Milius's brave attempt to get it all down is riddled with clichés. It's enormous fun to watch and has become the surfer's own *Rocky Horror Show*, filled with classic dialogue.

1981 **Storm Riders** by Dick Hoole and Jack McCoy. A great introduction to the power-surfing of the '80s, soundtracked by some of Australia's best bands of the time.

1990 **Surfers: The Movie** by Bill Delaney. A movie conceived to 'bring back the phenomenon of the surf film', it was very much welcomed by the media.

1996 **Litmus** by Andrew Kidman. Mellow, arty, grassroots-style nostalgia that reintroduced soul-surfing to the abrasive generation.

1997 **Endless Summer II** by Bruce Brown. Out of retirement, Brown put everyone in the mix – shortboarders and longboarders – to great effect.

2001 **Shelter** by Taylor Steele and Chris Malloy. The third and best part of the Moonshine Experiment series (*Thicker Than Water* and *September Sessions* being the earlier instalments). The use of 16mm film and a mellow soundtrack helps contrive an atmosphere of highly polished professional soul.

THE 1980s

After the golden era of the '70s, auditorium-filling surf films died a death as watch-at-home videos took over the market. As the pro scene got under way, backed in earnest by surf industry mega-bucks, the market became saturated by high-budget surf-corporation movies, usually little more than lengthy branding exercises.

2001 **Momentum Under the Influence** by Matt Beauchesne. Momentum lent its name to the first generation of pro surfers to blend the new school aerial attack with old school power surfing.

2002 **Dogtown and Z-Boys** by Stacy Peralta. A fascinating documentary about the birth of the new-school skaters in 1970s Southern California, a movement that fed into the shortboard revolution. *Dogtown* raised the bar in terms of thoughtful research and high production values.

2004 **Second Thoughts** by Timmy Turner. A tale of 21st-century feral surfers in Indonesia. They may come across as guys who have no food and little sense, but they do have professional camera gear and great waves and know exactly how to put them together.

2004 **Riding Giants** by Stacy Peralta. Another supremely well researched and presented documentary, this time about conquering the 'unridden realm' and the evolution of tow-surfing. Mind-blowing footage.

2003 **Billabong Odyssey** by Philip Boston. Notable mainly for its stunning opening sequence, essentially this is a long corporate advertisement masquerading as a genuine movie on general release.

2004 **Hungarian Surf Trip** by D. Profundo. Referencing the manufactured mystique of Hungarian-born Miki Dora, this is a scathing and trenchant critique of the casual imperialism of travelling Western surfers, and of the imposition of questionable cultural values by the globalising surf industry. The first surf film to be bitterly critical of the excesses of its own culture, it was consequently panned by the critics and buried by the distributors.

2006 **Sipping Jetstreams** by Taylor Steele. Steele hooks up with photographer Dustin Humphreys to produce a stunning-looking travelogue. The image and musical montages are undoubtedly beautiful but tend to the clichéd, and the surfing is often unexceptional.

2008 **Stranger Than Fiction** by Taylor Steele. This is more like it – explosive, progressive surfing and a fresher ironic approach after the art excesses of *Sipping Jetstreams*.

2009 **Waveriders** by Joel Conroy. Bringing into timely focus the new big-wave frontier of Ireland; rich in historical detail.

2012 **A Deeper Blue** by Jack McCoy. A lovingly crafted historical surf documentary by one of the old masters of surf movie-making, with the emphasis on environmental impact.

Ahrens, Chris. *The Surfer's Travel Guide: A Handbook to Surf Paradise* (Chubasco, 1995). A handy guide for your first venture overseas.

Barrett, Bradley Wayne. *Grannis: Surfing's Golden Age, 1960–1969* (Journal Concepts, Inc, 1998). Iconic images by one of the greats of early surf photography.

Blackburn, Mark A. *Surf's Up: Collecting the Longboard Era* (Schiffer, 2007). Captures all the style, grace and exoticism of the surfing in the '50s and '60s. A feast for nostalgia buffs.

Brown, David, and Ford, Nick. *Surfing and Social Theory: Experience, Embodiment and Narrative of the Dream Glide* (Routledge, 2006). An academic inquiry into the contemporary social and cultural meaning of surfing. Difficult, but rewarding.

Butt, Tony, and Russell, Paul. *Surf Science* (Alison Hodge, 2002). Written by surfers for surfers, this tells you all you need to know about meteorology, bathymetry and wave theory in an accessible and vivid style.

Capp, Fiona. *That Oceanic Feeling: A Surfing Odyssey* (Aurum, 2004). Reflects the uncertainty of a female writer delving into the surfing world, but does unearth some very interesting characters along the way.

Carroll, Nick (ed). *The Next Wave: A Survey of World Surfing* (Queen Anne Press, 1991). A fun neon overview from the great day-glo 1980s.

Coleman, Stuart Holmes. *Eddie Would Go: The Story of Eddie Aikau, Hawaiian Hero* (Mindraising Press, 2002). Coleman finds a way into the fascinating social and cultural intrigue that surrounds one of surfing's great tragedies.

Diamond, Paul (ed). *Surfing's Great Misadventures* (Casagrande, 2006). A patchy but fun collection of tall tales and hair-raising moments.

Doyle, Mike. *Morning Glass* (Manzanita, 1993). Doyle was at the forefront of so many of surfing's pivotal moments that this is essential reading for those interested in a personal view of the development of surfing from the 1950s onwards.

Duane, Daniel. *Caught Inside: A Surfer's Year on the California Coast* (North Point Press, 1996). A well-written, occasionally profound, account of an inland journalist whole-heartedly adopting the surfing lifestyle.

Finney, Ben, and Houston, James. *Surfing: A History of the Ancient Hawaiian Sport* (Pomegranate Artbooks, 1996). Recommended reading for those looking for a definitive history.

Fitzjohns, Ollie, et al. *The Stormrider Guide to Europe* (Low Pressure, 1992). More than just a travel guide, full of cultural and historical goodies too. Invaluable.

—— *The Stormrider Guide to the World* (Low Pressure, 1992). The sheer scope of the book limits the amount of finer detail, but this is a great book for flicking through, dreaming, then planning a surf trip.

Griggs, Matt. *Surfers* (Harpersports, 2007). Personal profiles of unique and inspiring surf characters.

Heller, Peter. *Kook: What Surfing Taught Me About Love, Life, and Catching the Perfect Wave* (Free Press, 2010). Like it's title, a little long-winded, but a mostly thoughtful and entertaining account of learning to surf.

Jarvis, Craig. *The Bluffer's Guide to Surfing* (Oval, 2008). This is a refreshingly concise and irreverent antidote to the portentous tone of too many of the coffee-table surf books.

Kampion, Drew. *Stoked: A History of Surf Culture* (General Publishing, 1997). In-depth, insightful and comprehensive.

—— *The Way of the Surfer* (Abrams Inc, 2003). Catering to the millennial explosion of mainstream interest in surfing, this is short on history but long on characters and lifestyles.

—— *Waves: From Surfing to Tsunami* (Gibbs Smith, 2005). A beautiful portfolio of the how, what and why of waves, mixing science with storytelling.

Kotler, Steven. *West of Jesus: Surfing, Science and the Origins of Belief* (Bloomsbury, 2006). An interesting book for those drawn to explore deeper philosophical aspects of committing to a life of riding waves.

Lopez, Gerry. *Surf Is Where You Find It* (Patagonia, 2008). Provides an insight into how Lopez has always seemed able to hover somewhere just above the circus that is professional surfing.

Mansfield, Roger. *The Surfing Tribe: A History of Surfing in Britain* (Orca, 2010). Painstakingly researched, and put together with a real sense of place. Lavishly illustrated too.

Marcus, Ben. *Extreme Surf* (Pavilion, 2008). Surfers constantly pushing the limits of what's possible and what's sensible, all presented in a fluid written style.

Motil, Guy. *Surfboards* (Globe Pequod Press, 2007). A lavish homage to the people who design, manufacture, ride and just appreciate the craft. Beautifully illustrated.

Muñoz, Mickey. *No Bad Waves – Talking Story With Mickey Muñoz* (Patagonia, 2011). Entertaining and fascinating tales from one of California surfing's great originals.

Noll, Greg, and Gabbard, Andrea. *Da Bull: Life Over the Edge* (North Atlantic Books, 1989). Outrageous, heartfelt tales of pioneer surfing told by one of the sport's biggest and most articulate characters.

Phillips, Jim. *Surf, Skate and Rock Art of Jim Phillips* (Schiffer, 2004). A mind-blowing and iconic collection of art from the mighty pen of Phillips, with an interesting narrative on how, thankfully, he was eventually able to make his art pay.

Power, Chris (ed). *Shooting The Curl* (Orca, 2009). Absolutely stunning images from some of the best surf photographers in the business.

Rensin, David. *All For a Few Perfect Waves* (Yellow Jersey Press, 2008). An insightful biography of Miki Dora, one of the most complex and enigmatic surfers of the last few generations. Like the character himself, the book is a little overblown.

Schiffer, Nancy. *Surfing* (Schiffer, 1998). A comprehensive collection of gorgeous surf design and imagery.

Walding, Murray. *Surf-o-rama: Treasures of Australian Surfing* (Miegunyah Press, 2008). A useful history of Australian surfing, with gorgeous illustrations of hundreds of collectable goodies.

Warshaw, Matt. *Above the Roar: 50 Surfer Interviews* (Waterhouse, 1997). This intriguing set of interviews reveals just what makes a professional surfer tick.

—— *Mavericks: The Story of Big-Wave Surfing* (Chronicle Books, 2000). Read this if you want to get either stoked or scared.

—— *The Encyclopedia of Surfing* (Harcourt, 2005). Incredibly well researched and thorough; all you could ever need to know.

—— *History of Surfing* (Chronicle Books, 2010). At 500 pages and a quarter of a million words, this is big, comprehensive and definitive.

Young, Nat. *The History of Surfing* (Palm Beach Press, 1983). Comprehensive and colourful overview of surf history by someone who should know: he was at the centre of a lot of it.

—— *Surf Rage* (Nymboida Press, 2000). A selection of thoughtful musings on the scourge of localism, collected by Young after he was badly beaten at his local beach by a bitter rival.

GLOSSARY

This is intended as an explanation of terms you'll come across in the surfing world. Some are cultural, some are technical. Remember that this is for reference and isn't a guide: you certainly don't have to speak like this in order to fit in, but it's handy at least to have a reference point.

A-frame Perfect triangular peak of a breaking wave, letting you surf either left or right.

Aerial Any manoeuvre above the surface of the wave.

Air drop An extremely steep take-off.

Alaia Wooden board from ancient Polynesia.

ASP Association of Surf Professionals, the current organising body of the world circuit.

Backhand Surfing with your back to the wave.

Backing off Waves that shape up to break but then don't quite manage it.

Backdoor To take off behind the peak.

Bail To abandon your board either in the face of an incoming wall of white water, or on a misjudged take-off.

Bank A sandbank that causes waves to break.

Barrel Tube.

Beach break Surf breaking on a sandy shore.

Blank The polystyrene or polyurethane block of foam out of which a board is shaped.

Blown out Describes surf conditions that have been ruined by an onshore wind.

Bomb A wave much larger than others that have preceded it.

Bombora, bombie Old term for a rare large wave breaking on a bank or reef far out from the shore.

Bonzer The original five-fin board (sometimes a tri-fin configuration) that features a large central fin and steeply canted outer fins, with deep concaves.

Booger Surfer's term for a body-boarder.

Bottom turn First turn on a wave after dropping in.

Bowl The result of refraction wrapping and focusing the wave into a steep and very powerful section.

Burn To cause someone to abort his or her ride, usually by dropping in.

Carve To execute powerful, full-rail turns.

Catalyst Liquid mixed with resin to make it set hard, or 'go off'.

Channel Deep-water access to surf break; or shaped concave on the bottom of a board designed to focus the release of water.

Clean Good glassy surf conditions; the opposite of 'blown out'.

Clean-up set An unusually large set of waves that catches everyone inside.

Close-out A wave, or section of a wave, that breaks too quickly along the line to be makeable.

Concave A design feature on the bottom of a board, to provide lift.

Cord Leash.

Corduroy Clean swell lines stacked to the horizon.

Cover-up To disappear in the white water in a ride but not into a clean barrel.

Cranking Surf that's going off; or, to carve a big turn.

Cruising Mellow, non-aggressive surfing.

Cutback Turning back on the face of the wave to head back towards the white water.

Dawn patrol To get in the surf early in an attempt to either beat the crowds or to catch the morning offshore breeze.

Deck The top of your board, where you stand.

Delamination An area of the board where the fibreglass cloth has lost its bonding to the foam.

Dialled To be in tune, either with a specific wave on a ride, or generally with local conditions.

Ding Board damage.

Drilled Hitting the bottom on a bad wipeout.

Double-up A wave that catches the slower, stalled wave in front of it, so combining their energies.

Down the line Surfing directly from the peak to the shoulder, with no manoeuvres.

Drop The free-fall take-off into a wave.

Drop-in To take the drop on a wave; or to take off in front of another rider.

Duck-dive Technique of sinking the board to get through the white water.

Dumping Heavy close-out waves breaking right on the shore.

Eat it To wipeout badly.

Egg A short rounded board, manoeuvrable but with great stability and paddling capacity; good for learners.

Elephant gun Same as a rhino-chaser, a board used for catching and riding huge waves.

Epoxy A lighter, harder resin type than polyester, but more difficult to work. Used with EPS.

EPS Expanded polystyrene. A lightweight beaded core foam for board blanks, for use with epoxy resins.

Eskimo roll Old term for rolling a larger board over to avoid the impact of white water. Also known as a T-roll or turtle roll.

EXPS Extruded polystyrene foam.

Face The green, unbroken front of a wave.

Fade To stylishly delay or draw out your turn.

Fetch The extent of ocean over which wind blows.

Fibreglass Woven cloth or mat used with polyester or epoxy resin.

Fins The keels on the bottom of your surfboard; or the flippers on your feet if you bodyboard.

Fish Very short, wide board with flat rocker.

Floater Beating a section by surfing across the top of the pitching lip.

Foamies Foam boards designed to be buoyant, forgiving and soft.

Foil Describes the cross-sectional distribution of thickness, from nose to tail of a board, for example, or from front to back of a fin.

Forehand Riding with your face to the wave.

Free surfing The opposite of competitive surfing.

Full If the tide's a little high for the waves to feel the bottom early enough to break well, the surf is said to be to full.

Glassy Windless, smooth conditions.

Gnarly Heavy, scary, intimidating.

Goat boat Derogatory term for any craft surfed sitting down.

Going off The surf is perfect; or, you're surfing extremely well.

Goofy-foot Someone who rides with the left foot at the back, right foot in front.

Grommet, grom Young, super-keen surfer.

Groundswell Ordered swell that has waves that come from some considerable distance.

Gun Longer narrow board used to catch and ride big swells.

Hack An especially aggressive turn.

Hang five A longboarding term for riding with the toes of your front foot right on the nose.

Hang ten Both feet on the nose, a manoeuvre that displays mastery and style on a longboard.

Hang time How long you stay in the air during an aerial manoeuvre.

Haole Hawaiian for 'foreign', but often used to describe somebody obviously out of his comfort zone.

Hawaiian janitor Stand-up paddleboarder.

Heavy Powerful waves; anything that has serious consequences.

Hog A wave hog is someone catching way more than his fair share of waves.

Hold-down The length of time you spend pinned underwater after a wipeout.

Hollow Waves breaking with enough power to make the lip pitch out into a barrel.

Hotdogging A term from the early 1960s used to describe a particular style of longboarding enabled by advances in surfboard manufacture.

Hybrid A compromise board shape that borrows and blends attributes from other shapes.

Impact zone The area where the waves are breaking with most power.

Inconsistent The waves are unpredictable, either in size or shape, making it difficult to judge where to surf or what to take off on.

Indicator A rock or a bank offshore that will break in a very large set providing a visual warning to those further inside that something big is on its way.

Inside The surfer closer to the peak is inside and has priority; or, to be caught inside is to be stuck shorewards of the breaking waves; or, to ride the barrel; or, the inside rail is the one nearest the wave face.

Jack Waves that suddenly rear up when they feel the bottom are said to 'jack'.

Kick out To turn out over the lip or shoulder and off the wave, ending your ride.

Kona A specific contrary wind in Hawaii, adopted to refer to any contrary winds.

Kook A surfer either just starting out or who doesn't heed the rules of surfing.

Layback A frontside turn made by dropping your inside arm to the face.

Leash Urethane cord tying you to your board. Also known as a kook-cord.

Left-hander A wave that breaks from your right to your left as you take off (left to right if you're looking from the shore).

Leg-rope Leash.

Lined-up Swell that has time to organise itself into nice lines; or, the act of getting yourself in the right place either at the peak of a surf break or on the wave itself.

Lip The pitching crest of a wave.

Localism Intimidation aimed at dissuading outsiders from surfing a break.

Low An atmospheric depression, an area of low barometric pressure.

Lull A period of relative calm in between sets, with few waves breaking.

Mal, Malibu Term given to a longer board, named in the '60s after the Californian break.

Maxed-out A break made unrideable by receiving more swell than it can handle.

Mushy Powerless, junk surf.

MPWC Motorised personal water craft.

Natural-foot Opposite of goofy-foot, a riding stance with the left foot forwards.

Pop-out Old derisory term for a factory-moulded board, usually heavy and crude.

Priority System for establishing who has right of way on a wave; regimented in pro surfing, less formal on the beach.

Prone-out To drop down from your feet to your belly to ride the white water back to shore.

PU Polyurethane foam.

Pumping Describes good, powerful groundswell; or, the method of generating speed by weighting and un-weighting.

Punt Aerial.

PWC Personal water craft, jetski, waverunner etc.

Quiver A selection of variously shaped boards for different conditions.

Noah Shark (Noah's Ark).

Nose Front of the board.

Nose-rider Longboard with extra volume and a concave in the nose for hanging five.

Off the lip, lip bash Top turn using the lip to bounce you back down the face of the wave.

Offshore Wind blowing from the shore to the sea.

Onshore Wind blowing from the sea to the land.

Outside Safely beyond the impact zone; or, where the largest waves will break.

Over the falls Getting pitched over with the lip.

Peak The apex of a breaking wave. Where you want to be to get priority.

Pearl Older term for falling by burying the nose of your board when taking off.

Peel The process of a wave breaking evenly across.

Pig-dog A way of tucking-in when surfing backhand, by crouching with one hand on the rail.

Pocket The most powerful part of the wave just under the lip.

Point break A jutting coastal feature refracting the swell and making waves peel evenly along the shore.

Poly Polyester resin, used with polyurethane foam.

Set A group of waves.

Shifty Term to describe conditions when waves aren't breaking in the same spot from one set to the next.

Shore break Waves that are breaking steeply very close to the shore, normally heavy and hazardous.

Shoulder The start of the wall or green part of the wave ahead of the white water and the pocket.

Shred To surf radically.

Sick Awesome surf, or especially impressive surfing.

Slab Sucky mutant wave breaking suddenly in very shallow water over a reef.

Slot The critical part of the wave with the most power; same as the pocket.

Snake The act of sneakily paddling inside another surfer who's nearest the peak to effectively give yourself priority.

Soup The foam, white water.

Spin-out When the fins of the board break free from the water and directional control is lost.

Sponge Bodyboard, or bodyboarder.

Spring suit Wetsuit with short legs and short or long arms.

Stall To slow the board down.

Steamer Full wetsuit.

Stoke The good feeling you get from surfing.

Radical Impressive, heavy, extreme.

Rail The edge of a board.

Rashie Smooth Lycra vest worn to prevent rashes from your wetsuit, or to protect from sunburn in the Tropics, or to identify learners as part of a surf school.

Rashtafarian Upper middle-class surfers who adopt the feral surfer style.

Reef break Waves breaking across a rock or coral reef or shelf.

Re-entry Top turn, coming back down with the lip, a big manoeuvre often used to finish off a ride when the wave closes out.

Reform A wave that's broken, backs off over some deeper water, then breaks again.

Resin Liquid petro-chemical that hardens when mixed with catalyst, used in fibreglass construction.

Rhino-chaser Same as an elephant gun, a board used for catching and riding huge waves.

Right-hander Wave that breaks from left to right as you take off, or from right to left viewed from the shore.

Rip A current of water moving out through the channel; or, to surf radically.

Rocker The curve in a board from tail to nose.

Roundhouse A full-rail manoeuvre that extends a cutback into a rebound off the foam.

Scratch To desperately paddle as fast as you can.

Section A portion of the wave breaking at once.

Stringer The thin wooden strip that runs down the length of the board to provide strength.

Stuff To cause a rider to lose position on a wave, usually by dropping in or snaking.

Sucky Very steep waves that draw water off the reef or sandbank before they break.

SUP Stand-up paddleboard.

Surfer's ear Medical condition of exostosis, a bony growth in the ear canal that develops in response to frequent exposure to cold water and wind.

Swellie, foamie Light, soft foam board used by beginners.

Switch-foot To ride opposite to your normal stance.

Tail The back third of the board.

Take off To commit yourself to the ride.

Template The outline of a board as seen from above; its plan shape.

Three-sixty A complete turn to face the way you were originally riding.

Thruster Three-finned board developed by Simon Anderson.

Tombstone After a heavy wipeout this describes the way the nose of your board sticks up vertically on the surface, with your dead weight buried six feet underwater at the end of your leash.

Trim To find the most efficient line for speed on a wave.

Turtle roll, T-roll To turn the board over in the face of oncoming white water.

Tube The hollow inside a steep breaking wave, behind the curtain of the lip.

Varial Any aerial manoeuvre with an inverted element to it.

Vee Design feature on the bottom of boards to facilitate rail-to-rail movement.

Waft Any turn where the fins break free of the water.

Wahine Hawaiian term for female surfer.

WCT World Championship Tour, surfing's competitive top flight.

Wedge Large, fast peak resulting from the energy of a cross-wave meeting the energy of an incoming wave.

Windswell Used to describe surf produced by wind with a very short fetch.

Wipeout To fall off.

Worked Beaten up during a wipeout.

WQS World Qualifying Series, a worldwide tour for surfers attempting to progress to the 44 places on the WCT.

Z-land A phrase used to describe (and disguise) any secret surfing spot.

AUTHORS ACKNOWLEDGMENTS

The author would like to acknowledge the work of Jacques Bely, Tony Butt and Paul Russell whose various publications provided the basis for much of the information contained in Chapter Two. It is very difficult to paraphrase work that has been presented with such clarity in its original form.

The author would also like to thank all those who patiently modelled or otherwise helped out for the photos: Alex W., Arthur at Surfboards Dalmeny, Calum F., Callum at Saltshots, Chris R., David at West Cornwall Adventure, George H., Jamie G., Jason at Leven Surfboards, Lucy at Lucy Aldridge Yoga, Malcolm at Snugg Westsuits, Ollie S., Stutes, Ross at Poldhu Café, Stef H., Trevor and Mark and the rest of the staff at Down the Line Surf Shop, and especially The Billies, Simon, and Stan.

And a big thankyou to Jason Feast and Alan Stokes for the surf shots.